BIBLE

THE

CHRISTIAN HOME,

AS IT IS IN THE

Sphere of Nature and the Church.

SHOWING

The Mission, Duties, Influences, Habits, and Responsibilities of Home its Education, Government, and Discipline; with Hints on "Match Making," and the Relation of Parents to the Marriage Choice of their Children; together with a consideration of the Tests in the Selection of a Companion, Etc.

BY

REV. S. PHILLIPS, A. M.

"Sweet is the smile of Home! the mutual look,
When hearts are of each other sure;
Sweet all the joys that crowd the household nook,
The haunt of all affections pure."

PUBLISHED BY GURDON BILL,
SPRINGFIELD, MASS.
H. C. JOHNSON, DETROIT, MICH.
1865.

PREFACE.

It is a fact conceded by all, that the constitution of the Christian family, and its social and spiritual relations, are not as fully developed as they should be. In this age of extreme individualism, we have almost left out of view the mission of home as the first form of society, and the important bearing it has upon the formation of character. Its interests are not appreciated; its duties and privileges are neglected; husbands and wives do not fully realize their moral relation to each other; parents are inclined to renounce their authority; and children, brought up in a state of domestic libertinism, neither respect nor obey their parents as they should. The idea of human character as a development from the nursery to the grave, is not realized. Home as a preparation for both the state and the church, and its bearing, as such, upon the prosperity of both, are renounced as traditionary, and too old and stale to suit this age of mechanical progression and "young Americanism."

As a consequence, the influence of home is lost; the lambs of the flock are neglected, grow up in spiritual ignorance, and become a curse both to themselves and to their parents. The vice and infidelity which prevail to such an alarming extent in the present day, may be ascribed to parental neglect of the young. The desolating curse of heaven invariably accompanies neglect of domestic obligations and duties; it was this that constituted that dreadful degeneracy which preceded the coming of the Messiah. The parents were alienated from the children, and the children from their parents. And the only way in which the Jews could avert deserved and impending ruin, was by "turning the heart of the fathers to the children, and the heart of the children to their fathers."

We must adopt the same method. We need in the present day a deeper and more scriptural sense, both in the state and church, of the importance of the family, and of its position in the sphere of natural and religious life. The attention of the people should be directed to the nature, the influences, the responsibilities, the prerogatives, duties and blessings of the Christian home.

Any work which contributes to this end is worthy of our high regard and subserves a noble purpose; for it is only when the details of home-life are given to the public, that proper interest in them will be developed, and we can hope for a better state of things in this first form of associated life.

The following work is an humble contribution to this important cause. It is intended to excite interest in the religious elements of family life, and to show that the development of individual character and happiness in the church and state, in time and in eternity, starts with, and depends upon, home-training and nurture. The author, in presenting it to the public, is fully conscious of its many palpable imperfections; yet, as it is his first effort, and as it was prepared amid the multiplied perplexities and interruptions of his professional life, he confidently expects that it will be received with charitable consideration. It is now published as an introduction to a work on the historical development of home, to which his attention has for years been directed. If this unassuming volume should be instrumental in the saving of one family from ruin, we shall feel ourself fully compensated.

THE AUTHOR.

CHAMBERSBURG, PA., 1859.

CONTENTS.

CHAPTER I.

WHAT IS THE CHRISTIAN HOME?

SECTION I.

HOME IN THE SPHERE OF NATURE.

"My home! the spirit of its love is breathing
  In every wind that plays across my track,
From its white walls the very tendrils wreathing
  Seem with soft links to draw the wanderer back.
There am I loved—there prayed for!—there my mother
  Sits by the hearth with meekly thoughtful eye,
There my young sisters watch to greet their brother;
  Soon their glad footsteps down the path will fly!
And what is home? and where, but with the loving?

Home! That name touches every fibre of the soul, and strikes every chord of the human heart as with angelic fingers. Nothing but death can break its spell. What tender associations are linked with home! What pleasing images and deep emotions it awakens! It calls up the fondest memories of life, and opens in our nature the purest, deepest, richest gush of consecrated thought and feeling.

> "Home! 'tis a blessed name! And they who rove,
> Careless or scornful of its pleasant bonds,
> Nor gather round them those linked soul to soul
> By nature's fondest ties, ...
> But dream they're happy!"

But what *is* home,—home in the sphere of nature? It is not simply an ideal which feeds the fancy, nor the flimsy emotion of a sentimental heart. We should seek for its meaning, not in the flowery vales of imagination, but amid the sober realities of thought and of faith.

Home is not the mere dwelling place of our parents, and the theater upon which we played the part of merry childhood. It is not simply a habitation. This would identify it with the lion's lair and the eagle's nest. It is not the mere mechanical juxtaposition of so many human beings, herding together like animals in the den or stall. It is not mere conventionalism,—a human association made up of the nursery, the parlor, the outward of domestic life, resting upon some evanescent passion, some sensual impression and policy. These do not make up the idea of home.

Home is a divine institution, coeval and congenital with man. The first home was in Eden; the last home will be in Heaven. It is the first form of society, a little commonwealth in which we first lose our individualism and come to the consciousness of our relation to others. Thus it is the foundation of all our relationships in life,—the preparation-state for our position in the State and in the Church. It is the first form and development of the associating principle, the normal relation in which human character first unfolds itself. It is the first partnership of nature and of life; and when it involves "the communion of saints," it reaches its highest form of development. It is an organic unity of nature and of interest,—the moral center of all those educational influences which are exerted upon our inward being. The idea of the home-institution rests upon the true love of our moral nature, involving the marriage union of congenial souls, binding up into itself the whole of life, forming and moulding all its relations, and causing body, mind and spirit to partake of a common evolution. The loving soul is the central fact of home. In it the inner life of the members find their true complement, and enjoy a kind of community of consciousness.

"Home's not merely four square walls,
Though with pictures hung and gilded;
Home is where affection calls—
Filled with shrines the heart hath builded."

Home may be viewed in a twofold aspect, as simply physical, and as purely moral. The former comes finally to its full meaning and force only in the latter. They are interwoven; we cannot understand the one without the other; they are complements; and the complete idea of home as we find it in the sphere of nature, lies in the living union of both.

By the physical idea of home, we mean, not only its outward, mechanical structure, made up of different parts and members, but that living whole or oneness into which these parts are bound up. Hence it is not merely adventitious, —a corporation of individual interests, but that organic unity of natural life and interest in which the members are bound up. By the moral idea of home, we mean the union of the moral life and interests of its members. This explodes the infidel systems of Fourierism, Socialism, Mormonism, and "Woman's Rights." These forms of Agrarianism destroy the ethical idea and mission of home; for they are not only opposed to revelation and history, but violate the plainest maxims of natural affection.

Love is an essential element of home. Without this we may have the form of a home, but not its spirit, its beating heart, its true motive power, and its sunshine. The inward stream would be gone, and home would not be the oneness of kindred souls. Home-love is instinctive, and begets all those silken chords, those sweet harmonies, those tender sympathies and endearments which give to the family its magic power. This home-love is the mother of all home delights, yea, of all the love of life. We first draw love from our mother's breast, and it is love which ministers to our first wants. It flashes from parent to parent, and from parent to child, making up the sunshine and the loveliness of domestic life. Without it home would have no meaning. It engenders the "home-feeling" and the "home-sickness," and is the moral net-work of the home-existence and economy. It is stronger than death; it rises superior to adversity, and towers in sublime beauty above the niggardly selfishness of the world. Misfortune cannot suppress it; enmity cannot alienate it; temptation cannot enslave it. It is the guardian angel of the nursery and the sick-bed; it gives an affectionate concord to the partnership of home-life and interest. Circumstances cannot modify it; it ever remains the same, to sweeten existence, to purify the cup of life, to smooth our rugged pathway to the grave, and to melt into moral pliability the brittle nature of man. It is the ministering spirit of home, hovering in soothing caresses over the cradle and the death-beds of the household, and filling up the urn of all its sacred memories.

But home demands not only such love, but ties, tender, strong, and sacred. These bind up the many in the one. They are the fibres of the home-life, and cannot be wrenched without causing the heart to bleed at every pore. Death may dissect them and tear away the objects around which they entwine; and they will still live in the imperishable love which survives. From them proceed mutual devotions and confiding faith. They bind together in one all-expanding unity, the perogatives of the husband, and the subordination of the wife, the authority of the parent and the obedience of the child.

> "O, not the smile of other lands,
> Though far and wide our feet may roam,
> Can e'er untie the genial bands
> That knit our hearts to home!"

The mother is the angel-spirit of home. Her tender yearnings over the cradle of her infant babe, her guardian care of the child and youth, and her bosom companionship with the man of her love and choice, make her the personal center of the interests, the hopes and the happiness of the family. Her love glows in her sympathies and reigns in all her thoughts and deeds. It never cools, never tires, never dreads, never sleeps, but ever glows and burns with increasing ardor, and with sweet and holy incense upon the altar of home-devotion. And even when she is gone to her last rest, the sainted mother in heaven sways a mightier influence over her wayward husband or child, than when she was present. Her departed spirit still hovers over his affections, overshadows his path, and draws him by unseen cords to herself in heaven.

Our nature demands home. It is the first essential element of our social being. The whole social system rests upon it: body, mind and spirit are concerned in it. These cannot be complete out of the home-relations; there would be no proper equilibrium of life and character without the home feeling and influence. The heart, when bereaved and disappointed, naturally turns for refuge to home-life and sympathy. No spot is so attractive to the weary one; it is the heart's moral oasis; there is a mother's watchful love, and a father's sustaining influence; there is a husband's protection, and a wife's tender sympathy; there is the circle of loving brothers and sisters,—happy in each other's love. Oh, what is life without these? A desolation!—a painful, glooming pilgrimage through "desert heaths and barren sands." But home gives to life its fertilizing dews, its budding hopes, and its blossoming joys. When far away in distant lands or upon the ocean's heaving breast, we pine away and become "home-sick;" no voice there like a mother's; no sympathy there like a wife's; no loved one there like a child; no resting place there like home; and we cry out, "Home! sweet, sweet home!"

Thus our nature instinctively longs for the deep love and the true hearts of home. It has for our life more satisfaction than all the honors, and the riches and the luxuries of the world. We soon grow sick of these, and become sick for home, however humble it may be. Its endearments are ever fresh, as if in the bursting joys of their first experience. They remain unforgotten in our memories and imperishable in our hearts. When friends become cold, society heartless, and adversity frowns darkly and heavily upon us, oh, it is then that we turn with fond assurance to home, where loved ones will weep as well as rejoice with us.

"Oh, the blessing of a home, where old and young mix kindly,
The young unawed, the old unchilled, in unreserved communion!
Oh that refuge from the world, when a stricken son or daughter
May seek with confidence of love, a father's hearth and heart;
Come unto me, my son, if men rebuke and mock thee,
There always shall be one to bless,—for I am on thy side!"

SECTION II.

HOME IN THE SPHERE OF THE CHURCH.

"A HOLY home,
Where those who sought the footprints of the Lord,
Along the paths of pain, and care, and gloom,
Shall find the rest of heaven a rich reward."

WHAT is the *Christian* home? Only in the sphere of christianity does the true idea of home become fully developed. Home with the savage is but a herding, a servitude. Even among many of the Jews it was little better than a Mahommedan seraglio. The most eminent of the heathen world degrade the family by making it the scene of lust, and introducing concubinage and polygamy. Plato, one of the most enlightened of the heathen, had base conceptions of home, and abused its highest and holiest prerogatives by his ideas of polygamy. We find too that in the ethics of Aristotle, the most lovely and sacred attributes of the family are totally discarded. The home which he holds up to view is unadorned with chastity and virtue. And Sophocles follows in the same path, stripping home of all that is sacred and essential to its true constitution. And when we come down to the present age, and view this divine institute in the light of Mormonism and Socialism, who will say that here we have unfolded its true idea and sacred character?

How different is the true Christian home! Here the marriage union is preserved "honorable," held sacred, and woman is raised to her true position. In the sphere of the Christian church, home is brought fairly and completely into view. Here it rises above the measure of natural affection and temporal interest. It enters the sphere of supernatural faith, and becomes the adumbration of our home in heaven.

The Christian home is a true type of the church. "The husband is the head of the wife, as Christ is of the church." The love of the family is self-denying and holy, like that between Christ and His church. The children are "the heritage of the Lord;" the parents are His stewards. Like the church, the Christian home has its ministry. Yea, the church is in the home, as the mother is in her child. We cannot separate them; they are correlatives. The one demands the other. The Christian home can have existence only in the sphere of the church. It is the vestibule of the church, bound to her by the bonds of Christian marriage, of holy baptism, and of the communion of saints, leading to her in the course of moral development, and completing her life only in the church-consciousness.

Home is, therefore, a partnership of spiritual as well as of natural life. The members thereof dwell "as being heirs together of the grace of life." "Heavenly mindedness," "the hidden man of the heart," and a "hope full of immortality," are the ornaments of the Christian home. Hers is "the incorruptibility of a meek and quiet spirit;" her members are "joint heirs of salvation;" they are "one," not only in nature, but "in Christ." They enjoy a "communion in spirit," that their "joy might be full." "What God, therefore, hath joined together, let not man put asunder."

Such a home, being "right with God," must be "full of good fruits, without partiality and without hypocrisy." Here the Christian shows his real character. In the sphere of the church, the family reaches its highest excellence and its purest enjoyment. Says the learned D'Aubigne,

"Without the knowledge and the love of God, a family is but a collection of individuals who may have more or less of natural affection for one another; but the real bond,—the love of God our Father, in Jesus Christ, our Lord,—is wanting."

We, therefore, abuse the idea of home when we divest it of the religious element. As the family is a divine institute and a type of the church and of heaven, it cannot be understood in its isolation from christianity; it must involve Christian principles, duties, and interests; and embrace in its educational functions, a preparation, not only for the State, but also for the church. The church gives to home a sacred religious ministry, a spiritual calling, a divine mission; investing it with prophetic, priestly and kingly prerogatives, and laying it under religious responsibilities.

This gives to the Christian home its true meaning, and secures for its members—

> "A sacred and home-felt delight,
> A sober certainty of waking bliss."

Such was the home of Abraham, who "commanded his children and his household to keep the way of the Lord, to do justice and judgment,"—of Joshua, who with "his house served the Lord,"—of David, who "returned to bless his household,"—of Job, who "offered burnt-offering according to the number of his sons," —of Cornelius, who "feared God with all his house,"—of Lydia, and Crispus, and the jailor of Philippi, who "believed in the Lord with all their house."

How many Christian parents practically discard this attribute of home! While all their temporal interests cluster around their home, and their hearts are fondly wedded to it as their retreat from a cold and repulsive world, they never think perhaps that God is in their family, that He has instituted it, and given those cherished ones who "set like olive plants around their table." They are faithful to all natural duties, and make ample provision for the temporal wants of their offspring; the mother bends with untiring assiduity over the cradle of her babe, and ministers to all its wants, watching with delight every opening beauty of that bud of promise, and willingly sacrificing all for its good. With what rapture she catches its first lispings of mother! The father toils from year to year to secure it a fair patrimony, a finished education, and an honorable position in life. How unremittingly these parents watch over the sick-bed of their children and of each other; and oh, what burning tears gush forth as the utterance of their agonizing hearts, when death threatens to blight a single bud, or lay his cold hand upon a single member!

This is all right, noble, and faithful to the natural elements of home. Natural affection prompts it, and it is well. But if this is all; if Christian parents and their children are governed only by the promptings of nature; if they are bound together by no spiritual ties and interests and hopes; if they are not prompted by faith to make provision for the soul, and for eternity; then we think they have not as yet realized the deepest and holiest significance of their home.

The Christian home demands the Christian consciousness,—the sense of a spirit-world with all its obligations and interests and responsibilities. Oh, is it not too often the case that even the Christian mother, while she teaches her babe the accents of her own name, never thinks of teaching it to lisp the name of Jesus,—never seeks to unfold its infant spirit,—never supplies it with spiritual food, nor directs its soul to the eternal world! In the same way the pious wife neglects her impenitent husband; and the pious husband, his reckless wife. There is too much such dereliction of duty in the homes of church members.

Our homes give us an interest in, and bind us by peculiar bonds to, the eternal world; those loved ones who have gone before us, look down from heaven upon those they have left behind; though absent from us in body, their spirits are still with us; and they come thronging upon glowing pinions, as ministering spirits, to our hearts. Mother! that little babe that perished in your arms, hovers over thee now, and is the guardian angel of your heart and home. It meets thee still! And oh, how joyful will your home-meeting be in heaven! Children! the spirit of your sainted mother lingers around your home to minister in holy things to thee. She has left you in body; she lies mouldering now in the humid earth; but she is with thee in spirit. Your home, dwelling in the sphere of the church on earth, has a spiritual communion with the sainted ones of the church in heaven. Thus, as the home-feeling can never be eradicated, so the home-meetings can never be broken up. Even the dead are with us there; their seats may be empty, and their forms may no longer move before us; but their spirits meet with us, and imprint their ministrations upon our hearts. The dead and the living meet in home!

"We are all here!
Father, mother,
Sister, brother,
All who hold each other dear,
Each chair is filled, we're all at home!
Let gentle peace assert her power,
And kind affection rule the hour—
We're all—all here!
Even they—the dead—though dead so dear,
Fond memory to her duty true,
Brings back their faded forms to view.
How life-like through the mist of years,
Each well-remembered face appears;
We hear their words, their smiles behold,
They're round us as they were of old—
We are all here!"

CHAPTER II.

THE MISSION OF THE CHRISTIAN HOME.

"If in the family thou art the best,
Pray oft, and be mouth unto the rest;
Whom God hath made the heads of families,
He hath made priests to offer sacrifice."

If home is a divine institution, and includes the religious element, moving in the sphere of nature and of the church, then its calling must be of God; its mission is divine; it is designed to subserve a spiritual purpose; it has a soul-mission. This was the view of David when he "returned to *bless* his household." To him his family was a church in miniature, and he its priest. Thus too Joshua felt that his service of God must include family worship.

What then is the mission of the Christian home? It is two-fold,—the temporal and eternal well-being of its members. It is the mission of home to provide for the temporal well-being of its members. They are parts of one great whole. Each must seek the welfare of all the rest. This involves obedience to the law of cooperation; and has special reference to that provision which the heads of families should make for the wants of those who are placed under their protection. As the parent sustains a physical, intellectual and moral relation to the child, it is his mission to provide for its physical, mental and moral wants. "He that provideth not for his own house hath denied the faith, and is worse than an infidel." Natural affection will prompt to this. Children are in a state of utter helplessness. The infant is at the mercy of the parent. Instinct impels the parent to provide for its wants. Even the brute does this.

That it is a part, therefore, of the home mission to provide for the physical wants of the dependents there, is very evident. To refuse to fulfill it is a crime against nature. This part of the home-mission includes the education of the body, by properly unfolding and directing its powers, and providing it with appropriate nutriment, raiment and shelter. In a word, we should make proper provision for the development and maturity of the physical life of our children. This is the mission of the parent until the child is able to provide for itself. This, says Blackstone, "is a principle of natural law;" and, in the language of Puffendorf, is "an obligation laid on parents, not only by nature herself, but by their own proper act in bringing them into the world." The laws of the land also command it. The child has a legal claim upon the parent for physical sustenance and education.

It is another part of the home-mission to provide for the intellectual wants and welfare of the child. Children have mind as well as body. The former needs nourishment and training as well as the latter. Hence it is as much the mission of the family to minister to the well-being of the mind of the child, as to that of its body. Civil law enforces this. Children have a legal as well as a natural claim to mental culture. In a word, it is the home-mission to provide for the child all things necessary to prepare it for a citizenship in the state.

Parents abuse this mission in two ways, either when they by their own indolence and dissipation compel their children to support them; or, on the other hand, when they become the willing slaves of their children, labor to amass a fortune for them, and, in the anticipation of that, permit them to grow up in ignorance, idleness, and prodigality, fit only to abuse and spend the fruit of parental servitude. In this way the misapplied provision made by parents often becomes a curse, not only to the members of the family, but to the state and church.

Another part of the home-mission is, the spiritual and eternal well-being of its members. This is seen in the typical character of the Christian family. It is an emblem of the church and of heaven. According to this, parents are called to administer the means of grace to their household, to provide for soul as well as for body, to prepare the child for a true membership in the church, as well as for a citizenship in the state, to train for heaven as well as for earth.

Parents are "priests unto their families," and have the commission to act for them as faithful stewards of God in all things pertaining to their everlasting welfare. Their souls, as well as their bodies, are committed to their trust, and God says to them,—

> "Go nurse them for the King of Heaven,
> And He will pay thee hire."

This is their great mission, and corresponds with the conception of the Christian home as a spiritual nursery. The family is "God's husbandry;" and this implies a spiritual culture. As its members dwell as "being heirs together of the grace of life," it is the function of each to labor to make all the rest "fellow-citizens with the saints, and of the household of God." Parents should provide for the religious wants of their children. Mere physical maintenance and mental culture cannot supersede the necessity of spiritual training. Children have a right to such training.

This religious provision is twofold; their moral and spiritual faculties should be developed; and their moral nature supplied with appropriate nutriment. All the wants of their moral nature are to be faithfully provided for. The home-mission involves the business of education of body, of mind, and of spirit;—of preparation for the state, for the church, for eternity. It is this which makes it so sacred and responsible. Strip the Christian family of its mission as a nursery for the soul; wrest from the parents their high prerogative as stewards of God; and you heathenize home, yea, you brutalize it! Tell me, what Christian home can accomplish its holy mission, when the soul is neglected, when religion is left out of view, when training up for God is abandoned, when the church is repudiated, and eternity cast off? You may provide for the body and mind of your children; you may amass for them a fortune; you may give them an accomplished education; you may introduce them into the best society; you may establish them in the best business; you may fit them for an honorable and responsible position in life; you may be careful of their health and reputation; and you may caress them with all the tender ardor of the parental heart and hand; yet if you provide not for their souls; if you seek not their salvation; if you minister only to their temporal, and not to their eternal welfare, all will be vain, yea, a curse both to you and to them. Husband and wife may love each other, and live together in all the peace and harmony of reciprocated affection; yet if the religious part of their home-mission remain unfulfilled, their family is divested of its noblest attraction; its greatest interests will fall into ruin; its highest destiny will not be attained; and soon its fruits will be entombed in oblivion; while their children, neglected and perishing, will look back upon that home with a bitterness of spirit which the world can neither soothe nor extract!

How many such homes there are! Even the homes of church members are too often reckless of their high vocation. Their moral stewardship is neglected; their dedications, formal and heartless. No prayers are heard; no bible read; no instructions given; no pious examples set; no holy discipline exercised. Their interests, their hopes and their enjoyments; their education, their labor and their rest, are all of the world, —worldly. The curse of God is upon such a home!

The importance and responsibility of the home-mission may be seen in its vicarious character, and in its influence upon the members. The principle of moral reproduction is manifest in all the home-relations. What the parent does is reproduced, as it were, in the child, and will tell upon the generations that follow them. Those close affinities by which all the members are allied, give to each a moulding influence over all the rest. The parents live, not for themselves alone, but for their children, and the consequence of such a life is also entailed upon their offspring. "The iniquity of the fathers shall be visited upon the children unto the third and fourth generation." If the parent "sow to the flesh," the child, with him, "shall of the flesh reap corruption;" but if he "sow to the spirit," his offspring, with him, shall "of the spirit reap life everlasting."

Sacred and profane history proves and illustrates this great truth. Did not God punish the first born of Israel, because their fathers had sinned? And is it not a matter of daily observation that the wickedness of the parent is entailed upon the child? Such is indeed the affinity between them that the child cannot, unless by some special interposition of Providence, escape the curse of a parent's sin. "If one member suffer, all the members suffer with it."

The guilt and condemnation of unfaithfulness to the home-mission may be inferred from its importance and responsibility. Those who are unfaithful are guilty of "blood." We see the curse of such neglect in that deterioration of character which so rapidly succeeds parental delinquency. They must answer before God for the loss which the soul, the state, and the church sustain thereby. "It shall be more tolerable for Sodom and Gomorrah in the day of judgment than for them."

The Christian home should be qualified for this mission. There can be no such qualification, however, where the marriage alliance involves inequality—one of the parents a Christian, the other not; for they cannot "dwell together as heirs of the grace of life," neither can they effectually dispense that grace to their offspring. When thus "the house is divided against itself, it must fall." "Be ye not, therefore, unequally yoked together." If one draws heavenward and the other hellward, there will be a halting between Baal and God, and the influence of the one will be counteracted by that of the other. "What communion hath light with darkness? What fellowship hath righteousness with unrighteousness? What part hath he that believeth with an infidel?" Thus divided, their home will be unfit for its high vocation. Hence parents, in their marriage alliance as well as in their individual character, should qualify themselves for the responsible mission of home. Can the ungodly wife or husband fulfill this mission? Can the irreligious parent bring up his offspring "in the nurture and admonition of the Lord?"

Many parents disqualify themselves for their home-mission by devoting too much attention to society,—by spending more time abroad, at parties, theaters and masquerade balls, in gossiping and recreation, than at home with each other and with their children. They commit their children, with all the family interests, to nurses and servants. They regard their offspring as mere playthings to be dandled upon the knee, brought up like calves in the stall, and then turned out to shape their own destiny.

This is a sad mistake! There is no substitute for home,—no transfer of a parent's commission, no adequate compensation for a parent's loss. None can effectually take the parent's place. Their influence is overwhelming and absolute.

> "With what a kingly power their love
> Might rule the fountains of the new-born mind!"

Not even the dark villainies which have disgraced humanity can neutralize it. Gray-haired and demon guilt will weep in his dismal cell over the melting, soothing memories of home. Their impressions are indelible, "like the deep borings into the flinty rock." To erase them we must remove every strata of their being. They give texture and coloring to the whole woof and web of the child's character. The mother especially preöccupies the unwritten page of its being, and mingles with it in its cradle dreams, making thus a deathless impress upon its soul.

> "The mother in her office, holds the key
> Of the soul; and she it is who stamps the coin
> Of character, and makes the being who would be a savage
> But for her cares, a Christian man!"

What a folly and a sin, therefore, for Christian parents to give over their holy mission to another, while they immerse themselves in the forbidden pleasures and recreations of the world! Oh, if you are loving, faithful parents, you will love the society of your household more than the fashions and the fashionable resorts of the world; you will not substitute the "nurse" and the "boarding school" for the more efficient ministrations of the Christian home.

> "If ye count society for past time,—what happier recreation than a nursling,
> Its winning ways, its prattling tongue, its innocence and mirth?
> If ye count society for good,—how fair a field is here,
> To guide these souls to God, and multiply thyself in heaven!"

"Walk, therefore, worthy of the vocation wherewith ye are called, with all lowliness and meekness." "Magnify your office." Be faithful to your home-mission. Draw your pleasure from it. Souls are committed to your trust and hang upon your hire. Your regard for the temporal and eternal welfare of your children should prompt you to faithfulness to the holy mission of your family. You love your children, and desire their welfare and happiness. But do what you will for them, if you are unfaithful to their souls, you wrest from them the means of safety and of happiness; you aid in their misery in this and in the world to come. You are more cruel to them than was Herod who slew the bodies of children. You murder their souls. He murdered the children of others; you murder your own; he employed others to do it for him; you do the work of slaughter yourself! If, then, you love your children; if their souls are committed to you; if your unfaithfulness to them may result in their ruin; if God blesses the holy mission of your home to their temporal and eternal welfare; if its fulfillment by you be "like words spoken in a whispering gallery, which will be heard at the distance of years, and echoed along the corridors of ages yet to come;" and if it will prove to them in life like the lone star to the mariner upon the dark and stormy sea,—should you not be faithful to your home-vocation!

Not only so, but your regard for your own comfort and happiness here and hereafter should impel you to this faithfulness. Do you love yourself? Do you regard your own comfort and welfare? Would you avoid painful solicitude, bitter reflection, heart-burning remorse, dreadful foreboding? Then be faithful to the home-mission. If you are, God will bless you for it through your children. What a comfort it will be to you to see them become Christians, enter the church, and, at their side around the Lord's Table, hold communion with them in the joys of faith and in the anticipations of heaven! And should God remove them from you by death, you will be cheered amidst the agonies of separation by their dying consolation. The hope of a speedy reunion with them in heaven would afford a sweet solace to your bereaved heart.

Or should you be taken before them, what a comfort would they afford you in your last moments! With the glow of Christian faith and hope, they would whisper to you the consolations of the gospel, and bless you for your faithfulness to them. And when you and they shall meet at the bar of God, they will rise up and call you blessed.

But, on the other hand, should you neglect them; and, as a consequence, they grow up in wickedness and crime; oh, what a source of withering remorse they would cause you! No sin more heavily punishes the guilty, and mingles for him a more bitter cup, than the sin of parental neglect. What if after the lapse of a few years, your neglected child be taken from you, and consigned to the cold grave, think you not that when you meet it before the bar of God, it will rise up as a witness against you, and pour down its curses upon your head!

But suppose that child grows up, unprovided for by you in its early life; and profligacy mark his pathway, and demon guilt throw its chains around him in the prison cell; and he trace back the beginning of his ruin to your unfaithfulness, oh, with what pungency would the reflection send the pang of remorse to your soul!

> "Go ask that musing father, why yon grave
> So narrow, and so noteless, might not close
> Without a tear?"

Because of the bitter and heart-stricken memories of a neglected, ruined child that slumbers there!

Or suppose that you die before your neglected children, think you not that the recollection of your past parental unfaithfulness will plant thorns in your pillow, and invest with deeper shades of horror your descent to the dark valley of death? And oh, when you meet them before the bar of the avenging judge, most fearful will be your interview with them. Tell me, how will you dare to meet them there, when the voice of their blood will cry out from the hallowed ground of home against you! And then, eternity, oh, eternity! who shall bring out from the secrets of the eternal world, those awful maledictions which God has attached to parental unfaithfulness?

Provide, therefore, for your family as the Lord commands. Remember that if you do not, you "deny the faith and are worse than an infidel;" and in the day of Judgment "it shall be more tolerable for Sodom and Gomorrah than for you."

CHAPTER III.

FAMILY RELIGION.

"Lo! where yon cottage whitens through the green,
The loveliest feature of a matchless scene;
Beneath its shading elm, with pious fear,
An aged mother draws her children near,
While from the Holy Word, with earnest air,
She teaches them the privilege of prayer.
Look! how their infant eyes with rapture speak;
Mark the flushed lily on the dimpled cheek;
Their hearts are filled with gratitude and love,
Their hopes are centered in a world above!"

THE Christian home demands a family religion. This makes it a "household of God." Without this it is but a "den of thieves." It is "the one thing needful."

What is "family religion?" It is not an exotic, but is indigenous to the Christian home. It is not a "new measure," but an essential ingredient of the home-constitution, — coëxistent with home itself. The first family "began to call upon the name of the Lord;" the first parent acted as high-priest of God in his family.

It is not individual piety as such, not simply closet devotion, but family service of God,—religion taken up in the home-consciousness and life. Hence a family, and not simply a personal religion.

Such religion, we say, is as old as the church. We find it in Eden, in the tents of the patriarchs and in the wilderness of the prophets. We find it in the tent of Abraham in the plains of Mamre, in the "house" of Moses, in the "service" of Joshua, in the "offerings" of Job, and in the palace of David and Solomon. It is also a prominent feature of the gospel economy. The commendation bestowed by Paul upon Timothy, was that "from a child" he enjoyed the "unfeigned faith" of his mother Eunice and his grandmother Lois. Paul exhorts Christians thus: "Rule well your own houses; speaking to yourselves in psalms and hymns and spiritual songs." The same family religion was a prominent feature of the homes of the primitive Christians. With them, every house was a sanctuary, and every parent a minister in holy things to its members. The bible was not only a parlor ornament, but a lamp to their feet and a guide to their path, used, meditated upon, prayed over. Says Turtullian of its members, "They are united in spirit and in flesh; they kneel down together; they pray and fast together; they teach, exhort and support each other with gentleness."

How, alas! have Christian homes degenerated since then in family piety! They received a reviving impulse in the Reformation; yet even this was meteor-like, and seemed but the transient glow of some mere natural emotion. The fire which then flashed so brilliantly upon the altar of home, has now become taper-like and sepulchral; and the altar of family religion, like the altar of Jehovah upon Mt. Carmel, has been demolished and forsaken. Only here and there do we find a Christian home erect and surround a Christian altar. Parents seem now ashamed to serve the Lord at home. They have neither time nor inclination. Upon the subject of religion they maintain a bashful, sullen, wonderful silence before their families. They seem to be impressed with the strange idea that their wives and children put no confidence in their piety, (and may they not have reason for it?) and that it would, therefore, be vain for them to pray, or exhort their households. "Many walk thus," says Paul, "of whom I have told you often, and now tell you even weeping, that they are the enemies of the cross of Christ!" Upon them shall be answered the prayer of Jeremiah, "Oh Lord, pour out thy fury upon the families that call not upon thy name!"

Thus, therefore, we see that the Christian home demands a family religion. The private devotion of the individual can be no effectual substitute for it.

"The parents pair their secret homage,
And offer up to heaven the warm request,
That He who stills the raven's clamorous nest,
And decks the lily fair in flowery pride,
Would, in the way His wisdom sees the best,
For them and for their little ones provide."

Family religion includes parental bible instruction, family prayer, and religious education, government, discipline and example. These involve the parent's position in his household as a prophet, priest, and king. "Thou shalt teach my words diligently unto thy children, and talk of them when thou sittest in thy house."

"Daily let part of Holy Writ be read,
Let as the body, so the soul have bread.
For look! how many souls in thy house be,
With just as many souls God trusteth thee!"

Thus felt and acted our primitive fathers. By every winning art, they sought to fill their children with the knowledge of God's Word. The entire range of nursery instruction and amusement was comprised in scripture pictures and hieroglyphics. They intermingled religion with all their home pursuits, and entwined it with their earliest and purest associations of childhood. If Christian parents would follow their example now, in these days of parental delinquency, we would not behold so many of their children grow up in religious ignorance and indifference.

The same may be said of the family altar and

prayer. A prayerless family is an irreligious, godless family. Says Henry, "They who daily pray in their houses do well; they that not only pray, but read the scriptures, do better; but they do best of all, who not only pray and read the scriptures, but sing the praises of God."

Besides, the religion of home implies that we "command our children and household to keep the way of the Lord,"—that we "bring them up in His nurture and admonition," and "train them up as He would have them go;" and that in things pertaining to their spiritual welfare we "go in and out" before them as their pattern and example, bidding them to "follow us even as we follow Christ," and living in their midst as "the living epistles of Christ, known and read" of them all.

Family religion must "show itself by its works" of Christian charity and benevolence to the poor, the sick and the distressed. We should "lay by" a certain amount each year of what God bestows, for the support of the church and the propagation of the gospel. Oh, how little do Christians now give to these benevolent objects! A penurious, close-fisted, selfish home cannot be a religious household. Family religion must be reproductive, must return to God as well as receive from Him. But as these characteristic features of the Christian home will be considered hereafter, we shall not enlarge upon them here. Suffice it to say that the mission of home demands family religion. Its interests cannot be secured without it.

Let our homes be divorced from piety, and they will become selfish, sensual, unsatisfactory, and unhappy. Piety should always reign in our homes, — not only on the Sabbath, but during the week; not only in sickness and adversity, but in health and prosperity. It must, if genuine, inspire and consecrate the minutest interests and employments of the household. It must appear in every scene and feeling and look, and in each heart, as the life, the light, the hope, and the joy of all the members.

The necessity of family religion is seen in the value of the soul. The soul is the dearest treasure and the most responsible trust of home. What shall it profit the family if its members gain the whole world and lose their own souls? What would Christian parents give in exchange for the souls of their little ones? Is it not more important that they teach them to pray than to dance, to "seek the kingdom of heaven" than the enjoyment of "the pleasures of sin for a season?" Oh, what is home without a title to, and personal meetness for, that kingdom? It is a moral waste; its members move in the putrid atmosphere of vitiated feeling and misdirected power. Brutal passions become dominant; we hear the stern voice of parental despotism; we behold a scene of filial strife and insubordination; there is throughout a heart-blank. Domestic life becomes clouded by a thousand crosses and disappointments; the solemn realities of the eternal world are cast into the shade; the home-conscience and feeling become stultified; the sense of moral duty distorted, and all the true interests of home appear in a haze. Natural affection is debased, and love is prostituted to the base designs of self, and the entire family, with all its tender cords, ardent hopes, and promised interests, becomes engulfed in the vortex of criminal worldliness!

But reverse the picture! See what home becomes with religion as its life and rule. Human nature is there checked and moulded by the amiable spirit and lovely character of Jesus. The mind is expanded, the heart softened, sentiments refined, passions subdued, hopes elevated, pursuits ennobled, the world cast into the shade, and heaven realized as the first prize. The great want of our intellectual and moral nature is here met, and home education becomes impregnated with the spirit and elements of our preparation for eternity.

The relations of home demand family religion. These are relations of mutual dependence, involving such close affinity that the good or evil which befalls one member must in some degree extend to all the other members. They involve "helps." Each member becomes an instrument in the salvation or damnation of the others. "For what knowest, O wife, whether thou shalt save thy husband? or how knowest thou, O man, whether thou shalt save thy wife?"—1 Cor. vii., 16. "If one member suffer, all the members suffer with it." They stimulate each other either to salvation or to ruin; and hence those children that go to ruin in consequence of parental unfaithfulness, will "curse the father that begat them, the womb that bare them," and the day they entered their home.

Many parents seek to excuse themselves from the practice of family religion, upon the ground that they have not the capacity nor the time. If so, you should not have married. But if you are Christians, you have the capacity, and you will take the time.

But some are ashamed to begin family religion. Ashamed of what? of your piety? of your children? of the true glory and greatness of your home? Then you are ashamed of Jesus! You should rather blush that you have not begun this good work.

The great defect of family religion in the present day is, that it is not educational. Parents wait until their children have grown up, and established habits of sin, when they suppose that the efforts of some "protracted meeting" will compensate for their neglect in childhood. They overlook the command of God to teach them His words. The influence of this defect and delusion has been most destructive. Many Christian homes are now altogether destitute of religious appliances. If the angel that visited the homes of Israel were to visit the Christian homes of this age, would he not be tempted to say, as Abraham said to Abimelech, "Surely the fear of God is not in this place!"

One great reason, perhaps, why there are so many such homes is, that there are now so many irreligious marriages, where husband and wife are "unequally yoked together," one a believer and the other not. "How can two walk together except they be agreed?" Can there be family religion when husband and wife are traveling to eternity in opposite roads? No! There will be hindrances instead of "helps." If they marry not "in the Lord," religion will not be in their home. Says the pious Jay, "I am persuaded that it is very much owing to the prevalence of these indiscriminate and unhallowed connections, that we have fallen so far short of those men of God, who are gone before us, in the discharge of family worship, and in the training up of our households in the nurture and admonition of the Lord."

Family religion is implied in the marriage relation and obligation. It is included in the necessities of our children, and in the covenant promises of God. The penalties of its neglect, and the rewards of our faithfulness to it, should prompt us to its establishment in our homes. Its absence is a curse; its presence a blessing. It is a foretaste of heaven. Like manna, it will feed our souls, quench our thirst, sweeten the cup of life, and shed a halo of glory and of gladness around our firesides. Let yours, therefore, be the religious home; and then be sure that God will delight to dwell therein, and His blessing will descend, like the dews of heaven, upon it. Your children shall "not be found begging bread," but shall be like "olive plants around your table,"—the "heritage of the Lord." Yours will be the home of love and harmony; it shall have the charter of family rights and privileges, the ward of family interests, the palladium of family hopes and happiness. Your household piety will be the crowning attribute of your peaceful home,—the "crown of living stars" that shall adorn the night of its tribulation, and the pillar of cloud and of fire in its pilgrimage to a "better country." It shall strew the family threshold with the flowers of promise, and enshrine the memory of loved ones gone before, in all the fragrance of that "blessed hope" of reunion in heaven which looms up from a dying hour. It shall give to the infant soul its "perfect flowering," and expand it in all the fullness of a generous love and conscious blessedness, making it "lustrous in the livery of divine knowledge." And then in the dark hour of home separation and bereavement, when the question is put to thee, mourning parents, "Is it well with the child? is it well with thee?" you can answer with joy, "It is well!"

CHAPTER IV.

THE RELATION OF HOME TO THE CHURCH.

THE Christian home sustains a direct relation to the church. This relation is similar to that which it sustains to the state. The nature and mission of home demand the church. The former is the adumbration of the latter. The one is in the other. "Greet the church that is in thine house." The church was in the house of Aquila and Priscilla, in the tent of Abraham, and in the palace of David. It must be in every Christian home, and every Christian home must be in the church. In a word, our families must be churchly.

This relation is vital and necessary,—a relation of mutual dependence. The family is a preparation for the church, subordinate to it, and must, therefore, throw its influence in its favor, be moulded by it, and labor with direct reference to the church in the way of training up for membership in it. As the civil and political relations of home involve the duty of parents to train up their children for efficient citizenship in the state.

so its moral and religious relations involve the duty of education for the church. Hence the Christian home is churchly in its spirit, religion, education, influence, and mission.

Family religion is an element of home, not only as a mere fact or principle in its subjective form, but in the form and force of the church. In its unchurchly form it is powerless. It must be experienced and administered in a churchly spirit and way, not as something detached from the organic embodiment of christianity. The relation of the church to the family forbids this. The church pervades all the forms of society. It includes the home and the state. It gives to each proper vitality, legitimate principles, proper direction, and a true destiny.

But home is not only a preparation for the church, but completes itself in the church,—never out of the church. By the "mystery" of marriage and the sacrament of holy baptism, home and the church are bound up into each other by indissoluble bonds. The one receives the mark and superscription of the other; the one is the type or emblem of the other.

The church, through her ordinances, ministry and means of grace, is brought directly "into the house," and operates there constantly as a spiritual leaven. It is the purpose of God that our homes be entrenched within the sacred enclosures of His church. The former, in its relation to the latter, is like "a wheel within a wheel,"—one of the parts which make up the great machinery of the kingdom of grace, operating harmoniously and in its place with all the rest, and for the same end. The former is built upon the latter, —receives her dedication and sanctity from it. They are correlatives. The one demands the other. Hence they cannot be divorced. The individual passes over to the church through the Christian home. The one is the step to the other. They have the same foundation. Home is not erected upon a quicksand, but reared upon the same rock upon which the church is built. Like the church, it rises superior to all the fluctuations of civil society, and will live and flourish in all its tender charities, in all its sweet enjoyments, and in all its moral force, in the humble cottage as well as in the costly palace, under the shadow of liberty as well as under the frowns of despotism, in every nation, age, and clime. Like the church of which it is the type, it can never be made desolate; break it up on earth, and you find it in heaven. Its nuptial union with the church is like that between the latter and Christ. Nothing can throw over our homes a higher sanctity, or invest them with greater beauty, or be to them a greater bulwark of strength, than the church. Home is the nursery of the church. "Those who are planted in the house of the Lord shall flourish in the courts of our God, and shall bring forth fruit in old age."

Thus, therefore, we see that the relation between the Christian home and the church is one of mutual dependence. The latter, as the highest form of religious association, demands the former, and the former looks to the latter as its completion. Where the religion of the family does not move in the element of the church, it is at best but sentimentalism on the one hand, and rationalism on the other. It is a spurious pietism. To be genuine it must be moulded by the church. Without this it is destitute of sterling principle, of a living faith, of well-directed effort and lofty aims. The family which does not move in the element of the church is a perversion of the true purpose of God in its institution. It will afford no legitimate development of Christian doctrine, and the whole scheme of its religion will rest for its execution upon unreliable agencies extraneous to home itself. Hence we find that the piety of those families or individuals that isolate themselves from the church, is at best but ephemeral in its existence, contracted in spirit, moving and operating by mere impulse and irregular starts, and withal destitute of vitality and saving influence. A death-bed scene may awaken a transient and visionary sense of duty; adversity may startle the drowsy ear, and cause the parents to turn for the time to the souls of their children; but these continue only while the tear and the wound are fresh, and the apprehensions of the eternal world are moving in their terrible visions before them!

The efficacy of the Christian home, therefore, depends upon its true relation to the church. The members should be conscious of this. Then both parents and children will appreciate the religious ministrations of home. Then the former will not grow weary in well doing, but will have something to rest upon, something to look to; and the latter will love the church of their fathers, and venerate the family as its nursery.

But the relation between the Christian home and the church implies reciprocal obligations and duties. The former should not only exist under the patronage of the latter, but in the spirit of a true subordination. Parents should teach and rule and appropriate the means of grace under the supervision of the church. They should take their household with them to her public service, send their children to her schools, and in all respects bring them up in her nurture and admonition.

Thus the family should exist as the faithful daughter of the church; and as the latter in the wilderness "leaned upon her beloved," so the former should repose itself upon her who is "the mother of us all," and in whom, as the "body of Christ," shall "all the families of the earth be blessed." As her loving and confiding daughter, the family should live under her government and discipline, listen to her maternal voice, and be led by her maternal hand. The minister in his pastoral functions, is the representative of the church in each of the families of his flock; and should, therefore, be received, loved, confided in and obeyed, as such. The home that repels his proffered ministrations in the name and according to the will of the church, throws off its allegiance to the latter, and through it, to Christ,—her glorious head, and is hence unworthy of the name of Christian home. The true Christian home yearns after the church, loves to lean upon it, to look up to it, to consecrate all to it, to move and develop its interests in the sphere of the church, and to labor to complete itself in it.

"For her my tears shall fall;
For her my prayers ascend;
To her my cares and toils be giv'n,
Till toils and cares shall end."

CHAPTER V.

HOME INFLUENCE.

"By the soft green light in the woody glade,
On the banks of moss, where thy childhood play'd;
By the gathering round the winter hearth,
When the twilight call'd unto household mirth,
By the quiet hour when hearts unite
In the parting prayer and the kind 'Good night;'
By the smiling eye and the loving tone,
Over thy life has the spell been thrown,
And bless that gift, it hath gentle might,
A guarding power and a guiding light!"

THE Christian home has an influence which is stronger than death. It is a law to our hearts, and binds us with a spell which neither time nor change can break. The darkest villainies which have disgraced humanity cannot neutralize it. Gray-haired and demon guilt will make his dismal cell the sacred urn of tears wept over the memories of home; and these will soften and melt into penitence even the heart of adamant.

The home-influence is either a blessing or a curse, either for good or for evil. It cannot be neutral. In either case it is mighty, commencing

with our birth, going with us through life, clinging to us in death, and reaching into the eternal world. It is the unitive power which arises out of the manifold relations and associations of domestic life. The specific influences of husband and wife, of parent and child, of brother and sister, of teacher and pupil, united and harmoniously blended, constitute the home-influence.

From this we may infer the character of home-influence. It is great, silent, irresistible, and permanent. Like the calm, deep stream, it moves on in silent, but overwhelming power. It strikes its roots deep into the human heart, and spreads its branches wide over our whole being. Like the lily that braves the tempest, and "the Alpine flower that leans its cheek on the bosom of eternal snows," it is exerted amid the wildest storms of life, and breathes a softening spell in our bosom even when a heartless world is freezing up the fountains of sympathy and love. It is governing, restraining, attracting and traditional. It holds the empire of the heart, and rules the life. It restrains the wayward passions of the child, and checks him in his mad career of ruin.

"Hold the little hands in prayer, teach the weak knees their kneeling,
Let him see thee speaking to thy God; he will not forget it afterward;
When old and gray, will he feelingly remember a mother's tender piety,
And the touching recollection of her prayers shall arrest the strong man in his sin!"

Home-influence is traditional. It passes down the current of life from one generation to another. Its continuity is preserved from first to last. The homes of our forefathers rule us even now, and will pass from us to our children's children. Hence it has been called the "fixed capital" of home. It keeps up a continuous stream of home-life and feeling and interest. Hence the family likeness, moral as well as physical,—the family virtues and vices,—coming from the family root and rising into all the branches, and developing in all the elements of the family history.

Home-influence is attractive. It draws us to home, and throws a spell around our existence, which we have not the power to break.

> "The holy prayer from my thoughts hath pass'd,
> The prayer at my mother's knee—
> Darken'd and troubled I come at last,
> Thou home of my boyish glee!"

Home-influence may be estimated from the immense force of first impressions. It is the prerogative of home to make the first impression upon our nature, and to give that nature its first direction onward and upward. It uncovers the moral fountain, chooses its channel, and gives the stream its first impulse. It makes the "first stamp and sets the first seal" upon the plastic nature of the child. It gives the first tone to our desires, and furnishes ingredients that will either sweeten or embitter the whole cup of life. These impressions are indelible, and durable as life. Compared with them, other impressions are like those made upon sand or wax. These are like "the deep borings into the flinty rock." To erase them we must remove every strata of our being." Even the infidel lives under the holy influence of a pious mother's impressions. John Randolph could never shake off the restraining influence of a little prayer his mother taught him when a child. It preserved him from the clutches of avowed infidelity.

The promises of God bear testimony to the influence of the Christian home. "When he grows old he will not depart from it!" History confirms and illustrates this. Look at those scenes of intemperance and riot, of crime and of blood, which throw the mantle of infamy over human life! Look at your prisons, your hospitals, and your gibbets; go to the gaming-table and the rum-shop. Tell me, who are those that are there? What is their history? Where did they come from? From the faithful Christian home? Had they pious fathers and mothers? Did they go to these places under the holy influence of devout and faithful parents? No! And who are they that are dying without hope and without God? Who are they that now throng the regions of the damned? Those who were "trained up in the way they should go?" No! if they are, then the promises of God must fail. You may perhaps find a few such. But these are exceptions to a general law. The damning influence of their unfaithful home brought them there.

Could they but speak to us from their chambers of wo, we should hear them pouring out curses upon their parents, and ascribing the cause of their ruin to their neglect. On the other hand, could we but listen to the anthems of the redeemed in heaven, we should doubtless hear sentiments of gratitude for a mother's prayer and a father's counsel.

Let us now briefly advert to the objects of home-influence. It is exerted upon the members of home, especially upon the formation of their character and destiny. It moulds their character. The parents assimilate their children to themselves to such an extent that we can judge the former by the latter. Lamartine says that, when he wants to know a woman's character, he ascertains it by an inspection of her home,—that he judges the daughter by the mother. His judgment rests upon the known influence the latter has over the former. It gives texture and coloring to the whole woof and web of character. It forms the head and the heart, moulds the affections, the will and the conscience, and throws around our entire nature the means and appliances of its development for good or for evil. Every word, every incident, every look, every lesson of home, has its bearing upon our life. Had one of these been omitted, our lives would perhaps be different. One prayer in our childhood was perhaps the lever that raised us from ruin. One omission of parental duty may result in the destruction of the child. What an influence home exerts upon our faith! Most of our convictions and opinions rest upon home-teaching and faith. A minister was once asked, "Do you not believe christianity upon its evidences?" He replied, "No; I believe it because my mother taught me!"

The same may be said of its influence upon our sympathies, and in the formation of habits. It draws us by magnetic power to home, and develops in us all that which is included in home-feeling and home-sickness.

> "I need but pluck yon garden flower,
> From where the wild weeds rise,
> To wake with strange and sudden power,
> A thousand sympathies!"

In this respect how irresistible is the influence of a mother's love and kindness! Her very name awakens the torpid streams of life, gives a fresh glow to the tablets of memory, and fills our hearts with a deep gush of consecrated feeling.

Our habits, too, are formed under the moulding power of home. The "tender twig" is there bent, the spirit shaped, principles implanted, and the whole character is formed until it becomes a habit. Goodness or evil are there "resolved into necessity." Who does not feel this influence of home upon all his habits of life? The gray-haired father who wails in his second infancy, feels the traces of his childhood-home in his spirit, desires and habits. Ask the strong man in the prime of life, whether the most firm and reliable principles of his character were not the inheritance of the parental home. What an influence the teachings and prayers of his mother Monica had upon the whole character of the pious Augustine! The sterling worth of Washington is a testimony to the formative power of parental instruction. John Quincy Adams, even when his eloquence thundered through our legislative halls, and caused a nation to startle from her slumber, bent his aged form before God, and repeated the prayer of his childhood. "How often in old age," says Bishop Hall, "have I valued those divine passages of experimental divinity that I heard from the lips of a mother!" Dr. Doddridge ever lived under the influence of those scripture instructions his mother gave him from the Dutch tiles of her fireside. He says, "these lessons were the instruments of my conversion." "Generally," says Dr. Cumming, "when there is a Sarah in the house, there will be an Isaac in the cradle; wherever there is a Eunice teaching a Timothy the scriptures from a child, there will be a Timothy teaching the gospel to the rest of mankind." By the force of this same influence, the pious wife may win over to Christ her ungodly husband, and the godly child may save the unbelieving parent. "Well," said a mother one day weeping, "I will resist no longer! How can I bear to see my dear child love and read the scriptures, while I never look into the bible,—to see her retire and seek God, while I never pray,—to see her going to the Lord's table, while His death is nothing to me! I know she is right, and

I am wrong. I ought to have taught her; but I am sure she has taught me. How can I bear to see her joining the church of God, and leaving me behind—perhaps forever!"

The Christian home has its influence also upon the state. It forms the citizen, lays the foundation for civil and political character, prepares the social element and taste, and determines our national prosperity or adversity. We owe to the family, therefore, what we are as a nation as well as individuals. We trace this influence in the pulpit, on the rostrum, in the press, in our civil and political institutions. It is written upon the scroll of our national glory.

The most illustrious statesmen, the most distinguished warriors, the most eloquent ministers, and the greatest benefactors of human kind, owe their greatness to the fostering influence of home. Napoleon knew and felt this when he said, "What France wants is good mothers, and you may be sure then that France will have good sons." The homes of the American revolution made the men of the revolution. Their influence reaches yet far into the inmost frame and constitution of our glorious republic. It controls the fountains of her power, forms the character of her citizens and statesmen, and shapes our destiny as a people. Did not the Spartan mother and her home give character to the Spartan nation? Her lessons to her child infused the iron nerve into the heart of that nation, and caused her sons, in the wild tumult of battle, "either to live behind their shields, or to die upon them!" Her influence fired them with a patriotism which was stronger than death. Had it been hallowed by the pure spirit and principles of christianity, what a power for good it would have been!

But alas! the home of an Aspasia had not the heart and ornaments of the Christian family. Though "the monuments of Cornelia's virtues were the character of her children," yet these were not "the ornaments of a quiet spirit." Had the central heart of the Spartan home been that of the Christian mother, the Spartan nation would now perhaps adorn the brightest page of history.

But the family, whether Christian or heathen, exerts an overwhelming influence over the state. It is on the family altar that the fire of patriotism is first kindled, and often, too, by a mother's hand.

> "It hath led the freeman forth to stand
> In the mountain battles of his land;
> It hath brought the wanderer o'er the seas,
> To die on the hills of his own fresh breeze."

The same, too, may be said of the influence of home on the church. It is the nursery of the church, lays the foundation of her membership, and conditions the character of her members. The most faithful of her ministers and members are those generally who have been trained up in the most faithful families. Wherever there is the greatest number of such homes, there the church enjoys the greatest prosperity.

What a fearful responsibility must rest, therefore upon the Christian home! If its influence is for good or for evil, for weal or for woe, for heaven or for hell; if it is either a powerful emissary of Satan for the soul's destruction, or an efficient agent of God for the soul's salvation, then how responsible are those who wield this influence!

> "Upon thy heart is laid a spell,
> Holy and precious—oh! guard it well!"

Are you not, Christian parents, responsible to God for the exercise of such sovereign power over the character and well-being of your dear children? And will not the day soon come when you must "give an account of your stewardship?" Oh! what if it be exerted for the ruin of your loved ones, and they "curse the day you begat them?" What if, in the day of final reckoning, you find your hands drenched in the blood of your offspring, and hear the voice of that blood cry out from the hallowed ground of home against you, saying, "How long, oh Lord, holy and true, dost thou not judge and avenge our blood on them that dwell on earth?" Oh see, then, that your influence be wielded for good.

> "For round the heart thy power hast spun
> A thousand dear mysterious ties;
> Then take the heart thy charms have won,
> And nurse it for the skies!"

CHAPTER VI.

HOME AS A STEWARDSHIP.

"Take this child away, and nurse it for me, and I will give thee thy wages."—Exodus ii., 9.

"For look, how many souls in thy house be,
With just as many souls God trusteth thee!"

The Christian home is a stewardship. The parents are stewards of God. A steward is a servant of a particular kind, to whom the master commits a certain portion of his interest to be prosecuted in his name and by his authority, and according to his laws and regulations. The steward must act according to the will of his master, in his dealing with what is committed to his care. Such was Eliezer in the house of Abraham; and such was Joseph in the house of Potiphar. One of the specific duties of a steward was to dispense portions of food to the different members of the household, to give servants their portion in due season, and to superintend the general interests of the master's household.

In a religious sense, a steward is a minister of Christ, whose duty is to dispense the provisions of the gospel, to preach its doctrines and to administer its ordinances. It is required of such that they be found faithful.—1 Cor., chap. iv.

In its application to the Christian home, it expresses its relation of subordination to God, and the kind of services which the former must render to the latter. The stewardship of home is that official character with which God has invested the family. In this sense the proprietorship of parents is from God. They are invested only with delegated authority. Their home is held by them only in trust. It belongs to them in the same sense in which a household belongs to a steward. It is not at their absolute disposal. It is the "household of the Lord," and they are to live and rule therein as the Lord directs. They are to appropriate it and dispose of its interests according to the known law and will of their divine Master, and in this sense, yield, with their whole household, a voluntary subordination to His authority.

As a stewardship, God has entrusted the Christian home with important interests. He has committed to her trust, body and soul, talents and means of grace. He has entrusted to the parents the training of their children both for time and for eternity. These children are the heritage of the Lord; they are not at the absolute disposal of their parents; but merely entrusted to their care to be educated and dealt with according to the will of God.

There is one great peculiarity in this stewardship of the Christian family,—the absolute identity of interest between the Master and the steward. The interest of the former is that also of the latter; and the latter, in promoting the interest of his Lord, is but advancing his own welfare. Such is the economy of the gospel, and it is this which makes the servitude of the Christian so delightful. Faithfulness to God is faithfulness to our own souls. Parents who are thus faithful to God must be faithful to themselves and to their children. Thus, then, the interest of God in our families is the welfare of all the members. When we act towards our children as God directs, we are but promoting their greatest welfare. This is one prominent feature of God's mercy towards us in all His dealings with us. He identifies His interest with the interest of His people. This is a powerful incentive to parental integrity, and is beautifully exemplified in the mother of Moses. When the daughter of Pharaoh said to her, "Take this child and nurse it for me, and I will pay thee thy wages," was not the interest of the queen and the nurse the same? In nursing him for the queen, that devoted mother nursed him also for herself; and in doing this, she was also promoting the welfare of her son, and executing the will of God concerning him. This illustrates the principle of stewardship in the Christian home. Of every child, God says to its parent,—

> "Go nurse it for the King of heaven,
> And He will pay thee hire."

Here is the important trust; here, too, is the duty of the steward. It is a trust from God, and the nursing is for God. The child is a tender plant, an invaluable treasure, more priceless than gold, or pearls, or diamonds. Your duty as a steward, is to nurse it, to cultivate it, to polish the lovely gem, to take care of it. And in doing this for God, are you not also doing it for the child,—yea, if you are Christian parents,—for yourselves? Will not even natural affection, as well as the discerning eye of faith, like that of the mother of Moses, detect in this stewardship an identity between the interest of the Master and that of the steward? It was not the simple compensation which stimulated the mother of Moses to accede to the proposition of Pharaoh's daughter. What cared she for the "hire," if she could but save her son! This was her great reward.

Thus the interest of the child should be the reward of the parent. God will, it is true, reward the faithful steward of the family; but He specially rewards and blesses parental faithfulness in making His purposes concerning home, identical with the parent's and the children's welfare. In this domestic stewardship,

"Like warp and woof, all interests
Are woven fast;
Locked in sympathy like the keys
Of an organ vast."

"Fear not, little flock; for it is your Father's good pleasure to give you the kingdom. Who, then, is that faithful and wise steward whom his Lord shall make ruler over his household, to give them their portion of meat in due season? Blessed is that servant whom his Lord, when He cometh, shall find so doing. Of a truth I say unto you, that He will make him ruler over all he hath. But and if that servant say in his heart, my Lord delayeth His coming, and shall begin to beat the men-servants and maidens, and to eat and drink, and to be drunken; the Lord of that servant will come in a day when he looketh not for him, and at an hour when he is not aware, and will cut him in sunder, and will appoint him his portion with the unbelievers. And that servant which knew his Lord's will and prepared not himself, neither did according to His will, shall be beaten with many stripes."

Here, then, we have the character and duties of the steward in the Christian home, the rewards of their faithfulness, and the penalties of their unfaithfulness. As the stewards of God, we must be faithful, giving the souls as well as the bodies of our children "their meat in due season;" we must not "waste the goods" of our Lord, but be "blameless, not self-willed, not soon angry, not given to filthy lucre, but a lover of hospitality, sober, just, holy, temperate, holding fast the faithful word as we have been taught." As the faithful stewards of God, we should dedicate our household in all respects to Him, and make it tributary to His glory. "Seek ye first the kingdom of heaven, and all these things shall be added unto you." The unjust steward will first seek the world and the things of the world, its gold, its pleasures and its honors; and after that seek the kingdom of heaven. But this is reversing the order of procedure as prescribed by the Master; it is running counter to His will, and, consequently, wasting His goods.

But the greatest trust committed to parents is, the souls of their children; and hence their most responsible duty, as the stewards of God, is to attend to their salvation. You should "give them the bread of life in due season." It will be of no avail for you to inquire, "What shall they eat, and what shall they drink, and wherewithal shall they be clothed;" if you neglect this their highest interest and your greatest trust? "What shall a man give in exchange for his soul?" It is not the wealth, nor the magnificence of life which will make your home happy; these are but the outward and fleeting ornaments of the world, and are too often the gaudy drapery in which demon guilt and misery are clothed.

> "The cobwebbed cottage, with its ragged wall
> Of mouldering mud, is royalty to me,"

if souls are there "fed upon the sincere milk of the word," and "trained up in the ways of the Lord." The training of the soul for heaven is both the duty and the glory of our homes. What if parents lay up affluence here for their children, and secure for them all that the world calls interest, while they permit their souls to famish, and do nothing for their redemption! Will not such parents be denounced in the day of judgment as unjust and unfaithful stewards? And yet alas! how many such Christian parents there are who prostitute this highest interest of home either at the altar of mammon or of fashion! The precious time and talents with which God has entrusted them, they squander away in things of folly and of sin, leaving their children to grow up in spiritual ignorance and wickedness, while they resort to balls and theaters and masquerades, in pursuit of unhallowed amusement and pleasure.

Such are unnatural parents as well as unjust stewards, and their homes will ere long be made desolate. Other parents prostitute the holy trust of home to money. They are "self-willed" stewards, "given to filthy lucre," who, for the sake of a few dollars, will "waste the goods" of their Lord, make their homes a drudgery, and work their children like their horses, bring them up in ignorance, like "calves in the stall," and contract their whole existence, and all their capacities, desires and hopes, in the narrow compass of work and money.

We would direct the attention of such parents to our last thought upon the stewardship of the Christian home, (the practical view of which we shall consider in the next chapter,) viz., that it involves the principle of accountability. It implies a settlement, a time when the Master and his steward shall meet together to close accounts.

"Give an account of thy stewardship; for thou mayest be no longer steward." That time will be when "the dead, both small and great, shall stand before God." Then He will examine into your stewardship. He will ask you how you employed your talents, and to what purpose you appropriated those interests He committed to your trust; and whether you were faithful to those souls which "hung upon your hire;" whether you "nursed them for him," and whether you provided them with "their meat in due season." And if you can answer, "Yea, Lord, here are those talents which thou hast given me; behold I have gained for thee five other talents. Here, Lord, are those children whom thou hast given me; I have brought them up in thy nurture, and trained them in thy ways." Your Lord will then answer, "Well done, thou good and faithful servant, thou hast been faithful over a few things; behold I will make thee ruler over many things; enter thou into the joy of thy Lord!"

But if you have been unfaithful as stewards, and have made your household unproductive for God, then you shall hear from his lips the dreadful denunciation, "Thou wicked and slothful servant!" "Take the talent from him, and cast ye the unprofitable servant into outer darkness; there shall be weeping and gnashing of teeth; for unto every one that hath shall be given, and he shall have abundance; but from him that hath not shall be taken away even that which he hath!"

CHAPTER VII.

RESPONSIBILITIES OF THE CHRISTIAN HOME.

> "What a holy charge
> Is theirs!—with what a kingly power their love
> Might rule the fountains of the new-born mind!
> Warn them to wake at early dawn, and sow
> Good seed before the world has sown its tares."

From the potent influence and moral stewardship of the Christian home, we may infer its responsibility. The former is the argument for the latter. The extent of the one is the measure of the other. "To whom much is given, of them much will be required." Our responsibilities are thus commensurate with our abilities. If the latter are properly devoted, we have our reward; if not, our curse. God will hold us accountable for the achievements we make by the abilities he has given us. If he gives us a field to cultivate, seed to sow, plants to train up, then we are responsible for the harvest, just in proportion to our agency in its production. If there is not a harvest of the right kind, because we neglected to cultivate the soil, to sow the proper seed, and to train up the plants, then He will hold us accountable, and "we shall not come out thence till we have paid the uttermost farthing."

This is an evident gospel principle. Who will doubt its application to the Christian home? The family is such a field; the seed of good or evil the parents can sow therein; their children are young and tender plants, entrusted to their care; their mission from God is to "bring them up in his nurture" and to "train them in his ways." And where God gives the command, he also gives the power to obey.

If, then, by their neglect, these tender plants are blighted, grow up in the crooked ways of folly and iniquity, and the leprosy of sin spread its dreadful infection over all the posterity of home; if, as a consequence of their unfaithfulness, the family becomes a moral desolation, and the anathemas of unnumbered souls in perdition, rise up in the day of judgment against them; or if, on the other hand, as the fruit of their faithful stewardship, blessings and testimonials of gratitude are now pouring forth from the sainted loved ones in glory, is it not plain that a responsibility rests upon the Christian home, commensurate with those abilities which God has given her, and with those interests he has entrusted to her care?

Let us look at the objective force of this. The family is responsible for the kind of influence she exerts upon her members Look at this in its practical light. There is a family. God has given children to the parents. How fondly they cling to them, and look up to them for support and direction. They inherit from their parents a predisposition to evil or to good; they imitate them as their example, in all things, take their word as the law of life, and follow in their footsteps as the sure path to happiness. These parents are members of the church, and, as such, have dedicated their children to the Lord at the altar of baptism, and there in the presence of God and a witnessing assembly, they vowed to bring them up in the nurture of their divine Master, and to minister in spiritual things to their souls.

Yet in this home, no prayer is offered up, no bible instructions given, no holy example set, no christian government and discipline instituted, no religious interests promoted. But on the other hand, sin is overlooked, winked at, and the world alone sought. These children behold their parents toil day after day to provide for their natural life; they notice the interest they take in their health and education, and the self-denial with which they seek to secure for them a temporal competency. And from all this they quickly and very justly infer that their parents love their bodies and value this world, and by the force of filial imitation they soon learn to do the same, and with their parents, neglect their souls and kneel at the altars of Mammon rather than bow in prayer before God. And thus they go on from one step in departure from God to another, until they die without hope and without salvation.

Tell me now, will not God hold these parents responsible for the ruin of their children? Will not the "blood of their destruction rest upon them?" Will not the "voice of that blood" cry out from their family against them? If, as a consequence of their negligence and of the unholy influence they exerted upon them, they become desperadoes in crime and villainy, and at last drench their hands in a brother's blood; and expiate their guilt upon the gibbet, and from there go down to the grave of infamy and to the hell of the murderer, will not their blood "cry unto them," and will not the woes and anathemas of Almighty God come in upon them like a flood?

Home-responsibility may be inferred from the relation of the family to God as a stewardship. We have seen that parents are stewards of God in their household, and that as such they are placed over their children, invested with delegated authority. God entrusts them to the care of their parents. Their nature is pliable, fit for any impression, exposed to sin and ruin, entering upon a course of life which must terminate in eternal happiness or misery, with bodies to develop, minds to educate, hearts to mould, volitions to direct, habits to form, energies to rule, pursuits to follow, interests to secure, temptations to resist, trials to endure, souls to save! Oh, how the parental heart must swell with emotions too big for utterance, when they contemplate these features of their important trust. What a mission this, to superintend the character and shape the destiny of such a being! Such is the plastic power you exert upon it, that upon your guidance will hinge its weal or its woe; and yours, therefore, will be the lasting benefit or the lasting shame. What you are now doing for your children is incorporated with their very being, and will be as imperishable as their undying souls. As the stewards of God, your provision for them will be "either a savor of life unto life or a savor of death unto death."

We have seen that God has given to you the ability and means of making them subservient to his glory; and hence from you he will require them as entrusted talents. If you have been unfaithful to them, your punishment will be in proportion to the wretchedness entailed upon your children. If, instead of the bread from heaven, you feed their souls with the husks of life, and lead them on by the opiates of bastard joys; if, "when they ask of you bread, you give them a stone, or for a fish, you give them a serpent," will it not be "more tolerable for Sodom and Gomorrah in the day of judgment than for you?"

Thus, therefore, you see, christian parents, how your responsibility is measured by the magnitude of those interests committed to your care, by the kind of influence you exert over them, and by the enormity of that guilt and wo which are consequent upon your unfaithfulness. Let this be an incentive to parental integrity. The day is rapidly approaching when you must give an account of your stewardship. Oh, what, if in that day you behold your children "fit for the eternal burning," and remember that that fitness is but the impress of a parent's hand!

Though it is painful to lose a child here; bitter tears are shed; pungent agonies are felt; there are heart-burnings kindled over the grave of buried love. But oh, how much more agonizing it is to bend over the dying bed of an impenitent, ruined child! And especially if, in that terrible moment, he turns his eyes, wild with despair and ominous of curses, upon the parents, and ascribes his ruin to their neglect! Let me ask you, would not this part of that sad drama add to your cup of bitterness, give a fearful emphasis to all your sighs, and burnings to your flooding tears? God would also speak to you, and say as he did to Cain, "the voice of thy" children's "blood crieth unto me!" "And now thou art cursed from the earth which hath opened her mouth to receive thy" children's "blood from thy hand."

But the scene would not close at the death-bed of your child; the second act would open at the bar of God. The maledictions of that ruined one would there be poured out with increased fury upon you. Parents of my home on earth! I am lost—lost forever! Soon I shall go where "the worm dieth not, and the fire is not quenched." Had you, in the home of my childhood, but instructed me, and been as faithful to my soul as you were to my body, I might stand here with a palm of victory in my hand, a crown of glory on my head, the joy of the redeemed in my heart, and with hosannas of praise upon my lips, rise upward to the untold felicities of God's eternal throne! But you did not! You fed my body, but you starved my soul, and left it to perish forever! Cursed be the day in which you begat me, and the paps that gave me suck! Cursed be the years that I lived under your roof, —cursed be you! Oh, parents, such rebuke would leave an undying worm in your souls; and would cry unto you from the very depths of hell.

This is no over-wrought picture. It is but the scripture prospectus of that terrible scene which shall be enacted "in the terrible and notable day of the Lord," when every Christian home shall be called to give an "account of her stewardship," and be dealt with "according to the deeds done in the body."

And let me say too, that a similar and corresponding responsibility rests upon those children who enjoy the benefits of a faithful Christian home. They must answer to God for every blessing there enjoyed. If they turn a deaf ear and a cold heart to all the entreaties of their parents, and resist those saving influences which are brought to bear upon them, and as a consequence, become outcasts from society and from heaven, then let me warn them that, every prayer they heard at the family altar, every lesson given, every admonition delivered, and every holy example set them, by their pious parents, will be ingredients in that bitter cup which it will take eternity for them to exhaust! Oh, children of the Christian home! think of this, and remember the responsibility of enjoying the precious benefits of a pious, faithful parent. They will be your weal or your woe,—your lasting glory or your lasting shame!

And, ye parents, be faithful to those little ones that are growing up "like olive plants around your table," so that in the day of judgment, you may say with joy, in the full assurance of reward, "Here are we, Lord, and the children whom thou hast given us!" And your reward shall be, "Well done, thou good and faithful servant! Enter thou into the joy of thy Lord!

CHAPTER VIII.

THE FAMILY BIBLE.

"What household thoughts around thee, as their shrine,
Cling reverently!—Of anxious looks beguiled,
My mother's eyes upon thy page divine,
Each day were bent; her accents, gravely mild,
Breathed out thy love; whilst I, a dreamy child,
Wandered on breeze-like fancies oft away,
. . . . . . Yet would the solemn Word,
At times, with kindlings of young wonder heard
Fall on my wakened spirit, there to be
A seed not lost; for which in darker years,
O, book of heaven! I pour with grateful tears,
Heart-blessings on the holy dead, and thee!"

The family bible! What sweet and hallowed memories cling like tendrils around that book of books! How familiar its sacred pages! How often in the sunny days of childhood, we were fed from its manna by the maternal hand! It was our guide to the opening path of life, and a lamp to the feeble, faltering steps of youth. Who can forget the family bible? It was the household oracle of our grandfathers and grandmothers,—of our dear parents. It bears the record of their venerated names; their birth, their baptism, their confirmation, their marriage, are here; and

> "Though they are with the silent dead,
> Here are they living still!"

How joyfully they gathered around the cheerful hearth to read this book divine. How often their hearts drew consolation from its living springs! What a balm it has poured into bleeding and disconsolate hearts. It has irradiated with the glories of eternal day, the darkest chamber of their home. What brilliant hopes and promises it has hung around the parental heart! And here too are the names of our parents,—long since gathered with their fathers. Here too are our names, and birth, and baptism, written by that parental hand, long since cold in death!

> "My father read this holy book
> To brothers, sisters dear;
> How calm was my poor mother's look,
> Who loved God's word to hear.
> Her angel-face—I see it yet!
> What thronging memories come?
> Again that little group is met
> Within the halls of home!"

That old family bible! Do we not love it? Our names and our children's names are drawn from it. It is the message of our Father in heaven. It is the link which connects our earthly with our heavenly home; and when we open its sacred page, we gaze upon words which our loved ones in heaven have whispered, and which dwell even now upon their sainted lips; and which when we utter them, there is joy in heaven! We would, therefore, say to the infidel, of this "family tree," as the returning child said to the woodsman, of the old tree which sheltered the slumbers and frolics of his childhood, "I'll protect it now."

The old family bible! What an inheritance from a Christian home! Clasp it, child, to thy heart; it was the gift of a mother's love! It bears the impress of her hand; it is the memento of her devotedness to thee; and when just before her spirit took its flight to a better land, she gave it as a guide for her child to the same happy home:

"My mother's hand this bible clasped;
She, dying, gave it me!"

And the spirit of that sainted mother shall still whisper to me through these sacred pages. In the light of this lamp I follow her to a better home. With this blessed chart I shall meet her in heaven.

"With faltering lip and throbbing brow,
I press it to my heart."

Every Christian home has a family bible. It is found in the hut as well as in the palace. It is an indispensable appendage to home. Without it the Christian home would be in darkness; with it, she is a "light which shineth in darkness." It is the chart and compass of the parent and the child in their pilgrimage to a better home.

> "Therein thy dim eyes
> Will meet a cheering light; and silent words
> Of mercy breathed from heaven, will be exhaled
> From the blest page into thy withered heart."

Like an ethereal principle of light and life, its blessed truths extend with electric force through all the avenues and elements of the home-existence, "giving music to language, elevation to thought, vitality to feeling, intensity to power, beauty and happiness."

The bible is adapted to the Christian home. It is the book for the family. It is the guardian of her interests, the exposition of her duties, her privileges, her hopes and her enjoyments. It exposes her errors, reveals her authority and government, sanctions her obedience, proclaims her promises, and points out her path to heaven. It makes sacred her marriages, furnishes names for her children, gives the sacrament of her dedication to God, and consecrates her bereavements. It is the fountain of her richest blessings, the source of her true consolation, and the ground of her brightest hope. It is, therefore, the book of home. She may have large and splendid libraries; history, poetry, philosophy, fiction, yea, all the works of classic Greece and Rome, may crowd upon her shelves; but of these she will soon grow wearied, and the dust of neglect will gather thick upon their gilded leaves; but of the bible the Christian home can never become weary. Its sufficiency for all her purposes will throw a garland of freshness around every page; its variety and manifoldness; its simplicity and beauty; its depth of thought and intensity of feeling, adapt it to every capacity and to every want, to every emergency and to every member, of the household. The little child and the old man, hoary with the frost of many winters, find an equal interest there. The rich and the poor, the learned and the ignorant, the high and the low, are alike enriched from its inexhaustible treasury.

It is a book for the mind, the heart, the conscience, the will and the life. It suits the palace and the cottage, the afflicted and the prosperous, the living and the dying. It is a comfort to "the house of mourning," and a check to "the house of feasting." It "giveth seed to the sower, and bread to the eater." It is simple, yet grand; mysterious, yet plain; and though from God, it is nevertheless, within the comprehension of a little child. You may send your children to school to study other books, from which they may be educated for this world; but in this divine book they study the science of the eternal world.

The family bible has given to the Christian home that unmeasured superiority in all the dignities and decencies and enjoyments of life, over the home of the heathen. It has elevated woman, revealed her true mission, developed the true idea and sacredness of marriage and of the home-relationship; it has unfolded the holy mission of the mother, the responsibilities of the parent, and the blessings of the child. Take this book from the family, and she will degenerate into a mere conventionalism, marriage into a "social contract;" the spirit of mother will depart; natural affection will sink to mere brute fondness, and what we now call home would become a den of sullen selfishness and barbaric lust!

The bible should, therefore, be the text-book of home-education. Where it is not, parents are recreant to their duty. It is the basis of all teaching, because it reveals "the truth, the way and the life," because it is God's testimony and message, and is "profitable for doctrine, for reproof, for correction, for instruction in righteousness," and was written "for our learning, that we, through patience and comfort of the scriptures, might have hope," and be made "wise unto salvation."

"While thou wert teaching my lips to move
And my heart to rise in prayer,
I learned the way to a home above;
And thou shalt meet me there!"

Its invaluable treasures, its manifoldness, its beautiful simplicity, its striking narrative, its startling history, its touches of home-life, its expansive views of human nature, of this life and of that which is to come, its poetry, eloquence, and soul-stirring sympathies and aspirations, make it the book for home-training. These features of its character will develop in beautiful harmony the whole nature of your child. Do you wish to inspire them with song? What songs are like those of Zion? Do you wish them to come under the influence of eloquent oration? What orations so eloquent as those of the prophets, of Christ, and of his apostles? Do you desire to refine and elevate their souls with beauty and sublimity? Here in these sacred pages is a beauty ever fresh, and a sublimity which towers in dazzling radiance far beyond the reach of human genius. This is evident from the fact that tributes of admiration have been paid to the bible by the most eminent poets, jurists, statesmen, and philosophers, such as Milton, Hale, Boyle, Newton and Locke. Erasmus and John Locke betook themselves solely to the bible, after they had wandered through the gloomy maze of human erudition. Neither Grecian song nor Roman eloquence; neither the waters of Castalia, nor the fine-spun theorisms of scholastic philosophy, could satisfy their yearnings. But when they wandered amid the consecrated bowers of Zion, and drank from Siloah's brook, the thirst of their genius was quenched, and they took their seats with Mary at the feet of Jesus, and like little children, learned of him!

Even deists and infidels have yielded their tribute of praise. What says the infidel Rosseau? Hear him: "The majesty of the scriptures strikes me with astonishment. Look at the volumes of the philosophers, with all their pomp, how contemptible do they appear in comparison with this! Is it possible that a book at once so simple and sublime, can be the work of men?" Thus

> "Learning and zeal, from age to age,
> Have worshiped, loved, explored the page."

How often is this precious book abused! In many would-be Christian homes, it is used more for an ornament of fashion than for a lamp to the Christian's path. We find the bible upon their parlor table, but how seldom in the family room! They make it a part of their fashionable furniture, to be looked at as a pretty, gilded thing. Its golden clasps and beautiful binding make it an attractive appendage to the parlor. Hence they buy the bible, but not the truth it contains. They place it upon the table as such; and indeed many do not even give it that prominence, but, yielding to the taste of fashion, place it under the parlor table, and there it rests, unmolested, untouched and unread even for years. In many professedly religious families this is their family bible! Ah! it is not so heartsome as that well-marked and long-used old bible which lies upon the table of the nursery room, speaking of many year's service in family devotion! The other unused bible seems like a stranger to the home-heart, and lies in the parlor just to show their visiting friends that they have a bible! Go into the nursery and other private apartments of that home, and you see no bible, while you behold piles of romance and filthy novels,—those exponents of a vitiated taste and a corrupt society, suited to destroy the young forever;—whose outward appearance indicates a studied perusal by both parents and children, and shows perhaps that they have been wept over; and whose inward substance must ever nauseate healthy reason, as well as poison the heart of youth, leading them from the sober realities of life into a world of nonentities.

But upon the family bible you cannot trace the hand of diligent piety. It is shoved back into some part of the room, as a worthless thing, obsolete and superfluous. And see! it is not even kept in decent order. The dust of many day's neglect has gathered thick upon its lids. Oh, Christian parents, when you thus close up the wells of salvation by the trash of degenerate taste and vitiated morals, you are despising the testimonies of the Lord, and leading your children step by step to the verge of destruction. You may buy them splendid bibles, gilt and clasped with gold, and have their names labeled in golden letters upon its lid; but if the good old family bible is neglected, and the yellow covered literature of the day substituted in its stead; if you permit them to buy and read love-sick tales in preference to their bible, and they see you do the same, you are but making a mock of God's Word, and must answer before Him for your children's neglect of its sacred pages.

Let me, therefore, affectionately admonish you

to be faithful to that precious book you call the family bible. Read it to your children every day. From its sacred pages teach them the way to live and the way to die. Let it be an opened, studied family chart to guide you and them in visions of untold glory to the many mansions of your Father's offered home in heaven. It will soothe your sorrows, calm your fears, strengthen your faith, brighten your hopes, and throw around the graves of the loved and the cherished dead, the light and promise of reunion in heaven!

"A drop of balm from this rich store,
Hath healed the broken heart once more.
Like angels round a dying bed,
Its truths a heavenly radiance shed;
And hovering on celestial wings,
Breathe music from unnumbered strings."

CHAPTER IX.

INFANCY.

"A BABE in a house is a well-spring of pleasure, a messenger of peace and love;
A resting place for innocence on earth; a link between angels and men;
Yet it is a talent of trust to be rendered back with interest;
A delight, but redolent of care, honey sweet, but lacking not the bitter,
For character groweth day by day, and all things aid it in unfolding,
And the bent unto good or evil may be given in the hours of infancy."

THE birth of each child constitutes a new era in the Christian home, and multiplies its cares, its pleasures and its responsibilities. The first-born babe, like

"The first gilt thing
That wears the trembling pearls of spring,"

throws the rainbow colors of hope and joy over the bowers of home, and awakens in the bosom of parents, emotions and sympathies, new-born and never before experienced; cords in the heart, before untouched, now begin to thrill with new joy; sympathies, before unfelt, now swell the bosom. Sleep on, thou little one, in thy "rosy mesh of infancy," in the first buddings of thy being! These hours of thy innocence are the happiest of thy life. Thou art "the parent's transport and the parent's care." Blessings are fondly poured upon thy head. Rest thee there in thy little bed, thou happy emblem of the loved and pure in heaven'

> "Visions sure of joy
> Are gladdening his rest; and ah, who knows
> But waiting angels do converse in sleep
> With babes like this!"

imparting to his infant soul unutterable things, whispering soft of bliss immortal given, and pouring into his new-born senses the dreams of opening heaven.

What charms and momentous interests surround the cradle of infancy! When the first wailing of dependence reaches the listening ear, what new-born sympathies spring up in the parent's bosom! What a thrill of rapture the first soft smile of her babe sends to the mother's heart! It is this, the parents' likeness unsullied by their faults and cares; it is this, their living love in personal being,—their love breathing and smiling before them, lisping their names; it is this,—their new-born hope and care,—that gives to infancy such a charm, such a never-dying interest, and causes the parent to cling to it with such fond tenacity. "Can a mother forget her sucking child?" Never, while she claims a mother's heart! The couch of her babe is the depository of all those fond hopes and joys and cares and memories to which a mother's heart is sacred.

The infant is the most interesting member of the Christian home. It is the first budding of home-life, disclosing every day some new beauty, "the father's lustre and the mother's bloom," to gladden the hearts of the family. "As the dewy morning is more beautiful than the perfect day; as the opening bud is more lovely than the full blown flower, so is the joyous dawn of infant life more interesting than the calm monotony of riper years." It is the most interesting, because the purest, member of the household. It is the connecting link which binds home to its great antitype above. "Ye stand nearest to God, ye little ones," nearer than those who have tasted the bitter cup of actual sin. They are the budding promises, the young loves, the precious plants of home; they are its sunshine, its progressive interest, its prophetic happiness, the first link in the chain of its perpetuity. Like the purple hue of the wild heath, throwing its gay color over the rugged hill-side, they cast a magic polish over the spirit of the parent, causing the home-fireside to glow with new life and cheerfulness.

Infants are emblems of the loved and sainted

ones in heaven. "Of such is the kingdom of heaven." "Except ye become as this little child, ye cannot enter into the kingdom of heaven." This is based upon proper principles. The heart of the child is purely devotional and confidential. It is a helpless dependent upon the parent. It abdicates its self-will with joy; silently do the laws of home control it; its reverence and love are the melody of its being; its life is an exchange of obedience for protection. Its path is chosen for it by the lamp of parental experience, and the calm pure light of a mother's love. How close it keeps to the heart that loves it, and to the hand that leads it! It looks without doubt or suspicion in the parent's eye, and makes the parent's home and interest its own.

Here is a picture of the true child of God in his tent-home on earth, and in his eternal home in heaven. For this they are given to us. As they are to us, their parents, so should we be to our Father in heaven, and so are all those loved and sainted ones who have gone before us.

"Little children, flowers from heaven,
Strewn on earth by God's own hand,
Earnest emblems to us given,
From the fields of angel-land!"

Hence it was that Jesus loved little children, took them in His arms, blessed them, and regarded them as "the lambs of His flock." "He shall gather the lambs with His arm." He gazed with pleasure into their sweet faces, invited their parents to bring them unto Him, and held them up as the type of the spirit and character of the admitted into heaven. And the aged John, having in view this typical character of children, addressed his followers as his little children!

Infants are helpless dependents upon others for subsistence and protection. If abandoned at their birth, their first breath would soon be succeeded by their last. Hence they demand all the attention which maternal love and tenderness can bestow. They live like the tender bud or the opening blossom, exposed to the blight of a thousand fortuitous events. Hence their existence is very precarious; in a moment they may sink like the frosted flower in its lovely blush. This may be said of the soul as well as of the body and mind. What an argument, therefore, we have here for parental diligence and promptness in duty to the eternal as well as to the temporal well-being of the child.

The infant is the first prophecy of the man. It is the germ of manhood. It is the man in a state of involution. It is the undeveloped man. Infancy is the twilight of life,—the first morning of an endless being, the age of germ and of mere sense. As the first dawn of spring is the season of the undeveloped harvest, so childhood is manhood in possibility. The infant is the vernal bud of life; it is a being of promise and of hope,—the prophecy of the future man. Hence the age of education. The mother, in the nursery, is ever evolving into the strength of maturity those powers of her child which will be wielded for happiness or for misery. Her babe is an "embryo angel, or an infant fiend." We behold in that fragile form, the bud of the strong man,—the possibility of one who may in a few years arouse with his thrilling eloquence a slumbering nation, or with the torch and sword of revolution, overturn empires and dethrone kings, or with his feet upon the walls of Zion, and the words of life upon his lips, overthrow the strongholds of Satan, and bring the rebel sinner in penitence to the feet of Jesus. Yea, we see in that wailing infant of a week, the outspringing of an immortal spirit which may soon hover on cherub-pinion around the throne of God, or perhaps, in a few years, sink to the regions of untold anguish. Oh, it is this which gives to the cradle of infancy such a thrilling interest. The star of those new-born hopes, which hangs over it, will set in eternal night, or rise with increasing splendor, till it is lost in the full blaze of eternal day!

Infants are a great, a dangerous and responsible trust. They are the property of God,—"an heritage from the Lord," given to their parents as a loan, a "talent of trust to be rendered back with interest." The infant is especially the mother's trust.

> "Though first by thee it lived, on thee it smiled,
> Yet not for thee existence must it hold,
> For God's it is, not thine!"

Given by its Creator in trust to her, it is her task

to bring it up for God. Here especially do we see the holy mission of the mother. None but the mother's heart and love can give security for this trust. The father is unfit by nature for the delicate training of infancy. The mother's hand alone can smooth the infant's couch, and her voice alone can sing him to his rosy rest. Her never-wearied love alone can watch beside him "till the last pale star had set,"

> "While to the fullness of her heart's glad heavings
> His fair cheek rose and fell; and his bright hair
> Waved softly to her breast."

She is the ministering angel of infancy, and the priestess of the nursery of home. She sets the first seal, makes the first stamp, gives the first direction, supplies the first want, and soothes the first sorrow. To her is committed human life in its most helpless and dangerous state. Touch it then with the rude hand of parental selfishness; let it grow up in a barren soil, amid noxious weeds, under the influence of unholy example; and the delicate tints of this blossom will soon fade; the blush of loveliness will soon give way to the blight of moral deformity.

Hence every babe will be the parent's glory or the parent's shame, their weal or their woe. If entrusted to them, God will hold them responsible for its moral training. He will require it from them with interest. Their trust involves the eternal happiness or misery of their child. The productions of art will perish; the sun will be blotted out, and all the glory and magnificence of the world will vanish away, but your babe will live forever. It will survive the wreck of nature, and either shine as a diadem in the Redeemer's crown of glory, or dwell in the blackness and darkness of perdition forever.

To you, Christian parents, as the stewards of God, this precious being is entrusted. The care of its body, mind and spirit is committed to you; and its character and destiny in after life will be the fruit of your dealings with it. It looks to you for all things. It confides in you, draws its confidence from your protection, relies on your known love, takes you as the pattern of its life, imitates you as its example, learns from you as its teacher, is ruled by you as its governor, is measured by you as its model, feels satisfied with you as its sufficiency, and rests its all upon you as its all and in all.

Thus you are the very life and soul of its being, and hence in its maturity, it will be a fair exponent of your character. You are the center around which its life revolves, the circumference beyond which it never seeks to go. What, therefore, if you are unfit to move and act in its presence! What, if in its imitation of you, its life be a progressive departure from God! Oh, what, if in the day of judgment, it be an outcast from heaven, and, as such, bear the impress of a parent's hand! God will then hold you accountable for every injury you may have done your child.

Begin, therefore, the work of training that infant, now, while its nature is pliable, susceptible, yet tenacious of first impressions. "With his mother's milk the young child drinketh education." What you now do for your child will be seen in all future ages. "Scratch the green rind of a sapling, or wantonly twist it in the soil, the scarred and crooked oak will tell of thee for centuries to come." "It will not depart from the ways in which you train it." If, therefore, you would be a blessing to your child, and avert those terrible judgments of God which rest upon parental delinquency, begin now, while your infant is in the cradle, to sow the seeds of life. Prune well the tender olive plants, and direct its evolving life in the way God would have it go.

> "Soon as the playful innocent can prove
> A tear of pity or a smile of love,"

teach it to lisp the name of Jesus and to walk in His commandments. But alas! how many Christian parents are recreant to this duty! How many destroy their children by the over-indulgence of a misdirected love and sympathy, and by procrastinating the period of home-education. Forgetful of the power of first impressions, they wait until their children are established in sin, and the seeds of evil are sown in their hearts.

This is the reason why so many reckless and wicked children come out of Christian homes. Their parents permit their misdirected fondness to absorb all their thoughts and apprehensions of danger and responsibility. Their love for the body and mind of their children seems to repel all love for, or interest in, their soul. The former they tenderly nurse, fondly caress, and zealously direct. But the soul of the infant is unhonored, unloved and uncared for. It is blighted in its first bursting of beauty. Oh, cruel and unthinking parents! why will you thus abuse the loveliest and noblest part of your child? Why make that babe of yours a mere plaything? If "out of the mouths of babes and sucklings God has perfected praise," then why not train them up to praise Him? "Take heed that ye despise not one of these little ones, for I say unto you, that in heaven their angels do always behold the face of my Father which is in heaven." Oh, you who are the nurse of infant innocence, have you ever thought of the deep curse that will attend your neglect of the babe which God has given you! Have you, pious mother, as you pressed your child to your bosom, ever thought that it would one day be a witness for or against you? Far better for thee and it that it were not born and you never revered as mother, than that you should nourish it for spiritual beggary here, and for the eternal burnings hereafter! Oh, look upon that babe! It is the gift of God,—given to thee, mother, to nurse for Him. Look upon that cherished one! See its smile of confidence turned to you! It is a frail and helpless bark on the tumultuous sea of life; it looks to you for direction,—for compass and for chart; your prayers for it will be heard; your hand can save it; the touch of your impressions will be a savor of life unto life, or of death unto death.

> "Then take the heart thy charms have won,
> And nurse it for the skies!"

CHAPTER X.

HOME DEDICATION.

"THE rose was rich in bloom on Sharon's plain,
When a young mother with her first born thence
Went up to Zion, for the boy was vowed
Unto the Temple-service; by the hand
She led him, and her silent soul, the while,
Oft as the dewy laughter of his eye
Met her sweet serious glance, rejoiced to think
That aught so pure, so beautiful, was hers,
To bring before her God!"

BEAUTIFUL thought, and thrice beautiful deed,—fresh from the pure fount of maternal piety! The Hebrew mother consecrating her first-born child to the Temple-service,—dedicating him to the God who gave him! What visions of unearthly glory must have been before her, as she led her little boy before the altar of the "King of kings!" Happy mother! thou hast long since gone to thy great reward. And happy child! to be led by such a mother. Ye are now together in that temple "not made with hands, eternal in the heavens," and with united voice swelling those anthems of glory which are poured from angelic lips and harps to Him who sitteth upon the throne.

What an example is this for the Christian parent! God is the Father of every home. From Him cometh down every good and perfect gift; and hence to Him should all the interests and the loved ones of the household be dedicated. This is essential to the very conception of a Christian home.

But especially should the children be dedicated to the Lord. That infant over which the mother bends and watches with such passionate fondness, is "an heritage of the Lord," given to her only in trust, and will again be required from her. As soon as children are given they should be devoted to Him; for "the flower, when offered in the bud, is no mean sacrifice." Then and then only will parents properly respect and value their offspring, and deal with them as becometh the property of God. By withholding them, the parents become guilty of the deed of Ananias and Sapphira. Like the Hebrew mother, every Christian parent will gratefully devote them to Him, and rejoice that they have such a pure oblation to "bring before their God."

"My child, my treasure, I have given thee up
To Him who gave thee me! Ere yet thine eye
Rested with conscious love upon thy mother,
Long ere thy lips could gently sound her name,
She gave thee up to God; she sought for thee

One boon alone, that thou mightest be His child;
His child sojourning on this distant land,
His child above the blue and radiant sky,
'Tis all I ask of thee, beloved one, still!"

Here is a dedication worthy of a Christian mother. Natural affection and human pride might lead the fond mother to dedicate her child at the altar of Mammon, to gold, to fame, to magnificence, to the world. But no, every wish of the pious mother's heart is merged in one great wish and prayer, "that thou may'st be His child."

The dedication of our children to the Lord is one of the first acts of the religious ministry of home. All the means of grace will be of no avail without it. What will the acts of the gospel minister avail if they are not preceded by an offering of himself to the Lord who has called him? His holy vocation demands such an offering. It is his voluntary response to and acceptance of his calling of God. Thus with Christian parents. What will baptism avail, so far as the parents are concerned, without this dedication of their children to Him in whose name they are baptised? No more than the form apart from the spirit. It would be but a mockery of God.

We have a beautiful example and illustration of this dedication, in the family of the faithful Abraham. "By faith Abraham, when he was tried, offered up Isaac: and he that had received the promises offered up his only begotten son."

We might at first view regard this act of his as an evidence of his want of parental sympathy and tenderness. But not so; it is rather an evidence of these. What he did was the prompting of a true faith, yielding implicit obedience to the Lord, and offering as an obligation to Him, what he loved most upon earth. Had he not loved him so dearly, God would not have chosen him as a means of testing his father's religious fidelity. Hence this oblation of his son was the best evidence of his supreme love to God, and that all he had was consecrated to his service. This act called for the subordination of natural affection to christian faith and love. "Take now thine only son Isaac, whom thou lovest, and get thee into the land of Moriah, and offer him there for a burnt offering!"

What a startling command was this! How it must have stirred up the soul of that parent, and for the time caused a bitter conflict between natural affection and christian faith! "Take thy son,"—had it been a slave, the command would not have been so stirring; but a son, an only son, the joy of his heart, and the pride and hope of his age,—the son he so much loved,—oh it was this that harrowed up such a revulsion in his soul, and, for the moment doubtless, caused him to shrink from the very thought of obedience. But the command was imperious,—it was from God; and though the parent shrunk from the deed, yet the faith of the faithful servant gained a signal triumph over all the protestations of natural affection, and silenced all its rising murmurs; for "Abraham rose up early in the morning, and saddled his ass, and took two of his young men with him, and Isaac his son, and clave the wood for the burnt offering, and rose up, and went unto the place of which God had told him." There he built an altar, laid the wood in order, bound Isaac, and laid him upon the wood on the altar. But when with uplifted sacrificial knife, he was about to slay his son, just at the point where God had the true test of his faith, a ministering angel stayed his hand, and prevented the bloody form in which he was about to offer his only son to God; "for now I know that thou fearest God, seeing thou hast not withheld thy son, thine only son, from me!" He needed now but dedicate him in the moral sense to God.

The case of Samuel is another instance of the offering of children unto the Lord. His mother had asked him of the Lord, and vowed, as she prayed, to "give him unto the Lord all the days of his life."—1 Sam. I., 11. Her prayer was answered, and in obedience to her holy vow, she took him, when very young, with her to the Temple, where she offered him up as an oblation to the Lord. "For this child I prayed, and the Lord hath given me my petition which I asked of him; therefore also have I lent him to the Lord; as long as he liveth shall he be lent unto the Lord!" David also consecrated all that he had to the Lord,—his possessions as well as his children. When he built a house, he dedicated it to the Lord, and prepared "a psalm and song at the dedication of the house."

Here in these examples of Old Testament family offerings to God, we have a type and illustration of the oblations of the Christian home. The Lord does not ask the Christian parent, as he did Abraham, to build an altar upon the summit of some lofty cliff, and there to thrust a sacrificial knife to the heart of his child, and offer his quivering flesh and bleeding body a burnt offering to him; but he commands him to bring his child to the altar of baptism in his church, and there dedicate his life, his talents, his all, as a living sacrifice "holy and acceptable unto God," vowing before witnessing angels and men that, as the steward of God and the representative of the child, he will hold it sacred as the property of the Lord, given to him only in trust; that he will consult and faithfully execute the will of the Lord concerning the child, and that in all his relations to it, he will seek to make it subserve his purposes and reflect his glory.

This is the most precious and acceptable oblation of the parent's heart and home,—more precious than gold or pearls, than rivers of blood or streams of oil; and where there is a corresponding dedication of all that belongs to home, it promotes and preserves the highest privileges and the greatest well-being of the child. With the deep and sublime feelings of faith we should, therefore, take our little ones, in infancy, before the Lord, as the free-will offering of the Christian home; and in all subsequent periods of their life under the parental roof, we should eagerly watch, in each expanding faculty, in each growing inclination, in the bent of each tender thought, in the warm glow of each feeling and desire, for some indications of the will of God concerning their mission in this life.

This leads us to remark finally, that, in the dedication of our children to the Lord, we should have reference to the highest function within the calling of man, viz: the christian ministry; or in other words, we should offer our sons to God with the hope and prayer that He may call them to the work of the ministry, and every indication of His answer to our prayer, given in their mental and moral fitness, should encourage the parent to train them up with special reference to that sacred office.

This, the state of the church and the many destitute and waste places of the earth, imperiously demand. Like the Hebrew mother, we should at least devote one of our sons to the Temple-service, direct his attention to it, favor it by all our intercourse with him, and use all proper means for his preparation for it. And you may be assured that God will answer your prayer. Your offering, if holy, will be acceptable.

> "Even thus, of old, a babe was offered up—
> Young Samuel, for the service of His Temple;
> Nor He refused the boon, but poured on him
> The anointing of all gifts and graces meet
> For his high office."

But alas! how many parents refuse thus to yield their sons unto God! They will formally and outwardly dedicate their children to Him in holy baptism; but afterwards obstruct their way to the ministry, yea, even discourage it for reasons the most worldly and infidel. They will remind them of its arduous duties and self-denials; they will remind them that it affords no money speculations, that the salary of ministers is so small, no wealth can be amassed by preaching, and besides, they will have to remove so far from home. And thus by urging such frivolous objections, they beget in their sons a prejudice against the ministry,—yea, a contempt for it. Ah, if preaching were a money-making business; if it opened the door to luxury and affluence and worldly ease, then I am sure every parent would show the outward piety of dedicating his sons (and daughters too) to the ministry. Here we see how natural affection, misdirected by the love of worldly gain, neutralizes the promptings of faith. Had Abraham lived under the same influence, he would not have obeyed the edict of God. It is because of the dominant spirit of worldliness in the Christian home, that the laborers upon the walls of Zion are inadequate to the great work to be done, that they are insufficient for the great harvest of souls. And this will ever continue so long as Christian parents refuse to make an offering of their sons to God, and turn their homes into a den of thieves.

Such parental reservation of children for filthy lucre and the pleasures of sin for a season, involves a guilt which no redeeming attribute can mitigate. If God gave his only Son to suffer and die upon the accursed tree, shall we, his professed followers, not give in turn our sons to Him, to proclaim the glad news of a purchased and offered redemption? Think of this, oh ye who profess to be the parents of a Christian home, and have with the lip had your children dedicated to God in baptism! Think that the gift of God has bought them with a price, and that as they belong to Him, you rob God when you withhold them, and deal with them as your own property, leaving out of view the great law of stewardship. Mistaken parents! methinks you would give your children to all save to God; you would devote them to any thing but religion. You fit them for this life, choose their occupation, labor to leave them a large inheritance, and rejoice when they rise to eminence in the world.

But in all this, God, religion and eternity are cast into the shade; you act towards them as if God had no claim upon them, and you were under no obligations to meet that claim. Think of this, ye who have been recreant to your duty, —ye who have not followed Abraham to the mount of oblation, nor brought up your sons as an offered Samuel. Oh think, that God will demand of you these children, and that if they are not now devoted to the Lord, you will not have them to return to Him in the great day of final reckoning. May the momentous interests and responsibilities of that coming day bring you with your children around the altar of consecration, and constrain you there to say—

"I give thee to thy God—the God that gave thee,
A well-spring of deep gladness to my heart!
And precious as thou art,
And pure as dew of Hermon, He shall have thee,
My own, my beautiful, my undefiled!
And thou shalt be His child!"

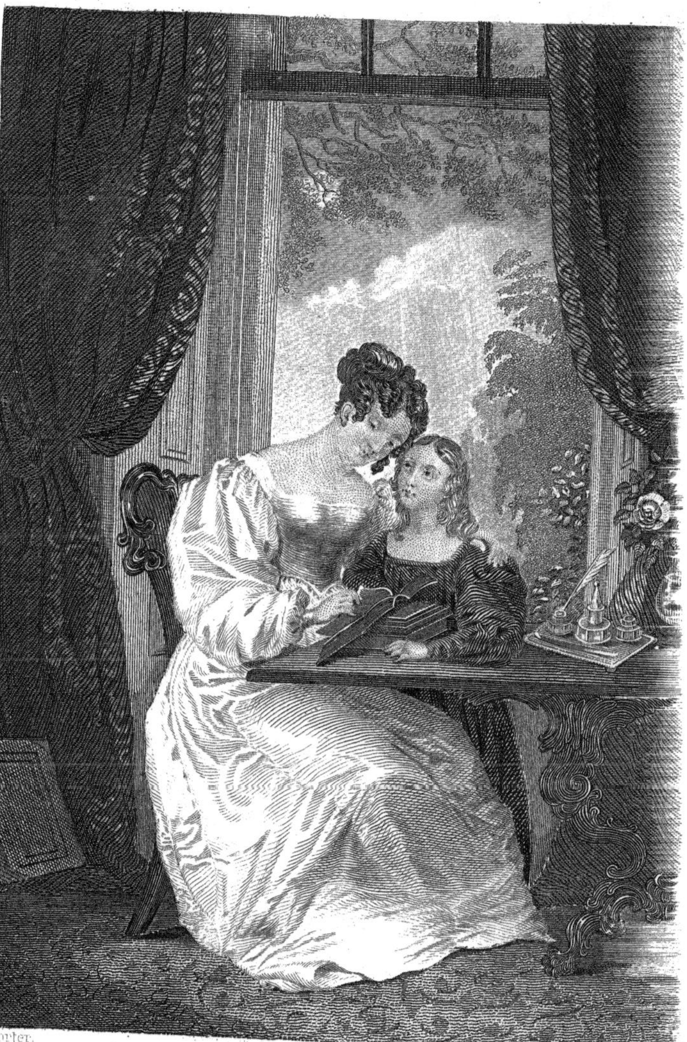

J. Porter.

T. Poll

TEACHING THE SCRIPTURES.

CHAPTER XI.

CHRISTIAN BAPTISM.

"WATER—of blest purity
Emblem—do we pour on thee;
Little one! regenerate be—
Only by the crimson flood
Of the Spotless, in the blood
Of the very Son of God!
Father, Son and Holy Ghost!
Take the feeble, take the lost,
Purchased once at Calvary's cost!"

WHAT delightful associations cluster around the baptismal altar! How tenderly does the pious mother fold her babe to her yearning heart, as she devoutly approaches that consecrated spot, and there dedicates in and through this holy sacrament, the child of her love and hope, to Him who gave it! What a holy charge she there assumes; what a sacred vow she there makes; what a solemn promise she there gives; what a momentous interest is entrusted to her there; what a weight of responsibility is there laid upon her!

Her charge is an infant soul; her vow is to be faithful to it; her promise is to train it up for God; and her's will be the lasting glory or the lasting shame! These very engagements and trusts elevate the pious parents; diffuse a tenderness and sympathy over all the domestic relations, and make better husbands, better wives, better parents, and better children, by the deep insight which is given to their faith in those mysterious relations and mutual obligations which bind them together. As the consecrated water falls upon the face of the devoted child, the parents feel the solemn vow sink deep into the soul, and realize the weight of that responsibility which God lays upon them.

God commands us not only to dedicate our children to Him, but to do so in the way He has appointed, viz., in and through Christian baptism. In this way we bring our children into the church, and train them up in a churchly way. We bring them to God through the church. In their baptism we have, as it were, a confirmation of their dedication by "the mighty Master's seal." It is the link which binds our children to the church, the rite of their initiation into the kingdom of Christ, the sign and seal of their saving relation to the covenant of grace. By it they are solemnly set apart to the service of God, enrolled among the members of His kingdom, entitled to its privileges and guardian care, and placed in the appointed way of salvation and eternal life, receiving the seal and superscription of the Son of God.

This is indispensable to the demands of the Christian faith. To deny that infants are thus included in the covenant of grace, destroys the purity and spiritual unity of the Christian compact, and subverts the foundations and harmony of the Christian home.

It is revolting to the parent's faith to forbid his little ones the privilege of the church, and to treat them as aliens from the covenant of promise. Does the gospel place them under such a ban of proscription? Surely not! He who instituted the family relation had special regard to the family in all the appointments of his grace. His command is like that of Noah, "Come thou and all thy house into the ark." "The promise is unto you and your children." This is the comfort of the parent, that his children are planted by the ordinance of God into the soil of grace, where they may grow up as a tender plant in the likeness of His death, and be "like a tree planted by the rivers of water, that shall bring forth his fruit in his season; his leaf shall not wither, and whatsoever he doeth shall prosper."

Baptism in the Christian home is eminently infant baptism. Take this away, and you sever the strongest cord that binds church and home. As the Jew was commanded to circumcise his child, and thus bring it into proper relations to the theocratical covenant, so the Christian has a similar command from Christ to bring his children, through the holy sacrament of baptism, to Him. It is not our purpose to discuss the baptistic question. When we shall have thrown sufficient light upon it to convince the Christian parent, that it is a duty to have little children dedicated to God in baptism, our plan shall be fully executed. We must either admit infant baptism, or deny that the Christian covenant includes children, and that the parent is bound to dedicate them to God. Hence the objection brought against infant baptism can, with equal propriety, be urged against circumcision; for the latter is the type of the former. In baptism Christ places Himself in true organic relations to the child, and thus opens up to it the sources from which alone the Christian life can proceed and develop itself.

The baptism of our children is grounded in their need of salvation at every age and stage of development. It is also based upon the very idea of Christ Himself; upon primitive christianity; upon the extent and compass of the Christian covenant; and upon those vital relations which believing parents sustain to their offspring. It might be proven from the commission given by Christ to His disciples to "preach the gospel to every creature;" from His language and conduct in reference to children; from the usage of the Apostles and of the apostolic church. The idea and mission of Christ Himself, we think, would be a sufficient argument in favor of infant baptism. He included in His life the stage of childhood, and came to save the child as well as the man. His own infancy and childhood are securities for this. He entered into and passed through all the various states and stages of man's development on earth, and thus became adapted to the wants of every period of our life,—man's infancy as well as man's maturity. Ireneus says, "Christ Jesus became a child to children, a youth to youth, and a man to man." The fact, too, that the blessings of the covenant of grace are extended to the children of believing parents, is sufficient to prove the validity of infant baptism. Peter said on the day of Pentecost, when he called upon his hearers to be baptized: "for the promise is to you, and your children, and all that are afar off, even as many as the Lord our God shall call."

Thus His gospel excludes none, neither is it restricted to a certain age or capacity. As the child, as well as the man, fell and died in the first Adam, so the child, as well as the man, can be made alive in the second Adam. As infants, therefore, are subjects of grace, why not subjects also of baptism? As they are included in the covenant, why not enter it by the divinely constituted sacrament of initiation? As they are included in the plan of salvation, why not receive it in a churchly way? If Christ is the Saviour of infants, why not bring them to Him through baptism?

Besides, the idea of following Christ reaches its full meaning only through infant baptism. His own infancy, as we have already seen, is a warrant of this. Without it He cannot penetrate and rule in every natural stage of human life. Hence a denial of infant baptism is a subversion of the fundamentals of Christian doctrine. The very constitution of the Christian family, its unity and mission must be overthrown; for infant baptism is incorporated with the nature of christianity itself, with the conception and necessities of the individual Christian life, and of the Christian family life.

And yet with the plainest teachings of the gospel before them, is it not strange that there are so many virulent enemies to infant baptism? Their rejection of it seems to rest mainly upon the untenable position that baptism has meaning and force only when it is the fruit of an antecedent, self-conscious faith on the part of the subject, and that it is but the outward demonstration of a separate and prior participation of some inward grace. As infants have not a self-conscious faith, it is believed, therefore, that they are not, of course, fit subjects of baptism.

There is a cunning sophistry in all this. It goes upon the supposition that faith necessarily demands the prior development of self-consciousness. It assumes that faith is bound to a particular age, and can be exercised only after the full and complete development of the logical consciousnes, and is dependent upon it; it also assumes that this faith must necessarily be exercised by the subject of Christian baptism.

Now this is all mere assumption. There is no scripture for it. In all this, the distinction is not made between faith in its first bud, and faith in its ripe fruit. The first may exist in the unconscious infant, just as undeveloped reason exists there; because natural powers do not generate supernatural faith. Faith is the gift of God; and its existence does not depend upon any particular stage of mental development. The enemies of infant baptism can see nothing in baptism. They can see no objective force in that holy sacrament; but regard it as something merely external, extraneous, unproductive,—a mere unmeaning form in which a prior faith is pleased to express itself, as the conclusion of a work already accomplished. The great error here lies just in this, that they mistake it as an act of faith, whereas it is an act of Christ. They think it is the formal rite through which they elect and receive Christ; whereas it is the sacrament in which Christ elects and receives them.

If, in church worship, man placed himself in a relation to God, without God placing Himself in a relation to man, then we might reject infant baptism. But this is not so. God, in baptism, places Himself in a relation to the subject, receives the subject until it become a part of the organism of grace in its subjective and objective force, and is recognized as a member of the church of Christ. Now the falsity of the position assumed by the enemies of infant baptism lies just here, that only the subjective side of baptism is held up, while its objective, sacramental character is left altogether out of view. It reverses the relative positions of faith and baptism, making the former to take the place of the latter, and holding that any one dissociated with the church, can receive and exercise a true living faith, which overthrows the very idea of the church itself. It makes faith first, baptism second, entering the church third; whereas baptism comes before the conscious faith of the subject. If so, then why object to infant baptism?

Baptism is that sacrament by means of which the order of divine grace is continued. It generates faith, and its development is from authoritative, to free, personal faith. "What the personal election of Christ was to the first circle of disciples, that baptism is for the successive church, the divine fact through which Christ gives to His church its true and eternal beginning in the individual." If so, then is it not plain that baptism goes before the self-conscious faith of the subject? And if this church-founding sacrament brings your child into a living and saving relation to the church, then why deny it that baptism? Dare you reverse the divine procedure which God has ordained for the salvation of His people? And if Christ is related to the individual only through the general; if He is related to the members only through the body, and having fellowship with them only as the Head of that body, then is it not plain that your children, in order to come to Him as such, to be incorporated with Him and related to Him in a saving way, must come to Him through the church,—must become a member of it, and that too in the manner and through the medium He has prescribed, viz., baptism?

He who, for the reason, therefore, that children can have no self-conscious faith, refuses to have them baptized, but exposes his ignorance of the divine procedure of grace as developed in the church, of the true moral relation between parent and child, and of the scripture idea of the Christian home. Why not for the very same reason refuse to teach them, to have them pray, to bring them up to church service? Yea, why not deny to them salvation itself? For the very same reason for which you reject infant baptism, you must also reject infant salvation; for faith is held up in the Word of God as a qualification for salvation with more emphasis than as a qualification for baptism. Hence if you say that infants cannot be baptized because incapable of faith, you must also say, by a parity of reasoning, that infants cannot be saved, because incapable of faith.

This is a dilemma, and to avoid it, some enemies to infant baptism have even confessed that they see no hope for the salvation of children. Thus Dr. Alexander Carson says, "The gospel has nothing to do with infants. It is good news, but to infants it is no news at all. None can be saved by the gospel who do not believe it! Consequently by the gospel no infants can be saved!" But if out of Christ there is no salvation, then tell me, how will infants be saved? We have no answer from these enemies, yea, there is no answer!

Christian parents! what think you of this? When bending over the grave of a beloved child, with the cherished hope of meeting it in heaven, how would such intelligence as this startle you from your dream of reunion there, and cast a deep pall of desolation around your sorrowing hearts? Does not the parent's faith forbid the intrusion of a doctrine so revolting as this? Though you have been in your home, the divinely appointed representative of your child, and in its baptism exercised faith in its behalf, on the ground of those natural and moral relations which the Lord has constituted between you and your child, yet in this startling dogma of the enemies of its baptism, you find a virtual denial of the existence of such moral relations and parental vicarage; yea, a denial of parental stewardship and of the religious ministry of the Christian home. The revulsion with which the Christian heart receives such a denial of infant baptism is at least a presumptive evidence against it. But we think enough has been said to lay the foundation of some practical comments upon the subject of Christian baptism.

If it is a fact that infants are proper subjects of baptism, then it is the duty of Christian parents to have them baptized. It is not only a duty, but a delightful privilege, to consecrate them to God in a perpetual covenant never to be forgotten, regarding them as the members of the kingdom of Christ, and so called to be God's children by adoption and grace.

Their baptism involves many parental duties and responsibilities. If it is both a sign and a seal of the covenant of grace, and a means of grace, so that the parent's faith, in their baptism, places the child in covenant relation to the Incarnate Word, through the life-giving Spirit, then it is plain that the parent is bound to secure for the child those blessings which that baptism contemplates, and which hang upon the exercise of a receiving faith. This sacrament gives the child a churchly claim upon parental interposition in its behalf, in all things pertaining to its spiritual culture,—in a true religious training, in a proper direction in the use of the means of grace, in a holy Christian example. Here it is the parent's duty to represent the church, to act for the church in religious ministrations to the child, to be the steward of the church in the Christian home, to rear up the child for a responsible membership.

No parent, therefore, who neglects the baptism of the child, can have "the answer of a good conscience towards God." If we are satisfied to have our homes separate from the church; if we are satisfied with individualistic, disembodied, unassociated christianity,—a religion that owns no church, but which has its origin, root and maturity in the self-conscious activity of the individual, we may then neglect this duty. But in doing so, to be consistent, we must also discard the sister ordinance of the Lord's supper, yea, all the churchly means of grace; yea, the church itself;

for why repudiate one ordinance, — one idea of associated christianity, and not all the others?

That baptism is greatly abused and neglected, none will deny. It is often abused by neglect of the proper time of its administration. The earliest period of infancy is the proper time; for then there will be a proper correspondence in time between the dedication and the baptism. In this we have an example from Jewish circumcision. The pious Jew took the infant when it was but eight days old, and had it circumcised. But many Christian parents defer the baptism of their children until late childhood, while their vows of dedication are left in mere naked feeling and resolution, having no sacramental force and expression; and as a consequence will grow cold and indifferent. When parents thus delay having their children brought within the fold of God and the bosom of the church, they presume to be wiser than God, and oppose their own weak reason to His word and promises.

Baptism is often abused, also, by being used as a mere habit, an unmeaning form, without a proper sense of its significance, importance, duties and responsibilities. It is administered because others do the same,—because customary among most church members, and because perhaps it looks like an adherence to the outward of christianity and the church at least. When they have thus obeyed the law of habit, and girded themselves with the formula of parental duty, they feel they have done enough; and perhaps neither their children nor the vows they assumed at their baptism ever after recur to them as objects of specific duty.

But we would remind such parents, that habit is not always duty, and our adherence to habit does not prove our sincerity and the truthfulness of our purpose. It does not always imply "the answer of a good conscience towards God." If having our children baptized is simple obedience to the law of habit, it is not the performance of a parental duty, but the abuse of a blessed privilege; there is in it all no living churchly expression of willing vows. In this way we only reach its outward form, and we do that, not because of its inherent worth, not because of a duty and privilege; but because we desire to cope with others, and decorate our religion in the popular dress of other people's habits.

Baptism is also abused by mistaking the object and design of its administration. Why do many parents have their children baptized? Because they wish to express their vows of dedication in that sacramental form and way which God has appointed? Because they desire to bring them into the fold and bosom of the church, and place them in saving relations to the means of grace? Alas, no! but too often because they make their baptism the mere occasion of giving them, in a formal, public way, their Christian names. They christen their children to give them a name; and often with them this holy sacrament is as empty as the name. Their baptism, in their view, is but the sealing and confirming the name they had before chosen for the child; and when this is done they have no more thought of the baptism. With them the baptism of their children is the ordinance of name-giving. Before it takes place they are busied about getting a name from the most approved and fashionable novels of the day. This takes the place of dedication. Their prior thoughts are all absorbed in getting a strange, new-fangled name,—such an one as will carry you away by association to some love-sick tale, or remind you of the burning of Rome, or some other deed which has disgraced humanity. And then as soon as this is done, they fix upon some auspicious occasion when either in the church or in the presence of a select company at home, (for children cry now-a-days too much to bring them to church) they have their pastor to baptize them.

Perhaps a great feast is prepared; godfathers and godmothers (if they have the warrant of some valuable presents) are chosen; and then in all the glare and parade of fashion, they have the ordinance administered. And what then is the first joyful cry of the fond parents, after the solemn ceremony is ended? Why "now, dear, you have your name!" And this is the end,—yes, the finale of the vows there made before God,—the end of all until God shall call them to account!

It requires but very little discrimination to see

that in all this the nature, design, and obligations of Christian baptism are left totally out of view. They do not here appreciate this ordinance as a channel for the communication of God's grace to their children. When baptized they do not regard them as having been received into gracious relation to God, as plants in the Lord's vineyard, as having put on Christ, and as having their ingrafting into Him not only signified but sealed. Thus being undervalued, it is, as a consequence, abused and neglected.

The great neglect of Christian baptism is doubtless owing to the low, unscriptural views of its nature and practical importance; for if they realized its relations to the plan of salvation, and its office in the appropriation of that salvation to their children, they would not permit them to grow up unbaptized, neither would they be recreant to the solemn duties which are binding upon the parent after its administration. But upon the subject of baptism itself, we have seen that there is great laxity of feeling and opinion.

The spirit of our fathers upon this point is becoming so diluted that we can scarcely discern any longer a vestige of the good old landmarks of their sacramental character. Instead of walking in them, Christians are now falling a prey to a latitudinarian spirit of the most destructive kind. They are, in leaving these old landmarks, falling into the clutches of rationalism and radicalism, which will ere long leave their homes and their church

"A wreck at random driven,
Without one glimpse of reason or of heaven!"

Even ministers themselves seem to grow indifferent to this wide-spread and growing evil. They hardly ever utter a word of warning from the pulpit against it. Their members may be known by them to neglect the baptism of their children; and yet by their silence they wink at this dereliction; and when they have occasion to speak of this ordinance, many advert to it as a mere sign, as something only outward, not communicating an invisible grace, not as a seal of the new covenant, ingrafting into Christ. No wonder when this holy sacrament is thus disparagingly spoken of, that Christian parents will neglect it practically, as a redundancy in the church, — as a tradition coming in its last wailing cry from ages and forms departed, — as a church rite marked obsolete, as an old ceremonial savoring of old Jewish shackles, embodying no substantial grace, and unfit for this age of railroad progression and gospel libertinism.

Will any one deny the extent of such a spirit in the church and homes of the present day? Let him refer to church statistics, where he may receive some idea of the magnitude of this evil. In them we can see the extent to which parents have neglected the baptism of their children. We take from a note in the "Mercersburg Review" the following statistical items: "The presbytery of Londonderry reports but one baptism to sixty-four communicants; the presbytery of Buffalo city, the same; the presbytery of Rochester city, one to forty-six; the presbytery of Michigan, one to seventy-seven; the presbytery of Columbus, one to thirty. In the presbytery of New Brunswick, there are three churches which report thus: one reports three hundred and forty-three communicants, and three baptisms; another reports three hundred and forty communicants, and two baptisms. In Philadelphia, one church reports three hundred and three communicants, and seven baptisms; another, two hundred and eighty-seven communicants, and one baptism."

These statistics speak volumes. They tell us how Christian parents neglect the baptism of their children, and also how the church winks at it. And from this neglect we can easily infer their indifference to it. If we refer to the statistics of all other churches, we shall witness a similar neglect. No branch of the church now is free from the imputation of such neglect. It is now difficult indeed, to induce parents to have their children baptized, because they think it is no use! "Let them wait," say they, "till they grow up, and then they will know more about it!" This shows us where the parent stands, viz., in an unchurchly state, and radical to the very core. It shows us what that influence is, which is at work upon his mind. "He will know more about it!"—just as if that in religion is worthless until we know all about it. Baptism then is not worth anything until the child understands all about it! In that parental utterance we hear the wildest shout of triumphant rationalism!

But again, baptism is often abused by parental unfaithfulness to its obligations. In the baptism of their children, parents solemnly vow to bring them up in the nurture of the Lord, to train them up in His holy ways, to teach them by precept and example, to pray for them and teach them the privilege of prayer. And yet how grossly are these solemn vows left unperformed, and even never thought of in all after life! Perhaps the very opposite course is taken even on the day of baptism. Parents! by this you endanger your own souls as well as the souls of your children. How will the memory of such neglected duty and privilege sink with deepening anguish in your souls, when you shall be called hence to answer to God for your parental stewardship! Be not deceived; God is not mocked; neither will he hold you guiltless when you thus outrage His holy sacrament.

Baptism is often abused by the unfaithfulness of children to its privileges, influences and blessings. Many children fight against these, prevent parents from performing their duties, and repel all the overtures of the Christian home, all the offers of the Spirit's baptism, abandoning the means of grace, refusing to assume the baptismal engagement taken for them by their parents; and thus, so far as they are concerned, undo and neutralize what their parents did for them. Oh, ye baptized children,—ye to whom the holy ministry of home has been faithfully applied,—know ye not that the frowns of abused heaven are upon you, and that the memory of your rebellion against the prerogatives of the family, will constitute an ingredient in your cup of woe? The privilege of baptism lays you under solemn requisition. If unfaithful to it, it will be your condemnation, and add new fuel to the flame of a burning conscience.

Parents and children! be faithful to this holy ordinance of God. It is a solemn service. You should approach the baptismal font with a trembling step and a consecrated heart. And what a solemn moment it is, when you take your child away from that altar! There you gave it up to God,—dedicated it to His service; and there in turn He commits it to you in trust, saying to you as Pharaoh's daughter said to the mother of Moses, "Take this child and nurse it for me, and I will pay thee thy wages," and you bore it away, as did that faithful mother, to bring it up for God. There you solemnly promised that in training that child, the will of God should be your will, and the law of all your conduct towards it. You can never forget that solemn transaction, and how you there vowed before witnessing men and angels that you would be faithful to the little one God has given you. What now has been the result? Eternity will answer.

CHAPTER XII.

CHRISTIAN NAMES.

"SHE named the child Ichabod."—1 SAMUEL.

"Thus was the building left
Ridiculous, and the work confusion named."

CHRISTIAN baptism suggests Christian names. This introduces us to an important topic, viz., the kind of names Christian parents should give to their children at their baptism. Baptismal names are indeed an important item of the Christian home. Much more depends upon them than we are at first sight of the subject, disposed to grant.

Christianity eminently includes the great law of correspondence between its inward spirit and its outward form. Its form and contents cannot be separated. The principle of fitness, it everywhere exhibits; and hence its nomenclature is the herald of its spirit and truth. The names that religion has given to her followers signify some principle of association between them. They were adopted to designate some fact in the history of the individual, or in his relation to the church. Hence the names adopted for the children of the Christian home should be the utterance of some fact or calling which belongs to that home. Their name is one of the first things which children know, and hence it makes a deep impression upon them. And as our Christian names are given to us at the time of our baptism, one would think that there is always a correspondence between the name and some fact or interest connected with the occasion. We should then receive a Christian name, a name which does not bind us by the laws of association to what is evil either in the past or the present, but which indicates a relation to some precious boon involved in the dedication of the child to God.

Is this always so? By no means. It once was. It was so in the Hebrew home and in the families of the apostolic age. But in this day of parental rage after new-fangled things and names, taken from works of fiction and novels of doubtful character, we find that parents care but very little about the baptismal name being the herald of a religious fact. "What is in a name?" was a question propounded by a poet. His answer was "nothing!"

> "That which we call a rose
> By any other name would smell as sweet."

The principle here evolved is false. There is much in a name; and at the creation names were not mechanically given to things; but there was a vital correspondence between the name and the thing named. Much depends upon the name. It exerts a potent influence for good or for evil upon the bearer and upon all around him.

Primarily, a name supposed some correspondence between its meaning and the person who bore it. Hence the name should not be arbitrary in its application, but should "link its fitness to idea," and with the person, run in parallel courses.

> "For mind is apt and quick to wed ideas and names together,
> Nor stoppeth its perceptions to be curious of priorities."

Nebuchadnezzar, king of Babylon, felt that practically there was much in a name, when he heathenized the names of the young Hebrew captives. By this he thought to detach them from their Hebrew associations. God was in each of their original names, and in this way they were reminded of their religion. But the names this Chaldee king gave them were either social or alluded to the idolatry of Babylon. Their Hebrew names were to them witnesses for God, mementoes of the faith of their fathers; hence the king, to destroy their influence, called Daniel, Belteshazzar, i. e. "the treasurer of the god Bel;" Hannaniah he called Shadrach, i. e. "the messenger of the king;" Mishael he called Meshach, i. e. "the devotee of the goddess Shesach." He showed his cunning in this, and a historical testimony to the potent influence of a name.

By this same rule of correspondence, Adam doubtless named, by order of his Creator, the things of nature as they struck his senses.

> "He specified the partridge by her cry, and the forest prowler by his roving,
> The tree by its use, and the flower by its beauty, and everything according to its truth."

The Hebrews obeyed the same law in naming their children. With them there was a sacred importance attached to the giving of a name. For every chosen name they had a reason which involved the person's life, character or destiny. Adam named the companion of his bosom, "woman because she was taken out of man." He called "his wife's name Eve, because she was the mother of all living." Eve called her first-born Cain (possession) "because I have gotten a man from the Lord." She called another son Seth (appointed,) "for God hath appointed me another seed instead of Abel, whom Cain slew." Samuel was so named because he was "asked of and sent to God." God Himself often gave names to His people; and each name thus given, conveyed a promise, or taught some rule of life, or bore some divine memorial, or indicated some calling of the person named. Says Dr. Krummacher on this point: "Names were to the people like memoranda, and like the bells on the garments of the priests, reminding them of the Lord and His government, and furnishing matter for a variety of salutary reflections. To the receivers of them they ministered consolation and strength, warning and encouragement; and to others they served to attract the attention and heart of God." This was right, and fully accorded with the economy of the Hebrew home, and with the conception of language itself.

Would that the Christian home followed her pious example! But Christians now are too much under the influence of irreligious fashion. Instead of giving their children those good old religious names which their fathers bore, and which are endeared to us by many hallowed associations, they now repudiate them with a sneer as too vulgar and tasteless. They are out of fashion, too common, don't lead us into a labyrinth of love-scrapes and scenes of refined iniquity, and are now only fit for a servant.

Hence instead of resorting to the bible for a name, these sentimental parents will pore over filthy novels, or catch at some foreign accent, to get a name which may have a fashionable sound, and a claim upon the prevailing taste of the times, and which may remind one of the battles of some ambitious general, or of the adventures of some love-sick swain, or of the tragic deeds of some fashionable libertine!

And when such a name is found to suit the ear of fashion and of folly, it is applied to the child, and reiterated by the minister before the baptismal font; and as often as it is afterwards repeated it reminds one perhaps of deeds which put modesty to blush, and startle the ear of justice and humanity. What a burning shame is this to the Christian home! The child who is cursed with such a name has ever before him the momorandum of his parent's folly, and as a recognized example, the character of him after whom he has been named. As often as he is hailed by it, he blushes to think that he has been called by pious parents after one who, perhaps, has turned many a home into desolation, and disgraced and blighted forever the fond hopes and joys of the young and old.

Have thoughts and associations like these no demoralizing influence? How can parents admonish their children against novel reading after they have taken their names from novels? The giving of Christian names at the present time is indeed a ridiculous farce, an insult to christianity, and a representation of stoical infidelity before the baptismal altar. It is there an act of the Babylonish king to heathenize the child. We might almost say that the folly has become a rage. The rage for new names especially,—names which do not adorn the sacred page, nor carry us back to the times and faith of our fathers, but which have gained notoriety in the world of fiction, and associate us with the lover's affrays and with the desperado's feats,—these are the names which Christian parents too often seek with avidity for their children. If you were to judge their homes by these names, you would think yourself in a Turkish seraglio, or amid the voluptuous scenes of a Parisian court, or in the bosom of a heathen family. What, for instance, is there about such names as Nero, Cæsar, Pompey, Punch, that would remind you that you were in a Christian home?

It is often disgusting, too, to see how some Christian parents, who live in humble life, seek to ape, in their children, the empty sounding titles of the world. They only show their vanity and weakness, and often bring ridicule upon their children; for—

> "To lend the low-born noble names, is to shed upon them ridicule and evil;
> Yea, many weeds run rank in pride, if men have dubbed them cedars,
> And to herald common mediocrity with the noisy notes of fame,
> Tendeth to its deeper scorn, as if it were to call the mole a mammoth."

When we thus give our children names associated with battle-fields, empty titles, brilliant honors, and lucrative offices,—positions in life which they can never expect to reach, and which, if they did, would not do honor to the child of a Christian family, we do them great injury; we fasten in them feelings the most disastrous, and draw out propensities unbecoming the child devoted to the Lord, breeding in his soul a peevish repining at his station. Alas! that Christian homes should ever become so servile in their devotions to the rotten sentiments and flimsy interests of misguided and perverted fashion! Her smile in your home is that of a harlot; her touch is the withering blight of corruption; her dominion is the desolation of family hopes and the extermination of those sacred prerogatives with which the Lord has invested the Christian fireside. The ball will take the place of prayer; novels will take the place of the bible; favorites will take the place of husbands and wives; and the children will regard their parents only as their masters.

Christian parents should, therefore, give suitable names to their children, that is, such names as will correspond with their state, character and relations to God,—names which do not suggest the idea of war, rapine, humbug, romance, and sensuality, but which are associated with the Christian life and calling, and which serve as a true index to the spirit and character of the parental fireside. Reason, as well as faith, will dictate such a choice; for

> "There is wisdom in calling a thing fitly; names should note particulars
> Through a character obvious to all men, and worthy of their instant acceptation."

Our name is the first and the last possession at our disposal. It determines from the days of childhood our inclinations. It employs our attention through life, and even transports us beyond the grave. Hence we should give appropriate names to our children,—such as will interest them, and neither be a reproach, on the one hand, nor reach to unattainable and unworthy heights, on the other; for the mind of your child will take a bias, from its name, to good or to evil.

Why not adopt scriptural names for them? Are they not as beautiful as other names? They are. And is not their influence as salutary? It is. And are they not more suitable for the Christian home than any other? They are. Where is there a more lovely name than Mary,—lovely in its utterance, and thrice lovely in the glowing memories which cluster around it, and in the hallowed home-associations it awakens in the Christian heart, drawing us at once to the feet of Jesus, where a Mary sat in confiding pupilage, and sealed her instructions and gratitude with the tear-drop that glowed like early dew upon her dimpled cheek? Would Christian parents desire to give their children more beautiful names,—beautiful in the light of history and of heaven,—than that of Benjamin, "son of the right hand;" of David, "dear, beloved;" of Dionysius, "divinely touched;" of Eleazar, "help of God;" of Eli, "my offering;" of Enoch, "dedicated;" of Jacob, "my present;" of Lemuel, "God is with them;" of Nathan, "given, gift;" of Nathaniel, "gift of God;" of Samuel, "asked of God and sent of God," &c.?

Besides, there are names of distinguished Christians, such as Wilberforce, Howard, Page, Martyn, Paul, Peter, John, Fenelon, Clement, Baxter, &c.,—bright as dew-drops on the page of history, and as beautiful in their enunciation as any chosen from the world of heartless fashion, —as beautiful in sound, and infinitely more so in associations which bind them to deeds of humanity and Christian love. The utterance of such names would be more becoming the Christian home; because they aid in developing the purest, holiest and loftiest idea of its nature and calling. Such names will bind your little ones to pure and holy persons and deeds, and will suit the book of life in which you hope to have them enrolled.

"Then, safe within a better home, where time and its titles
are not found,
God will give thee His new name, and write it on thy heart;
A name, better than of sons, a name dearer than of daughters,
A name of union, peace and praise, as numbered in thy God."

CHAPTER XIII.

HOME AS A NURSERY.

"The Ostrich, silliest of the feathered kind,
And formed of God without a parent's mind,
Commits her eggs, incautious, to the dust,
Forgetful that the foot may crush the trust;
And, while on public nurseries they rely,
Not knowing, and too oft not caring why,
Irrational in what they thus prefer
No few, that would seem wise, resemble her."

To nurse means to educate or draw out and direct what exists in a state of mere involution. It means to protect, to foster, to supply with appropriate food, to cause to grow or promote growth, to manage with a view to increase. Thus Greece was the nurse of the liberal arts; Rome was the nurse of law. In horticulture, a shrub or tree is the nurse or protector of a young and tender plant. We are said to nurse our national resources. Isaiah, in speaking of the coming Messiah and the glory of his church, says, "Thy daughters shall be nursed at thy side." "Kings shall be thy nursing fathers, and their queens thy nursing mothers."

The place or apartment appropriated to such nursing is called a nursery. Thus a plantation of young trees is called a nursery. Shakspeare calls Padua the nursery of arts. We call a very bad place the nursery of thieves and rogues. Dram-shops are the nurseries of intemperance. Commerce is called the nursery of seamen. Universities are the nurseries of the arts and sciences. The church on earth is called the nursery of the church in heaven. Christian families are called the nurseries of the church on earth, because in the former its members are nursed and propagated for the purpose of being transplanted into the latter.

In the same sense and for the same reason, the Christian home is the nursery of the young,—of human nature in its normal state. And as home is the nursery of the state as well as of the church on earth and in heaven, we must see that it is a physical, intellectual and religious nursery. We shall briefly consider it in these aspects. Indeed the Christian home cannot be considered in a more interesting and responsible light. The little child, dedicated to God in holy baptism, is entirely helpless and dependent upon the ministrations of the nursery. There is the department of its first impressions, of its first directions, of its first intellectual and moral formation, of the first evolution of physical and moral life. There the child exists as but the germ of what is to be. It grows up under the fostering care and plastic power of the parents. God's commission to them in the nursery is, to bring up these germs of life, in His nurture and admonition."

> "Take the germ, and make it
> A bud of moral beauty. Let the dews
> Of knowledge, and the light of virtue, wake it
> In richest fragrance and in purest hues."

The nursery is the department of home in which the mother fulfils her peculiar mission. This is her special sphere. None can effectually take her place there. She is the center of attraction, the guardian of the infant's destiny; and none like she, can overrule the unfolding life and character of the child. God has fitted her for the work of the nursery. Here she reigns supreme, the arbitress of the everlasting weal or woe of untutored infancy. On her the fairest hopes of educated man depend, and in the exercise of her power there, she sways a nation's destiny, gives to the infant body and soul their beauty, their bias and their direction. She there possesses the immense force of first impressions. The soul of her child lies unveiled before her, and she makes the stamp of her own spirit and personality upon its pliable nature. She there engrafts it, as it were, into her own being, and from the combined elements of her own character, builds up and establishes the character of her offspring. Hers will, therefore, be the glory or the shame.

> "Then take the heart thy charms have won,
> And nurse it for the skies."

The nursery is that department of home in which the formation of our character is begun. Infancy demands the nursery. It is not full-formed and equipped for the battle of life. It lies in the cradle in a state of mere involution, and in the hands of its parents is altogether passive, and susceptible of impressions as wax before the sun. The germ of the man is there; but it has yet to be developed. Its indwelling life must be nurtured with tender and assiduous care. It demands an influence suited to the expansion of its nature into bloom and maturity. It demands physical development, mental evolution, moral training, and spiritual elevation. In order to these it must live amidst the sweet and plastic socialities of maternal relationship. It must come under the fostering influence of a mother's heart, and be reared up by the tender touches of a mother's hand. This idea is embodied in home as a nursery. This is fourfold in its conception and relation to the child.

The nursery is physical. This involves the means of keeping the child in health, and the appliances of a vigorous physical development. The Christian mother, to this end, should make herself acquainted with the physiology of the infant body. Many well-meaning mothers, from sheer ignorance, destroy the health of their children; and it is on this account perhaps that four-tenths of them die under five years of age. They should also consider the bearing of the body upon the mind and morals of their children. How often do ignorant and indolent parents, by giving their children over to the care of sickly and immoral nurses, ruin forever the health and souls of their offspring. Much, then, depends upon the physical nurture of your child. If you would not injure its mind and soul, you must nurse its body with tender care and wisdom. A vital bond unites them; they reciprocally influence each other, and hence what affects the one must have a corresponding influence upon the other. Neglect the body of your child; destroy its health either by extreme and fastidious care, or by a brutal neglect, and you at the same time do lasting injury to its mind and morals; for the body as the vehicle of mind and spirit, is used for spiritual ends, and should, therefore, be nurtured with direct reference to these.

Your child, in the nursery, is like the tender plant. The storm of passion and the chill of indifference and the oppression of parental tyranny should not be heard and felt there; for where the storm rages and coldness freezes and the hand of cruelty oppresses, we can have no beautiful and vigorous development of physical or moral powers. There will be a stinted and one-sided growth. At best it will be dwarfish, and tend to counteract the spontaneous outflow of mental and moral life. The tender plant, when, cramped and clogged by existing impediments, cannot spring up into beauteous maturity. Neither can your child, when crammed with sweetmeats, and oppressed and screwed into monstrous contortions by the cruel inquisition of fashion and fashionable garments.

In this way the misdirected love and cruel pride of mothers often destroy the health and beauty of their children. They cause a sickly and dwarfish growth by too much confinement and mental taxation, by a too rigid choice of diet, by daily, uncalled for decoctions of medicine, and by fitting the body in a dress as the Chinese do their children's feet in shoes; in a word, by making the entire nursery life too artificial, and substituting the laws of art for those of nature. The result must be a delicate, artificial constitution, too fragile for the trials and duties of life. The body of your child has not the blooming, blushing form of nature, but the cold marble cast of a statue; and it imprints itself upon the disposition, the spirit, the mental faculties. It shows itself in peevishness, in imbecility, in such a passive, slavish subjection to the rules and interests of mere artificial life, as to admit no hope almost of spiritual progression.

The nursery is also intellectual. The mind of your child is unfolding as well as its body; and hence the former, as well as the latter, demands the nursery. How much of the mental vigor and attainments of children depend upon the prudent management of the nursery. Hence parents should

> "Exert a prudent care
> To feed our infant minds with proper fare;
> And wisely store the nursery by degrees
> With wholesome learning, yet acquired with ease.
> And thus well-tutored only while we share
> A mother's lectures and a nurse's care."

Parents may abuse the minds of their children in the nursery, either by total neglect, or by immature education, by too early training and too close confinement to books at a very early age, thus taxing the mind beyond its capacities. This is often the case when children betray great precocity of intellect; and the pride of the parent seeks to gratify itself through the supposed gift of the child. In this way parents often reduce their children to hopeless mental imbecility.

Again, parents often injure the minds of their children by their misguided efforts to train the mind. Even in training them to speak, how imprudent they are in calling words and giving ideas in mutilated language. It is just as easy to teach children to speak correctly, and to call all things by their proper names, as to abuse their vernacular tongue. Such mutilations are impediments to the growth of the intellect. The child must afterwards be taught to undo what it was taught to do and say in the nursery. But as this subject will be fully considered in the chapter on Home Education, we shall refrain from further comment here.

The nursery is moral and spiritual. The first moral and religious training of the child belongs to the nursery, and is the work of the mother. Upon her personal exhibition of truth, justice, virtue, &c., depends the same moral elements in the character of her child. In the nursery we receive our first lessons in virtue or in vice, in honesty or dishonesty, in truth or in falsehood, in purity or in corruption. The full-grown man is the matured child morally as well as physically and intellectually. The same may be said of the spiritual formation and growth of the child. Spiritual culture belongs eminently to the nursery. There the pious parent should begin the work of her child's salvation.

From what we have now seen of the nursery, we may infer its very common abuse by Christian parents in various ways. They abuse it either by forsaking its duties, or giving it over to nurses. The whole subject warns parents against giving over their children to dissolute nurses. What a blushing shame and disgrace to the very name of Christian mother, it is for her to throw the whole care and responsibility of the nursery upon hired and irreligious servants. And why is this so often done? To relieve the mother from the trouble of her children, and afford her time and opportunity to mingle unfettered in the giddy whirl of fashionable dissipation. In circles of opulent society it would now be considered a drudgery and a disgrace for mothers to attend upon the duties of this responsible department of home. But the nurse cannot be a substitute for the mother.

> "Then why resign into a stranger's hand
> A task so much within your own command,
> That God and Nature, and your interest too
> Seem with one voice to delegate to you?"

The same may be said of boarding schools, to which many parents send their children to rid themselves of the trouble of training them up. They are sent there at the very age in which they mostly need the fostering care of a parent. There they soon become alienated from home, and lose the benefit of its influence; and there too they often contract habits and are filled with sentiments the most degenerating and corrupt. They grow up and enter society without any conscious relation to home, and as a consequence, regard society as a mere heartless conventionalism. To this part of the subject we shall, in another chapter, devote special attention. It demands the prayerful consideration of Christian parents.

> "Why hire a lodging in a house unknown,
> For one whose tenderest thoughts all hover round your own?
> This second weaning, needless as it is,
> How does it lacerate both your heart and his!"

CHAPTER XIV.

HOME-SYMPATHY.

"Sweet sensibility! thou keen delight!
Unprompted moral! sudden sense of right!
Perception exquisite! fair virtue's seed!
Thou quick precursor of the liberal deed!
Thou hasty conscience! reason's blushing morn!
Instinctive kindness, ere reflection's born!
Prompt sense of equity! to thee belongs
The swift redress of unexamined wrongs!
Eager to serve, the cause perhaps untried,
But always apt to choose the suffering side!"

Where shall we find a more exquisite picture of home-sympathy than this, from the pen of that truly pious woman, Hannah More! We consider the home-sympathy as an argument against the neglect and abuse of the nursery. It is the instinctive impulse of the parent's heart to be faithful to the trust of home. What mother, prompted by such sympathy, can be recreant to the duties of her household? Can she, keenly sensible to the danger of her children, anxious for their welfare, prompt to do them justice, eager to procure them interests and joys, yearning to alleviate their misfortunes, push them from her arms, and give them over to the care of unfeeling and immoral nurses? If among all the members of the Christian home

> "There is a holy tenderness,
> A nameless sympathy, a fountain love,—
> Branched infinite from parents to children,
> From husband to wife, from child to child,
> That binds, supports, and sweetens human life,"

then the law of sympathy is the standard of faithfulness to the loved ones of home, and its violation is an abuse of the affections and faith of the heart. We shall now consider the natural and spiritual sympathy of home.

What are the natural elements of home-sympathy? The original meaning of sympathy is "harmony of the affections." As such it is an instinctive element of human nature. "Sympathy," says Adams in his Elements of Christian Science, "is a natural harmony by which, upon matters especially that concern the affections, one human being shall, under certain conditions, feel, feel in despite of all concealment of language, the real state of the other." It is, in a word, that law of our nature which makes the feeling of one become affected in the same way as are the feelings of another, so that, in obedience to this law, "we rejoice with them that rejoice, and weep with them that weep." In order to this the motive need not be the same in those in whom the feeling is the same; for that feeling engenders a feeling of its own kind in the other, independent of similar motive. Home-sympathy is that primary power of the heart by which all the affections of one member are extended to all the other members. It awakens in each for all the others, those delicate sensibilities which impel to the most self-denying and benevolent acts. The parent who sympathizes with the child, will extend to it all the aids within a parent's ability.

Its nature is to yield more of itself to weeping than to rejoicing, to misery than to joy. The parent will exert more power and do more for the wretched child than for those of his children who are not in the same condition. He will leave the latter in their security, and seek the one lost sheep of his little flock. Thus it exerts a sheltering influence against the dangers and miseries of human life. It is the law of home-preservation, written upon the heart, obeyed by the affections, and impelling each member to yield a voluntary devotion to the welfare of all the others. It is this which makes it one of the most lovely attributes of home. It is one of the golden chains that link its members together in close unity, making one heart of the many that are thus fused together, and blending into beautiful unison their specific feelings, and hopes and interests.

It is, therefore, the law of oneness in the family, weaving together, like warp and woof, the existence of the members, and locking each heart into one great home-heart, "like the keys of an organ vast," so that if one heart be out of tune, the home-heart feels the painful jar, and gives forth discordant sounds. By it we are not only bound to our kindred, but to our friends, our nation, our race. It impels us to all our acts of benevolence even to an enemy. Earth would be a dreary scene, and society would be a curse, if it did not reign in human nature.

Sympathy was a rich and interesting theme with the ancients. It entered into all their philosophy and religion, and gave rise to numerous fables. They believed that sympathy was a miraculous principle, and that it reigned in irrational and inanimate things. Thus they thought that "two harps being tuned alike, and one being played, the chords of the other would follow the tune with a faint, sympathetic music." It was also believed that precious stones sympathized with certain persons, that the stars sympathized with men, that the efficacy of ointment depended upon sympathy, that "wounds could be healed at a distance by an ointment whose force depended upon sympathy, the ointment being smeared upon the weapon, not upon the wound."

Upon this belief many erroneous, superstitious and dangerous systems of philosophy and religion were established. The natural philosophy of Baptista Porta, or Albertus Magnus, was founded upon the principle of sympathy. Plato applied this principle to marriage, and maintained that "marriage was the union of two souls that once, in their preëxistent state, were one, and that sympathy urges them to union again, and sends them unconsciously seeking it over the world." In the middle ages it was maintained that two friends could be so moved with mutual sympathy as to have, under certain conditions, a true and perfect knowledge of one another's state, even when at a great distance apart. To the revival of this erroneous view of the law of sympathy may be ascribed the theories of Mesmerism and spiritual rappings at the present day.

Home-sympathy, viewed as a feeling and a faculty, is twofold in its nature, viz., passive and active. As passive, it is the mere sense of harmony of feeling among all the members, producing the idea and feeling of the oneness of home. It makes a unity of affection, so that the temper, hopes and interests of each member have a living echo and response in all the others. It gives to home its unitive heart, preserves its vital coherence, fuses all the hearts together, makes each a thread in the web of home-being, where each finds its true measure, is inspired with the home-feeling when all is right, and oppressed with home-sickness when separated from it.

But home-sympathy is also active. As such it is "the active power that one person has naturally of entering into the feelings of another, and being himself affected as that other is." Each member of home has the power in his feelings of making the feelings of all the other members his own, though he may not have the causes of the feelings of the one with whom he sympathizes. Thus one friend may feel the grief of another, actually and really, though he may not suffer the loss of that friend. He can make the emotion which that loss caused, his own. We may weep with the mother who pours her floods of anguish upon the grave of her child, though we may not have sustained the same loss. The husband weeps with his wife, though he may not be able to feel the pangs which penetrate her heart. The child can enter into the feelings of the parent, and be affected to tears or to joy by them.

And thus the home-sympathy demands that all the emotions of home, whether joyful or painful, must affect all,—must vibrate from heart to heart. It involves the power of home-transference, by which each member conveys to his own affections, all within home. It is thus the law of adaptation and assimilation, for the home-affections. In obedience to this law the hearts and interests of the members are bound up in beautiful harmony. The necessities of one are supplied by all. It is this which makes the members faithful to each other, and prompts them to deeds of disinterested love.

It is, therefore, only when the home-sympathy, as a feeling and a faculty, is carried out and acted upon according to its instinctive impulses, that it becomes an effective agent of good. This, however, is not always done. Often it is neutralized by not being permitted to express itself according to the laws of its own operation. Many members have acute feelings and great powers of sympathy, but it exists in them only as feeling, only as a stimulus, a sentiment, and is, therefore, nothing but home-sentimentalism,—a disease of home-sympathy. Thus, for instance, parents may weep over the wickedness of their children, and the pious wife may lament the impenitence of her husband; but if they go no further, their sympathy is really false, because it does not share in and feel the state of others, nor seek to alleviate their impending miseries. The home-sympathy is not simply the look of the priest and Levite upon the half-dead traveler, but also the help of the good Samaritan. Its language is not only, "Be ye clothed and fed," but also, "I will clothe and feed thee." The mere indulgence in the feeling of sympathy is but to harden the heart in the end. Such were the sympathies of Rosseau, — mere heart-stimuli, without legitimate deeds and objective force, existing only as a love-sick sentiment. And this was both the theme of his eloquence and the cause of his misery. Such, too, were the sympathies of Robespierre, — a mere ebullition of disembodied sentiment, borne up like a floating bubble upon muddy waters, and exploding upon the slightest depression.

But, on the other hand, when home-sympathy is issued in faithful action as its emotions prompt, it becomes an efficient agent in the happiness and peace of the family. It not only gives eloquence to the tongue, tears to the eye, but faithfulness to the life. It serves as a key-note to the mind and heart, framing the home-energy, revealing to us our real state, and prompting, by the instinct of love, the means for our highest welfare.

> "How glows the joyous parent to descry,
> A guileless bosom true to sympathy!
> A long lost friend, or hapless child restored,
> Smiles at his blazing hearth and social board;
> Warm from his heart the tears of rapture flow,
> And virtue triumphs o'er remembered woe!"

Sympathy is excited and measured by the power of natural affection. In proportion to the strength of the latter will be the attractive power of the former. That soothing voice which calms the wailing infant; that fond bosom from which the child draws its subsistence, and on which it pillows its weary head; that smile which throws a sunshine around its existence, and all those acts of kindness administered by the hand of love, draw the child instinctively to the parent's heart, and blend in sweetest union its very being with theirs.

The principle of home-sympathy reigns in some degree in every household whose members have not sunk below the level of the brute. Its nature demands that it be mutual. It should glow with peculiar warmth in the wife, the mother, and the sister; because it is a more prominent instinct of woman. It is an intuition of the mother's heart.

> "When pain and anguish wring the brow,
> A ministering angel thou!"

Who but she can smooth the pillow and soothe the anguish of the child of affliction? There is a tenderness in her nature, a softness in her touch, a lightness in her step, a soothing expression in her face, a tender beam in her eye, which man can never have, and which eminently fits her for the lead in home-sympathy. The want of it is a libel upon her sex. It is her prerogative,—the magic power she wields in the formation and reformation of character.

But her sympathy should find response in the bosom of her husband, the father, the brother; for, if true, it must be mutual. Their joys and their sorrows must be common. Thus heart must answer to heart, and face. "The cruelty of that man," says J. A. James, "wants a name, and I know of none sufficiently emphatic, who denies his sympathy to a suffering woman, whose only sin is a broken constitution, and whose calamity is the result of her marriage." Without such mutual sympathy, the members of the family would be cold and repulsive, and society would be deprived of its most lovely attributes; its members would lose the connecting link which brings them together, and its entire fabric would fall to pieces and degenerate into barbaric individualism.

> "Had earth no sympathy, no tears would flow,
> In heart-felt sorrow, for another's woe;
> The joyous spirit then would weary roam,
> A stranger to the dear delights of home."

We shall now consider briefly the religious elements of home-sympathy. These involve harmony of the spiritual affections, and a transfer to all the members, of the religious experience and enjoyment of each. As natural sympathy arises out of and is measured by natural affection, so spiritual sympathy is the product of faith and love. Hence the latter is purer, more refined and efficient than the former. If the members of the family are the children of God, they will live together in the unity of the Spirit as well as of natural affection. The sympathy of the pious portion will be interposed in behalf of the salvation of the impenitent members. There will be an identity of soul-interest. The pious mother will make the everlasting interests of her husband and child, her own; and will labor with the same assiduity to promote them as she does to promote her own salvation. She will thus enter into the spiritual emotions of her kindred, and bear them vicariously, making thus her religious sympathies the law of preservation to all the members of her household.

The living stream of this sympathy is given by Christ in His address to the weeping daughters of Jerusalem: "Daughters of Jerusalem, weep not for me, but weep for yourselves and for your children!" The following is also its living utterance: "My son, if thy heart be wise, my heart shall rejoice, even mine." We have also a beautiful exhibition of it in the touching history of Ruth, in the life of Joseph, and in the mother of

Samuel. Peter describes it when he says, "Be all of one mind, having compassion one of another; love as brethren, be pitiful, be courteous." Esther expresses it in the exclamation, "How can I endure to see the destruction of my kindred!" Paul gives utterance to it when he says, "I would be accursed for my brethren and kindred's sake." Jesus exemplifies it in His intercourse with the family of Lazarus; He shows its emotion and its active charities when He stands on the grave of that friend, and weeps, and calls him from the dead. His sympathy for a lost world is the true pattern of home-sympathy. It was disinterested, superior to all selfishness, self-denying, active, and prompting Him to do and suffer all that He did. It was not measured by the merits of the object after which it yearned. He sympathized with all,

"For each He had a brother's interest in His heart."

And its softening influence fell, like morning dew, upon the heart of adamant, melting it into contrition and love.

"In every pang that rends the heart,
The Man of sorrows had a part;
He sympathizes in our grief,
And to the sufferer sends relief."

See Him bend over the bed of Jairus's daughter; see Him opening the eyes of the blind, healing the paralytic, comforting and feeding the poor widow, and cheering the bereaved and troubled heart. Wherever He went He was "a brother born for them in adversity." See Him on the cross, when weltering in blood and struggling with the pangs of a cruel death, He casts His languid eye upon His aged mother who is there weeping her pungent woes, and makes provision for her comfort. His sympathy now for all is the same.

> "None ever came unblest away;
> Then, though all earthly ties be riven,
> Smile, for thou hast a Friend in heaven!"

It is this sympathy which makes Him a member of every Christian home. And when the sympathy of its members is the reproduction of His, they will, like Mary, sit in loving pupilage at His feet, each becoming the agent of blessings for all the rest. The wife will seek the salvation of her husband; the mother will labor with unwearied diligence for the redemption of her child.

Thus when home-sympathy is purified and developed by Christian faith and love, it opens up the most elevated of all home-feeling and solicitude, and becomes the most effectual safeguard against impending ruin. No family can be true to its privileges and mission without it. It allures to the cross, leads all the members in the path of the sympathizing one, and prompts them to say, "Entreat me not to leave thee, or to return from following after thee; for whither thou goest I will go, and where thou lodgest, I will lodge; thy people shall be my people, and thy God my God; where thou diest I will die, and there will I be buried; the Lord do so to me, and more also, if aught but death part thee and me."

What would the Christian home be, therefore, without such sympathy? Powerless, a moral desolation! We read in God's Word, of men losing natural affection, and of mothers forgetting their sucking children. But these were worse than brutes. What shall we then say of Christian parents being devoid of spiritual sympathy,—shedding no tear of anguish over their moral ruin, nor showing the least concern about their salvation? Such parents do not rejoice even over the return of their children to God. They are a disgrace to the Christian name, and bring infamy upon the Christian home.

Some parents do not proceed quite so far. They indulge in the feeling of sympathy for their children; but alas! that feeling is never expressed in efforts to save them. It is all expended in vain and fruitless lamentations, and is, therefore, at best but a morbid sentimentalism,—but a cloak behind which are lurking parental hard-heartedness and religious apathy; proving plainly the great truth advanced by Adams, in his Elements of Christian Science, "that an indulgence in the feelings of sympathy without carrying them out to the relief of actual distress, produces hardness of heart to such a degree that the most pitiless and cruel, the most licentious and unnatural, and ungrateful conduct shall be joined with the most overflowing and deeply thrilling sentiment."

Let those parents who are ever lamenting the wickedness of their children, but do nothing to make them better, ponder well this sentiment, and see it in the grin of their own hypocrisy, and the desolation of their injured home and children. Let the other members, as well as the parents, take the timely warning. Let the pious wife here see the character of her sympathy for her impenitent husband. And let each see that their pious sympathy "always issue forth in actions." Let that sympathy give not only eloquence to the tongue, tears to your eye, and sighs to your heart, but also faithfulness to your life and holy calling. As the cry of hunger from your children, and their shivering cold in winter, prompt you to provide for their natural wants, so let their moral wants impel you to fidelity to their souls. All will be vain without this. The stern demands of a father's authority, and the formal teachings of a mother's lip, will fall like the frost of a winter's morning, upon their tender hearts, —only to sear and to harden and to freeze up the heart against God. For

> "He will not let love's work impart
> Full solace, lest it steal the heart."

But when pure and holy sympathy goes out, in its softening influence after the young;—

> "Then, feeling is diffused in every part,
> Thrills in each nerve, and lives in all the heart."

Such sympathy has a saving influence upon both

the parent and the child. It softens and refines the former, while it forms and allures the latter. The child fondly leans upon the parents, looks up to them for support and enjoyment, and is led by them in whatever path they choose. By its influence the feeling of natural and spiritual helplessness becomes developed in the child; the sense of dependence on a superior is awakened; and with these, all those feelings of confidence and veneration, which lay the foundation of religious affections, are unfolded. The parent's influence, both as to kind and degree, depends, therefore, upon the character of home-sympathy. If it is but natural, the parental influence will not extend beyond the worldly gain and temporal welfare of the child. The parent will exert no power over the soul. But if it be spiritual, and extend beyond the mere instincts of natural affection, it will expand the mind, and develop all the melting charities of our nature. It will pass with a new transferring and transforming power, from husband to wife, from parent to child, from kindred to kindred. Wherever it finds its way; whatever fiber of the heart it may touch, it begets a new and holy affection, unites the energies, lightens the toils, soothes the sorrows, and exalts the hopes, of all the members. It reflects a softening luster from eye to eye, goes with electric flash from heart to heart, glows in its warmth throughout all its moral courses, accumulates the home-endearments, stimulates each member to religious exertions for all the rest, and lays the foundation in each heart for an unbroken home-communion of their sainted spirits in heaven! It cements them together in their tent-home, creating a sweet concord of hearts and hopes and joys; and then elevates them unitedly in fond anticipation of reunion in their eternal home. They blend their tears together over the grave of buried love, and enjoy the saintly sympathy of loved ones gone before them.

This is its most lovely feature. Tell me, is there not a bond of sympathy between Jesus and His people here,—between loved ones in heaven and their pious kindred on earth? Do not the tears of the Christian home reflect the tears of Jesus? These are to the heart like the dews of Hermon,—like the dews that descended upon the mountains of Zion.

"No radiant pearl which crested fortune wears,
No gem that, sparkling, hangs from beauty's ears,
Not the bright stars which night's blue arch adorn,
Nor rising sun that gilds the vernal morn,
Shine with such luster as the tear that breaks
For others' woe, down virtue's lovely cheeks."

Is such, Christian brother, the sympathy of your home? It will be a safeguard against the follies and the false interests of life. It will restrict the fashionable taste and sentiments of the age. It will teach wisdom to the pious mother, and be a sure defense against the dangers and indiscretions of the nursery and fashionable boarding school. Under its influence, mothers will not trust the souls of their children to the guardianship of irreligious nurses, nor expose them to the perils of a corrupted and heartless fashion. They will deny themselves the ruinous pleasures of a gay and reckless association with the world; and with maternal solicitude, attend upon the opening of those buds of life which God has committed to them. The pious mother will wield her power over her children, by the force of this sympathy; for her's is the deepest, purest, and most saving of all home-sympathy:

"Earth may chill
And sever other sympathies, and prove
How weak all human bonds are—it may kill
Friendship, and crush hearts with them—but the thrill
Of the maternal breast must ever move
In blest communion with her child, and fill
Even heaven itself with prayers and hymns of love!"

CHAPTER XV.

FAMILY PRAYER.

"Hush! 'tis a holy hour,—the quiet room
Seems like a temple, while yon soft lamp sheds
A faint and starry radiance through the room
And the sweet stillness, down on yon bright heads,
With all their clustering locks, untouched by care,
And bowed, as flowers are bowed with night,—in prayer.
Gaze on, 'tis lovely—childhood's lip and cheek
Mantling beneath its earnest brow of thought!"

Home-sympathy will prompt to family devotion. The latter is the fruit of the former. A prayerless home is destitute of religious sympathy. The family demands prayer. Its relation to God, its dependence and specific duties, involve devotion. Communion with God constitutes a part of the intercourse and society of home. The necessity of family prayer arises out of the home-constitution and mission. Family mercies and blessings; family dangers and weaknesses; family hopes and temptations,—all bespeak the importance of family worship. If you occupy the responsible station of a parent; if God has made you the head of a religious household, and you profess to stand and live on the Lord's side, then, tell me, have you not by implication vowed to maintain regular family worship? Besides, the benefits and privilege of prayer develop the obligation of the family to engage in it. Is not every privilege a duty? And if it is a duty for individuals and congregations to pray, is it not, for a similar reason, the duty of the family to establish her altar of devotion? As a family we daily need and receive mercies, daily sin, are tempted and in danger every day; why not then as a family daily pray?

But what is family prayer? It is not simply individual prayer, not the altar of the closet; but the home-altar, around which all the members gather morning and evening, as a family-unit, with one heart, one faith and one hope, to commune with God and supplicate his mercy. "In the devotion of this little assembly," says Dr. Dwight, "parents pray for their children, and children for their parents; the husband for the wife, and the wife for the husband; while brothers and sisters send up their requests to the throne of Infinite Mercy, to call down blessings on each other. Who that wears the name of a man can be indifferent here? Must not the venerable character of the parent, the peculiar tenderness of the conjugal union, the affectionate intimacy of the filial and fraternal relations;

must not the nearest of relations long existing, the interchange of kindness long continued, and the oneness of interests long cemented, — all warm the heart, heighten the importance of every petition, and increase the fervor of every devotional effort?"

What scene can be more lovely on earth, more like the heavenly home, and more pleasing to God, than that of a pious family kneeling with one accord around the home-altar, and uniting their supplications to their Father in heaven! How sublime the act of those parents who thus pray for the blessing of God upon their household! How lovely the scene of a pious mother gathering her little ones around her at the bedside, and teaching them the privilege of prayer! And what a safeguard is this home-devotion, against all the machinations of Satan!

"Our hearths are altars all;
The prayers of hungry souls and poor,
Like armed angels at the door,
Our unseen foes appal!"

It is this which makes home a type of heaven, the dwelling place of God. The family altar is heaven's threshold. And happy are those children who at that altar, have been consecrated by a father's blessing, baptized by a mother's tears, and borne up to heaven upon their joint petitions, as a voluntary thank-offering to God. The home that has honored God with an altar of devotion may well be called blessed.

"Child, amidst the flowers at play,
While the red light fades away;
Mother, with thine earnest eye
Ever following silently;
Father, by the breeze of eve
Called thy warmest work to leave;
Pray!—ere yet the dark hours be,
Lift the heart and bend the knee."

The duty thus to establish family prayer is imperative. It is a duty because God commands it, and the mission of home cannot be fulfilled without it. It is a duty because a privilege and a blessing, and the condition of parental efficiency in all other duties;—because the moral and spiritual growth of the child depends upon it. It is one of the most effectual means of grace. All the instructions, all the discipline and example, of the parent will be in vain without it. Hence both natural affection and christian faith should suggest its establishment. Parents are bound to do so by their covenant vows, by the obligations of baptism, by all the interests and hopes of their household. They have dedicated their children to God, and pledged themselves to educate them for Him, and to train them up in His ways. Tell me then, can you be faithful to these vows and obligations without family prayer? Can you fulfil your covenant engagements, hope to receive your reward, and see your children grow up in the nurture of the Lord's vineyard, without rearing up a family altar?

The promised blessings of family prayer show

that every faithful Christian home must have its family altar. These are unspeakable. It is a sure defence against sin; it sanctifies the members, and throws a hallowed atmosphere around our household. The child will come under its restraining and saving influence. A mother's prayer will haunt the child, and draw it as if by magic power towards herself in heaven:

> "He might forget her melting prayer,
> While pleasure's pulses madly fly,
> But in the still, unbroken air,
> Her gentle tones come stealing by,—
> And years of sin and manhood flee,
> And leave him at his mother's knee!"

It affords home security and happiness, removes family friction, and causes all the complicated wheels of the home-machinery to move on noiselessly and smoothly. It promotes union and harmony, expunges all selfishness, allays petulant feelings and turbulent passions, destroys peevishness of temper, and makes home-intercourse holy and delightful. It causes the members to reciprocate each other's affections, hushes the voice of recrimination, and exerts a softening and harmonizing influence over each heart. The dew of Hermon falls upon the home where prayer is wont to be made. Its members enjoy the good and the pleasantness of dwelling together in unity. It gives tone and intensity to their affections and sympathies: it throws a sunshine around their hopes and interests: it increases their happiness, and takes away the poignancy of their grief and sorrow. It availeth much, therefore, both for time and eternity. Its voice has sent many a poor prodigal home to his father's house. Its answer has often been, "This man was born there!" The child, kneeling beside the pious mother, and pouring forth its infant prayer to God, must attract the notice of the heavenly host, and receive into its soul the power of a new life.

"Who would not be an infant now,
To breathe an infant's prayer?
O manhood! could thy spirit kneel
Beside that sunny child,
As fondly pray, and purely feel,
With soul as undefiled.
That moment would encircle thee,
With light and love divine;
Thy gaze might dwell on Deity,
And heaven itself be thine."

And yet the neglect of family prayer is a very general defect of the Christian home. No home-duty has indeed been more grossly neglected and abused. Some attend to it only occasionally; some only in times of affliction and distress, as if then only they needed to pray to God; some only on the Sabbath, as if that were the only day to commune with Him. Some perform it only in a formal way, having the form without the spirit of prayer, as if God did not require the fervent, in order to the effectual, prayer that availeth much.

As a general thing, at the present day, not more than three or four families out of a whole congregation, have established the family altar. The parents may engage in closet prayer, but their children are strangers to the fact. Their devotions they seem zealous to conceal, as if they were ashamed of their piety. Can this be right? Is this the will of God? No! methinks if the parent is faithful to the duty of private prayer, he cannot omit the duty and privilege of family devotion. But why neglect family prayer? Are you ashamed of your children? Have you no time? Then you are unworthy of a family, and should not profess to act towards them as the steward of God. Think you that God will not answer and bless your prayers? What more could you do and hope for your children than to offer up supplications for them to God?

> "What could a mother's prayer,
> In all the wildest ecstacy of hope,
> Ask for her darling like the bliss of heaven?"

Many seek by the most frivolous excuses, to justify their neglect of family prayer. Some will urge the press of other duties, alleging that other engagements prevent it. This is false. God lays upon you no engagement that is designed to supersede the necessity of prayer. Besides, you will find that you really waste more time than it would require for family devotion. And further, can you spend your time to better purpose than in family prayer? I think not. It is the best husbandry of time. Says Philip Henry to his children, "Prayer and provender hinder no man's journey." But another pleads incapacity. He has not the gift of speech, and cannot make an eloquent prayer. This is no excuse. Prayer is the gift of the Holy Spirit; and if you have the spirit of prayer, you will find words for its utterance. Besides, eloquence does not condition the efficacy of prayer. "Where there is a willing mind, it is accepted according to that a man hath, and not according to that he hath not."

> "When we of helps or hopes are quite bereaven,
> Our humble prayers have entrance into heaven."

We have the capacity to ask for what we earnestly desire and feel the need of. The anger of God will kindle against you for this excuse, as it kindled against Moses for a similar one. When He called him to be his messenger to Israel, Moses said, as you do, "O my Lord, I am not eloquent,—I am slow of speech, and of a slow tongue. And the Lord said unto him, who hath made man's mouth? or, who maketh the dumb, or deaf, or the seeing, or the blind? Have not I the Lord? The anger of the Lord was kindled against him."

Let me, therefore, urge upon you, Christian parents, to make prayer a prominent element of your home. You should be a priest unto your family,—a leader in home-communion with God.

Your children have a right to expect this from you. If you are a church member, how strange and startling must be the enunciation in heaven, that you are a prayerless christian, and your home destitute of the altar! And do you think that, continuing thus, you will be admitted into that heavenly home where there is one unbroken voice of prayer and praise to God? Do you not tremble at the prospect of those tremendous denunciations which the Lord has uttered against those who neglect and abuse the privilege of prayer? "Pour out thy fury upon the families that have not called upon thy name." Oh then, make your home a house of prayer; lead your little flock in sweet communion with God. Establish in them the habit of devotion: Shape their consciences by prayer. In this way you shall secure for yourself and them the blessing of God: His smile shall ever rest upon your household: Salvation shall be the heritage of your children; they will grow up in the divine life; and will live amid the blessings of prayer, and be faithful to its requisitions:

"Hold the little hands in prayer, teach the weak knees their kneeling;
Let him see thee speaking to thy God; he will not forget it afterwards;
When old and gray will he feelingly remember a mother's tender piety,
And the touching recollection of her prayers shall arrest the strong man in his sin!"

CHAPTER XVI.

HOME-EDUCATION.

SECTION I.

THE CHARACTER OF HOME EDUCATION.

"SCRATCH the green rind of a sapling, or wantonly twist it in the soil,
The scarred and crooked oak will tell of thee for centuries to come;
Wherefore, though the voice of instruction waiteth for the ear of reason,
Yet with his mother's milk the young child drinketh education."

WE come now to consider one of the most important features of the Christian home, viz., as a school for the education of character. This is important because of its vital bearing upon the interests of home. The parent is not only king and priest, but prophet in the family. It is the first school. We there receive a training for good or for evil. There is not a word, nor an emotion, nor an act, nor even a look there, which does not teach the child something. Character is ever being framed and moulded there. Every habit there formed, and every action there performed, imply a principle which shall enter as an element into the future character of the child.

What is home-education? It is the physical, mental, moral, and religious development of the child. To educate means to draw out as well as to instil in. It means the evolution of our nature as well as the communication of facts and principles to us. The home training does not, therefore, consist of simple information, but is a nurture of body, mind and spirit. From this we may infer the frequent mistakes of parents, in substituting mere book-learning for a training up and nurture, dealing with their children as if they had no faculties, and making the entire education of their children mechanical and empirical. Home training involves the development of all their faculties as a unit and in their living relation, causing the body to move right, the mind to think right, the heart to feel right, and the soul to love right; changing your children from creatures of mere impulse, prejudice and passion, to thinking, loving and reasoning beings. To educate them is to bring out their hidden powers, to form their character, and prepare them for their station in life. Thus home-education means a drawing out and also a bringing up,—a training for man, and a bringing up for God; a training and nurture for the family, the state, and the church,—for time and for eternity. These must be done together; they involve but one process, and are conditioned by each other. We cannot separate a secular from a religious education, neither can we separate a training from a bringing up. While those faculties of the child which exist in a state of mere involution, are being developed, its nature must be supplied with appropriate food; and every element of its education must possess the plastic power of evolving and giving specific form to its future character and destiny. Thus the parent, in teaching, must have a forming influence over the child; and his instructions must correspond in character, kind and extent, with the nature, wants, and destiny of the child.

What are now the different kinds or parts of home-education?

It must be physical. The child has a physical nature, physical wants, and is related to the material world; and should, therefore, receive a physical education. The object of this is to ensure that sound, vigorous frame of body which is not only a great blessing in itself, but an essential concomitant of a sound state and vigorous development of mind. It refers to the proper management of the health of the child, its diet, habits of exercise and recreation. Parents should teach their children the nature of the body, its dangers, and bearing upon their future happiness. They should teach them to govern their appetite, and train them up to habits of exercise and early rising. This part of home-education begins in the nursery,—in the cradle, and is not complete till the body is brought to maturity in all its functions. Neglect of it will result in physical imbecility, and often in mental derangement. The object secured by it is, the preservation of the health and constitution of the child. In this we see its importance. What is your wealth, your station, your influence, if through your neglect of your children, they are deprived of health, and grow up with the seeds of immature death springing up in their system?

In the physical training of children due regard should be had to cleanliness, exercise, diet and dress. Without this all will be vain. Many parents keep them within doors, never let them enjoy the pure air, nor exercise the muscular system, keep their bodies cooped in clothing too small, and feasted upon a diet unwholesome; and as a consequence, they show a sickly growth, and become unfit either for the burdens or for the enjoyments of life.

The importance of exercise in the open air, and abstemiousness in diet, is proven from the health of those nations that train their children in all the exercise of riding, leaping, running and fencing, and subject them from infancy to the most frugal diet. Thus the perfect forms and vigorous health of the Greeks, the Romans and Persians were the fruit of national attention paid to physical education. Every home should have its suitable gymnasium. How many parents, by their violation of the laws of health, prostitute the strength of their children to profligacy and indolence.

Home-education must be intellectual. Much of human character and happiness depends upon the education of the mind, both as respects the development of its faculties and the application of legitimate truth. The mind is the man. It is not, as Locke declares, like a blank sheet of paper or a chest of drawers; but has an intuitional as well as a logical consciousness, innate ideas as well as capacities of receiving truth; while all its faculties involve a unity, and exist in the child in a state of involution; the abuse and neglect of one of which will have their bearing upon all the rest; and the mind without proper culture in its undeveloped state in the child, will show the symptoms of its abuse in the man. The character of the mind in the man will indicate the character of its education in the child. This education should begin properly with the first symptoms of consciousness. All the powers of the intellect should be unfolded. Parents should be the Principals in the mental training of their children. The manner and means of such training will be considered in another place. Our purpose here is simply to state this as a part of home-training. From the important part which the mind acts in the great drama of human life and destiny, we think that no intelligent parent would presume to repudiate its education.

Home-education must be moral. The family should develop the moral nature of the child. The will should be educated; the sense of right and wrong trained; the emotions cultivated; the passions and desires ruled; the conscience and faith developed. The necessity of this is seen in the fact that our nature is fallen and perverted. The means of educating the moral nature of the child, are natural and revealed. Both are of divine appointment. The former are those which lie within the circumference of our abilities, and will be of no avail without the latter, which are found in the scriptures and church. What are some of these means?

1. Parents should place their children in circumstances calculated to form a good moral character. They should surround them with a moral atmosphere, that they may, with their first breath, inhale a pure moral being, and escape the contamination of evil. This has been called "the education of circumstances." Much of character depends upon position and the circumstances in which we are placed. This is seen in the difference between those children who have enjoyed the true christian home, and those who have not. Hence the first thing parents should consider in the moral training of their children is, the home in which they are to be trained. This home should afford them circumstances the most favorable to their moral culture.

2. They should remove all temptation. Evil propensities are called forth by temptation; and

a child loses the power to resist in proportion to the frequency of the temptation. Hence the exposure of our children to temptation but educates and strengthens their propensities to evil. On the other hand, if we remove temptation, these propensities will not be called into activity, and will lose their tenacity. Never allow your children to tamper with sin in any form; teach them how to resist temptation; inspire them with an abhorrence and a dread of all evil. In this way you prepare them for the reception and reproduction of moral truth.

3. Another means of moral education is example. This has been styled the "education of example." This has more power than precept. The efficiency of this means is based upon the natural disposition of the child to imitate. Children take their parents as the standard of all that is good, and will, therefore, follow them in evil as well as in good. Hence the parent's example should be a correct model of sound morality. The child will be the moral counterpart of the parent. You can see the parent's home in the child. He is the moral daguerreotype of his parent. This but shows the importance of good example in his moral training.

4. But one of the most effectual means is, by moral training, by which we mean, to draw out and properly direct the moral faculties, and to habituate them to the exercise of moral principle. Without this, all mechanical education will be fruitless. To call forth muscular power you

must exercise the muscles. So you give the child moral stamina by developing its moral faculties, and establishing in them the habit of moral action. This training has its foundation in the law of habit. It is given, with its results, in the Word of God. "Train up a child," &c. Also in the old maxim, "Just as the twig is bent, the tree is inclined."

> "Scratch the green rind of a sapling, or wantonly twist it in the soil,
> The scarred and crooked oak will tell of thee for centuries to come!"

The power and pleasure of doing a thing depends much upon habit. Our nature may become habituated to good or evil; we become passive in proportion to the habit. How important, then, that the moral powers of our children be trained up to principles and action until habits of good thought, feeling, and conduct, are established. Then they will not depart from them; and their moral life will be spontaneous and a source of enjoyment.

The feelings, appetites and instincts of children should be thus specially trained. According to Dr. Gall, there are two classes of feelings,—the selfish, yet necessary for the preservation of the individual; and the unselfish, or those which are directed to objects apart from self, yet liable to abuse and misdirection. Both of these demand a home-training. The parent should give to each its true direction, restrain and harmonize them in their relations and respective spheres of activity, and bring them under law, and place before each its legitimate object and end. Then, and then only, do they become laws of self-preservation. The natural appetites are subject to abuse, and when unrestrained, defeat the very ends of their existence. Thus the appetite for food may be over-indulged through mistaken parental kindness, until habits of sensualism are established, and the child becomes a glutton, and finds the grave of infamy.

How many children have been thus destroyed in soul and body by parental indulgence and neglect of their natural feelings and appetites. The feeling of cruelty, revenge, malice, falsehood, tale-bearing, dishonesty, vanity, &c., have, in the same way and by the same indulgence, been engendered in the children of Christian parents. The same, too, may be said of the unselfish feelings. These have been called the moral sentiments; and upon their proper training depends the formation of a positive moral character. The conscience comes under this head. The parent should train that important faculty of the child. It should be taught to act from the standpoint of conscience, and to form the habit of conscientiousness in word and deed. This includes the training of the motives also, and of all the cardinal moral virtues, such as justice, honor, chastity, veneration, kindness, &c. "Teach your children," says Goodrich in his Fireside Education, "never to wound a person's feelings because he is poor, because he is deformed, because he is unfortunate, because he holds an humble station in life, because he is poorly clad, because he is weak in body and mind, because he is awkward, or because the God of nature has bestowed upon him a darker skin than theirs."

This early education should commence as soon as the necessities of the child demand it. A child should be taught what is necessary for it to know and practice as soon as that necessity exists and the child is capable of learning. Scripture sanctions this. Our fathers did so. It was the injunction of Moses to the children of Israel: Deut. vi., 6–9. God commands you to break up the fallow ground and sow the good seed at the first dawn of the spring-life of your children, and then to pray for the "early and the latter rain,"

> "Teaching, with pious care, the dawning light
> Of infant intellect to know the Lord."

Home-education should be religious. As the child has a religious nature, religious wants, and a religious end to accomplish, it should receive from its parents a religious training. Religion is educational. We are commanded to teach religion to our children. The admonition to "train up a child in the way he should go," and to "bring him up in the nurture and admonition of the Lord," is a scripture sanction of religious education. Nature and the bible are the text-books for such a training. The child should be taught natural and revealed religion. Such education involves the development of the child's religious nature, and the diligent use of those means by which it may become an adopted child of God.

Education should be suited to the wants and the destination of the child. Religion is its first want,—the one thing needful, the chief concern; and should, therefore, be the first object of attention in home-training. The fear and love of God should be the first lesson taught. This is the beginning of wisdom. Teach your children to love Him above father and mother, sister and brother. The child is capable of such ideas of God. Children can possess the sentiment of God; and when this is instilled and developed as a rudiment of their character, they have a preparation for the grace of God. What is the mere secular, without such a religious education? It is education without its essence; for piety is the essence of all education. Irreligious training is destructive,—a curse rather than a blessing,—only a training up to crime and to ruin. "The mildew of a cultivated, but depraved mind, blights whatever it falls upon." "Religion," says Dr. Barrow, "is the only science, which is equally and indispensably necessary to men of every rank, every age, and every profession." "The end of learning," says Milton, "is to repair the ruins of our first parents, by requiring to know God aright, and out of that knowledge, to love Him, and to imitate Him."

We see, therefore, that religious training is the only true palladium of your children's happiness and destiny; and should be the great end of all home-teaching. Tinge all their thoughts and feelings with a sense of eternity. Train them up to build for another world. Stamp the impress of a future life upon their tender hearts. Beget in them longings after immortality. See that their designs extend beyond this world. As the Spartan mother gave character to her nation by the instructions she gave her child, so you give character to your religion, your church, your home, by the spiritual culture of your offspring. Let the jewels you give them be the virtues and the gifts of the Holy Ghost,—the ornaments of a meek and quiet spirit.

> "Take the germ, and make it
> A bud of moral beauty. Let the dews
> Of knowledge and the light of virtue, wake it
> In richest fragrance and in purest hues."

Childhood is the period in which the principles of christianity can be the most effectually engrafted in our nature. Its pliability at that period insures its free assimilation to the spirit and truth of religion. "Would to God," says St. Pierre, "I had preserved the sentiment of the existence of the Supreme Being, and of His principal attributes, as pure as I had it in my earliest years!" It is the heart more than the head that religion demands; and you can fill the young heart with sentiments of God better than if you wait till it grows hard as adamant in sin. You can elevate the soul of your child to God, and teach it to raise its little hands and voice in prayer to the Most High. You can teach it this from the book of nature and of revelation,—from the daisies that spring up among the grass upon which it frolics, by the mellow fruits after which it longs, by the stars that shine in unclouded luster above it, and by the breezes which ruffle its silken curls, and bring perfume to its smiling face.

To the mother especially, is committed the religious education of the child at home. She is eminently adapted, if herself a Christian, for such a work. Her love, her piety, which breathes in every word, in every look, makes her instructions effectual and pleasing.

> " 'Tis pleasing to be schooled by female lips and eyes,
> They smile so when one's right, and when one's wrong,
> They smile still more; and then there
> Comes encouragement in the soft hand
> Over the brow, perhaps even a chaste kiss—
> I learned the little that I know by this."

They can better reach and train the heart. Religion is heart-wisdom. "My son, give me thy heart!" We may use the head as an avenue to the heart, yet nothing is done in the religion of our children until the heart be carried. It is only in that inner shrine that there can be deposited the wisdom that is from above, and only then will they be made wise unto salvation. And who is better able to storm and carry that inner citadel, and lead its subdued inmates to the Cross, than the pious, tender-hearted, soliciting mother!

Some parents object to the religious training of their children, "because," say they, "there is danger of having their minds biased by some particular creed; they should be left, therefore, to themselves till they are capable of making a choice, and then let them choose their creed." This is all a miserable subterfuge, and in direct opposition to the explicit command of God and the whole tenor of the gospel plan of salvation. It goes upon the assumption that religion is but an opinion—a subscription to a certain creed, learning certain doctrines—a mere thing for the head. Tell me, is it worse to bias their minds to a particular creed, than to let them grow up biased to the world, to the Devil and all his works? Is it all of home, religious culture to bias them to a particular creed? Besides, is it not the right, yea, the duty of parents to bias their children in favor of the religious creed of the parental home? It shows, therefore, that those parents who, for this reason, object to religious training, have but little love for, and confidence in, their own creed, or they would not shrink from biasing their children to it.

To encourage Christian parents to give their children a good religious education, God has given them numerous examples, from both sacred and profane history, of conversion and eminent piety in the age of childhood, as the direct fruit of early parental instruction. Look, for instance, at the child Samuel worshiping the Lord. Look, too, at the case of Moses and of David, of

Joseph and of John the Baptist. Dr. Doddridge, we are told, "was brought up in the early knowledge of religion by his pious parents." His mother "taught him the history of the Old and New Testaments before he could read, by the assistance of some Dutch tiles in the chimney of the room where they commonly sat; and her wise and pious reflections on the stories there represented were the means of making some good impressions on his heart, which never wore out." An eminently pious minister thus writes to his parents, confirming by his own blessed experience the early fruits of religious training: "I verily believe that had my religious training been confined to the gleanings of the Sabbath school, instead of the steady enforcement of the Mosaic arrangement at home by my parents, I might now be pursuing a far different course, and living for a far different end. Many, very many times, as early in childhood as I can recollect, has the Spirit of God convicted me of sin, as my father at home has taught me out of the scriptures, and I cannot easily forget that the same high-priest of the home-church once tore from me the hypocrite's hope. And that dear place had another to carry on the work, gentler but not weaker; and memory recalls a mother pressing her face close to mine as she often knelt with me before the mercy-seat. I will not cast reproach on any institution which has been productive of good to myself and to others, but with profound gratitude will say, home was the place of my spiritual nativity, and my parents were God's instruments in leading me to Christ!"

The eminent piety of Dr. Dwight stands on record as the fruit of a mother's faithful religious training; for "she taught him from the very dawn of reason to fear God and keep His commandments, and the impressions then made upon his mind in infancy, were never effaced." The mother of young Edwards is another example of early piety as the fruit of religious home-culture. The aged Polycarp, when under arrest during the persecution under Marcus Aurelius, in reply to the injunction of the pro-consul, "Swear, curse Christ, and I release thee!" exclaimed, "Six and eighty years have I served Him, and He has done me nothing but good; and how could I curse Him, my Lord and Saviour?" Thus showing himself to have been a Christian at the early age of four years! It was through the instructions of his grandmother Lois, and his mother Eunice, that young Timothy "knew from a child the holy scriptures, which made him wise unto salvation."

And what an effectual antidote are such instructions against vice and temptation! How many have by them been arrested from the devouring jaws of infidelity and ruin! Thus it was with John Randolph, who said that in the days of the French revolution, when infidel reason took the place of God and the bible, and infidelity prowled unmolested throughout France, he would have become an infidel himself, had it not been for the remembrance of his childhood days, when his pious mother taught him to kneel by her side, and to say, "Our Father, who art in heaven!" Thus, too, with the pious and learned J. Q. Adams, who daily repeated the little prayers his mother taught him when a child.

Thus, then, we see that parents are encouraged by the most brilliant examples of history, to teach their children religion at the home-fireside, "when thou liest down and risest up." Oh, let the gentle courtesies and sweet endearments of home engrave the Word and Spirit of God upon their tender hearts. Wait not until they are matured in rebellion, and sin lay beds of flinty rock over their hearts; but let them breathe from infancy the atmosphere of holiness, and drink from the living fountains of divine truth. See that your homes become their birth-place in the spiritual kingdom of Christ.

Such religious training will be the guardian of their future life, and will fortify them against impending evil. What made Daniel steadfast amidst all the efforts to heathenize him during his captivity in Babylon? His early religious culture. It was the means of his preservation. The truth had been deeply engraven upon his heart when young, and nothing could ever efface it. His early home-impressions glowed there with pristine freshness and power amid all the terrors which surrounded him in the den and before the throne of his implacable foe. These home-instructions may be silenced for a time, but never destroyed. They may be overshadowed, but not annihilated. Says Dr. Cumming, "The words spoken by parents to their children in the privacy of home are like words spoken in a whispering-gallery, and will be clearly heard at the distance of years, and along the corridors of ages that are yet to come. They will prove like the lone star to the mariner upon a dark and stormy sea, associated with a mother's love, with a father's example, with the roof-tree beneath which they lived and loved, and will prove in after life to mould the man and enable him to adorn and improve the age in which he is placed."

Be faithful, therefore, in the spiritual culture of your children. Give them "line upon line and precept upon precept, here a little and there a little." Lead them on by degrees to Christ until each indelible impression becomes an established habit. In the morning of their life sow the seed; and God will give the increase; and then in the day of judgment your children will rise up and call you blessed!

SECTION II.

NEGLECT AND ABUSE OF HOME-EDUCATION.

"ACCOMPLISHMENTS have taken virtue's place,
And wisdom falls before exterior grace;
We slight the precious kernel of the stone,
And toil to polish its rough coat alone.
A just deportment, manners graced with ease,
Elegant phases, and figure formed to please,
Are qualities that seem to comprehend
Whatever parents, guardians, schools intend;
Hence all that interferes, and dares to clash
With indolence and luxury, is trash!"

HOME-EDUCATION in all its parts is most sadly neglected and abused at the present day. Many parents think that the office of teacher is not included in the parental character and mission. The neglect of home-training seems to arise out of an existing prejudice against it. Some think that education will unfit their children for industry,—will make them indolent and proud. They regard mental culture as an enemy to both industry and virtue. Strange delusion! The mind is given to use, not to abuse; and its abuse is no argument against its proper use. God has given the mind, and intends it to be developed and cultivated. If, therefore, its training has made it indolent and dissipated, it only proves its education to be spurious. You might, by a parity of reasoning, blindfold the eye that it might not be covetous, or tie up the hand lest it pick a man's pocket, or hobble the feet lest they run into evil ways, as to keep the mind in ignorance lest it become wicked.

Besides, we find more real indolence and wickedness among the ignorant than among the educated; for man will be educated in something. If you do not educate your child in the truths of nature and religion, be assured he will become trained in falsehood and in the ways of Satan. "Uneducated mind is uneducated vice." A proper education is a divine alchemy which turns all the baser parts of man's nature into gold. Without it all is discord and darkness within and without. Besides, ignorance leads to misery because it leads to wickedness. Dr. Johnson was once asked, "Who is the most miserable man?" He replied, "That man who cannot read on a rainy day!" It has well been said by Edmund Burke that "Education is the cheap defense of nations." Why? Because it prevents vice, poverty, misery, and relieves the state of the support of paupers and criminals. "A good education," says Miss Sedgwick, "is a young man's best capital." Says Governor Everett to parents, "Sow the seed of instruction in your son's and daughter's minds. It will flourish when that over-arching heaven shall pass away like a scroll, and the eternal sun which lightens it, shall set in blood." Says the Rev. Robert Hall, "I am persuaded that the extreme profligacy, improvidence, and misery, which are so prevalent among the laboring classes in many countries, are chiefly to be ascribed to the want of education."

What indeed can we look for but wretchedness and guilt from that child that has been left by its cruel parents to grow up "darkening in the deeper ignorance of mankind, with all its jealousies, and its narrow-mindedness, and its superstitions, and its penury of enjoyments, poor amid the intellectual and moral riches of the universe; blind in this splendid temple which God has lighted up, and famishing amid the profusions of Omnipotence?" And, parents, let me ask you, if you thus neglect the proper education of your children, and as a consequence, such pauperism of estate, of mind, and of morals, come upon them, will you not have to answer for all this to God?

> "Oh, woe for those who trample on the mind,
> That fearful thing! They know not what they do,
> Nor what they deal with!"

Your children, thus neglected, will become victims to inordinate passion, without power to discern between reality and illusion, ignorant of what is true happiness, living for mere sense, with their moral nature enclosed in the iron mail of superstition, while the good seeds of truth sown upon their hearts "wither away, because they have no depth of earth."

Parents cannot, therefore, neglect the education of their children without incurring disgrace and guilt before God and man. They will meet a merited retribution both here and hereafter. The justice of this is forcibly illustrated in a law of the Icelanders, which makes the court inquire, when a child is accursed, whether the parents have given the offender a good education? And if not, the court inflicts the punishment on the parents. This but expresses the higher law of God which holds parents responsible for the training of their children. Listen to the threatening voice of God in history. Crates, an ancient philosopher, used to say that if he could reach the highest eminence in the city, he would make this proclamation: "What mean ye, fellow-citizens, to be so anxious after wealth, but so indifferent to your children's education? It is like being solicitous about the shoe, but neglecting entirely the foot that is to wear it!"

We would reiterate that proclamation in this age of superior intelligence. To the pious parent there is a pleasure in training the young and tender heart for God. What a beautiful tribute did Thompson yield to this pleasure in the following lines:

> "Delightful task! to rear the tender thought,
> To teach the young idea how to shoot,
> To pour the fresh instruction o'er the mind,
> To breathe enlivening spirit, and to fix
> The generous purpose in the glowing breast!"

But home-education, at the present day, is as

much abused as it is neglected. The criminality of the former is perhaps greater than that of the latter. This may have more reference to the female than to the male portion of the family. The abuse here consists of the want of a training up to wisdom. We see this in what is called the fashionable, instead of the Christian, education, received at some of our fashionable boarding schools. Here the child is sent with no home-training whatever, to be trained up a fashionable doll, fit to be played with and dandled upon the arms of a whining and heartless society, with no preparation for companionship in life, destitute of substantial character, with undoctrinated feelings of aversion to religion, fit only for a puppet show in some gay and thoughtless circle; kneeling before fashion as her God, and giving her hand in marriage only to a golden and a gilded calf.

According to this abuse of home-education, "a young maiden is kept in the nursery and the school room, like a ship on the stocks, while she is furbished with abundance of showy accomplishments, and is launched like the ship, looking taut and trim, but empty of everything that can make her useful." Thus one great abuse of home-education is to substitute the boarding school for home-culture,—to send our children to such school at an age when they should be trained by and live under the direct influence of the parent. This generally ends in initiated profligacy, and alienation from home, while at best but a dunce after his course of training is ended.

> "Would you your son should be a sot and a dunce,
> Lascivious, headstrong, or all these at once?
> Train him in public with a mob of boys,
> Childish in mischief only and in noise."

Too often is it the case that the artifices and refinements of our fashionable boarding schools, have a most withering influence upon body, mind and soul, enfeebling and distorting the body, producing depraved stomachs, whimsical nerves, peevish tempers, indolent minds, and depraved morals. They become but wrecks of what they were when they first entered the school. This has been called "the stiff and starched system of muslin education," and is the nursery of pale, sickly, listless, peevish children.

But this is not the only abuse of home-education. Even when the training is begun at home, the very idea of education is often abused, because inefficient, destitute of true moral elements, and partial both as to the mode and as to the substance of it. The true resources of life are not developed; there is no instruction given in the principles and conditions of temporal and eternal well-being; there is no discipline of the mind, or body or morals. But the great idea and aim of education with many parents now, is to teach the child to read and write and cipher as a means of making money and getting along in this world, —not, of course, to prevent them from cheating others, but others from cheating them. All is prostituted to money and business. Character and happiness are left out of view. What have our schools now to do with the propensities, appetites, temperaments, habits and character of the pupils? And how are the parents who send their children to school to have them trained up with reference to these! All that is now looked at, is that learning which will fit the child for business. As a consequence most of our schools are a disgrace to the very name of education. More evil actually results from them than good. The mind and heart are injured,—the one but half trained; the other corrupted. Mental and moral training are divorced; hence one-sided, and the very end of education defeated. The child has no incentive to a virtuous and a noble life, and sinks down to the groveling drudgery of money-making. It is educated for nature, but not for God,—for this, but not for the next life.

If we would not abuse home-education we must not separate the moral from the mental,—the secular from the religious; for in doing so, we expose the child to rationalism and infidelity on the one hand, and to superstition and spiritualism on the other. This course is generally taken by parents when they educate their children for mere worldly utility and fashion, when they have not the welfare of the soul in view, and look only to the advantage of the body.

The duty then of Christian parents to give their children a true home-education may be seen from the consequences of its neglect and abuse on the one hand, and from its value and importance on the other. They should furnish them with all the necessary means, opportunities, and directions, of a Christian education. Give them proper books. "Without books," says the quaint Bartholin, "God is silent, justice dormant, science at a stand, philosophy lame, letters dumb, and all things involved in Cimmerian darkness." Bring them up to the habit of properly reading and studying these books. "A reading people will soon become a thinking people, and a thinking people must soon become a great people." Every book you furnish your child, and which it reads with reflection is "like a cast of the weaver's shuttle, adding another thread to the indestructible web of existence." It will be worth more to him than all your hoarded gold and silver. Make diligent use of those great auxiliaries to home-education, which the church has instituted, such as Sabbath schools; bible classes and catechisation.

Home-education does not imply a system of parental training isolated from the educational ministrations of the church; but is churchly in its spirit and in all its parts, and should in all respects be connected with the church. Home-training is a duty you owe to the church. By virtue of your relation to her, she has the authority to demand of you such a training of your child; and by virtue of your relation to the child, he has a right to such an education, and can demand it from you. It stands on the basis of parental duty imposed on you by God Himself. It is a prime necessity. It is your children's birthright, which they themselves cannot sell with impunity, for the pottage of gold or silver or pleasure : neither can you neglect or abuse it without guilt before God.

It is, therefore, a duty which you cannot shake off, and which involves both for you and for your child, the most momentous consequences. Christian parents! be faithful to this duty. Magnify your office as a teacher; be faithful to your household as a school. Diligently serve your children as the pupils that God has put under your care. Educate them for Him. Teach them to "walk by faith, not by sight." Cultivate in them a sense of the unseen world,—the feeling of the actual influence of the Spirit of God, the guardianship of his holy angels, and of the communion of saints. Teach them how to live and how to die; and by the force of your own holy example allure them to the cross, and lead them onward and upward in the living way of eternal life. You are encouraged to do so by the assurance of God that "when they grow old they will not depart from it."

CHAPTER XVII.

FAMILY HABITS.

"Dost thou live, man, dost thou live, or only breathe and labor?
Art thou free, or enslaved to a routine, the daily machinery of habit?
For one man is quickened into life, where thousands exist as in a torpor,
Feeding, toiling, sleeping, an insensate weary round;
The plough, or the ledger, or the trade, with animal cares and indolence,
Make the mass of vital years a heavy lump unleavened."

Much of the character, usefulness and happiness of home depend upon home habits. No one is without habits, good or bad. They have much to do with our welfare here and hereafter. Hence the importance of establishing proper habits.

Habit is a state of any thing, implying some continuance or permanence. It may be formed by nature or induced by extraneous circumstances. It is a settled disposition of the mind or body, involving an aptitude for the performance of certain actions, acquired by custom or frequent repetition. There are habits of the body, of the mind, of action; physical, mental, moral and religious habits. All these are included in the term home-habits.

Habit has been considered an "ultimate fact," that is, one of those qualities of life which are found to exist, and beyond which no investigation can be made. Habit may be referred to the law of action which pervades all vital being. Nature demands the repetition of vital action, and habit arises from this demand and from the manner in which it is supplied. It is the fruit of the operation of the law of repetition of action in all life. Hence it is, that habit becomes a part of our very existence, and that the well-being and happiness of our existence depend so much upon it.

The facility of action depends upon habit. In proportion as the actions of life become a habit, they will be easily performed, and performed with pleasure. The capacity to establish habits is the consequence of the power given us to promote our own welfare. This capacity is designed to bind us to that course of action which will accomplish the purposes of our existence. If rightly used, it is the guardian of our happiness; but if misused it will be our certain ruin. It will delight and fascinate until it subjugate our will, and lead us on, as in the case of the drunkard and the gambler, to infamy and to hell.

Home-habits are easily formed and established.

some kind, either good or bad, are being established every day. They are often secretly and unconsciously formed. All the principles and rules of conduct there introduced become at once the nuclei of future habits. These increase in power and supremacy as they are formed. We see this in the use of tobacco and intoxicating drink. These are, at first, disagreeable, and the victim has the power of repelling and overcoming them; but soon the habit is formed, when their use becomes pleasant, and he is made a willing slave to them.

The same may be said of the habits of industry, of study, of frugality, yea, of all the moral and religious acts of the Christian. It is easy to form such habits in children. Evil habits are more easily established, because we are naturally inclined to all evil; and when once formed, no parental interposition can break them up. Hence the importance of an early training up to good. If parents but leave their children to their own ways, they will run into evil habits; for sin is an epidemic. Profanity and falsehood and all other outrages against God will soon become the controlling habits of their lives. But when taken early, parents have complete power over their offspring. It is, therefore, a gross abuse of the Christian home when parents become indifferent to the formation of habits. It is their duty to crush every evil habit in its incipient state.

The forming of a good habit may not at first be congenial with our feelings. It may be irksome.

But if we persevere in it, that which at first was painful and difficult will soon be a source of enjoyment. Thus the habit of family prayer may at first be repulsive even to the Christian parent; a feeling of delicacy and the sense of unworthiness may, at the family altar, repress the feelings of enjoyment experienced in the closet; but soon the habit of this devotion will be formed, when it will be enjoyed as an essential part of home. To abandon it would be like breaking up the tenderest ties which bind the members together. The same may be said of the omission of a duty. How easily can the Christian form the habit of omitting family prayer or any other duty! Every such omission but forms and increases the habit, until it gains an ascendancy over our sense of duty, and at last exhibits its sovereign power in our total abandonment of the duty. Each omission has the power of reproducing itself in other and more frequent omissions. In this way Christian homes insensibly become unfaithful to their high vocation, and degenerate finally into complete apathy and estrangement from God. That indulgence which the misguided sympathy of too many parents prompts to, and which does away with all parental restraint, is the cause of children coming under the curse of evil habits. In this way parents often contribute to the temporal and eternal ruin of their offspring. This indulgence is no evidence of tender love, but of parental infatuation. It shows a blind and unholy love,—a love which owns no law, which is governed by no sense of duty, and which excludes all discipline; and hence unlike the love of God, who "chastiseth every one whom He loveth and receiveth."

The force and influence of home-habits will teach us the importance of establishing such only as receive the sanction of God. Habits, as we have seen, are much more easily formed than broken. When once established they enslave us to them, and subject our character to their iron despotism. They become the channel through which our life flows. The stream of our existence first forms the channel, and then the channel rules, guides and controls the current of the stream. The deeper the channel is wrought, the greater is its moulding and controlling influence over the stream. Thus our habits become our masters, and are the irrevocable rulers of our life. This is true of good as well as of bad habits. We come into voluntary subjection to them, until we shrink from the first proposal to depart from them.

"Habit," says the Rev. C. C. Colton, "will reconcile us to everything but change, and even to change, if it recur not too quickly. Milton, therefore, makes his hell an ice-house, as well as an oven, and freezes his devils at one period, but bakes them at another. The late Sir George Staunton informed me, that he had visited a man in India, who had committed a murder, and in order not only to save his life, but what was of much more consequence, his caste, he submitted to the penalty imposed; this was, that he should sleep for seven years on a bedstead, without any mattress, the whole surface of which was studded with points of iron resembling nails, but not so sharp as to penetrate the flesh. Sir George saw him in the fifth year of his probation, and his skin then was like the hide of a rhinoceros, but more callous. At that time, however, he could sleep comfortably on his bed of thorns, and remarked that at the expiration of the term of his sentence, he should most probably continue that system from choice, which he had been obliged to adopt from necessity."

This illustrates the force of established habit, and the pliability of our nature in yielding a voluntary subjection to it. What is at first involuntary, painful, and a self-denial to us, will, when it passes into a habit, become agreeable, because the habit bends our nature to it, chains us down to it, infatuates the will, and thus becomes, as it were, a second nature. If so, it is very plain that our habits are either a blessing or a curse. When good, they are a safeguard against evil, give stability to our character, and are the law of perseverance in well-doing. Such habits in the Christian home form an irresistible bulwark against the intrusions of temptation and iniquity. But when they are bad, they chain us to evil, and impel us onward and downward to ruin. Hence from his habits we can easily estimate the merit or demerit of a person, know all his weak points and idiosyncrasies, and what will be the probable termination of his existence.

The same may be said of the habits of a family. They enter into its very constitution, rule and direct all its activities and interests. They cling to each member with more than magic power, and become interwoven with his very being; and by them we may easily ascertain the moral and spiritual strength of that family; we can tell whether the parents are faithful to their mission, and whether its members will be likely to pass over from the home of their childhood to the church of Christ. Who has not felt this power of habit? Who has not wept over some habits which haunt him like an evil spirit; and rejoiced over others as a safeguard from sin and a propellor to good? Is it not, therefore, a matter of momentous interest to the Christian home, that it establish habits of the right kind and quality?

It should never be forgotten by Christian parents, and they cannot be too careful to impress it upon their children, that habit engenders habit,—has the power of reproducing itself, and begetting habits of its own kind, increasing, according to the laws of growth, as it is thus reproduced. A habit in one member of a family may produce a like habit in all the other members. The habits of the husband may be engendered in the wife, and those of the parents, in their children. If so, then are we not responsible for our habits? And shall any other kind save Christian habits, be found in the Christian home? These we cannot give in detail. It is plain that those habits only are Christian, which receive the sanction of God's Word and Spirit, and find a response in the Christian faith and conscience. Here, for instance, is a habit being formed,—habit of thought: is it pure? Here is a habit of conversation: is it holy? Here is a habit of action: is it godly? And if not, it does not belong to the Christian home.

See, then, ye members of the Christian home, to the habits you are forming. Form the habit of "doing all things decently and in order." Let the work and duties of each day be done according to method. This is essential to success in your pursuits and aims. Without this, your Christian life may be blustering and stormy, but you will accomplish little, and will be as unstable as water. One duty will interfere with another. You may have family prayer and instruction to-day, but something will prevent it to-morrow. Establish the habit of Christian industry. Be diligent; not slothful in business. Industry must be the price of all you obtain. You must be instant in season. The Christian home cannot be an indolent, idle home. Whatsoever thy hand findeth to do, do it with all thy might. Press forward.

It is said of Rutherford that "such was his unwearied assiduity and diligence, that he seemed to pray constantly, to preach constantly, to catechise constantly, and to visit the sick, exhorting from house to house, to teach as much in the schools, and spend as much time with the students, in fitting them for the ministry, as if he had been sequestered from all the world, and yet withal, to write as much as if he had been constantly shut up in his study." Such should be the industry of each Christian home. Without it, temptation will beset the members. "A busy man is troubled with but one devil, but the idle man with a thousand."

Establish the habit also of perseverance in well-doing. "Be steadfast, immovable, always abounding in the work of the Lord." "Be not weary in well-doing." Let the strata of your home be made up of the immovable Rock. He only that continueth unto the end shall be saved. Having done all, stand! Let your motto be, *Perseverando vinces.* Form the habit of contentment with your home and condition in life. "Godliness with contentment is great gain." If your home is humble, and not adorned with the embellishments and luxuries of life, yet it may be holy, and hence, happy. Avoid all castle-building. Do not fancy a better home, and fall out with the one you enjoy. Never permit the flimsy creations of a distorted imagination to gain an ascendancy over your reason and faith. Live above all sentimentalism and day-dreaming; and in all the feelings and conduct of your household, submit to the guidance of a superintending Providence, walking by faith and not by sight, assured that your present home is but probationary and preparatory to a better home in heaven.

CHAPTER XVIII.

HOME-GOVERNMENT.

"Alas! for a thousand fathers, whose indulgent sloth
Hath emptied the vial of confusion over a thousand homes;
Alas! for the palaces and hovels, that might have been nurseries for heaven,
By hot intestine broils blighted into schools for hell;
None knoweth his place, yet all refuse to serve,
None weareth the crown, yet all usurp the scepter;
The mother, heart-stricken years agone, hath dropped into an early grave;
The silent sisters long to leave a home they cannot love;
The brothers, casting off restraint, follow their wayward wills."

Home is a little commonwealth jointly governed by the parents. It involves law. The mutual relation of parent and child implies authority on the one hand, and obedience on the other. This is the principle of all government. Home is the first form of society. As such it must have a government. Its institution implies the prerogatives of the parent and the subordination of the child. Without this there would be no order, no harmony, no training for the state or the church; for—

"Society is a chain of obligations, and its links support each other;
The branch cannot but wither that is cut from the parent vine."

The relation of the parent to the child is that of a superior to an inferior. The right of the parent is to command; the duty of the child is to obey. Hence it is the relation of authority to subordination. This relation includes the principles of home-government. The parent is not the author of his authority. It is delegated to him. Neither can he make arbitrary laws for home; these must be the laws of God. It is as much the duty of the parent to rule as it is for the child to be ruled.

The principle of home-government is love,—love ruling and obeying according to law. These are exercised, as it were, by the instinct of natural affection as taken up and refined by the Christian life and faith. This government implies reciprocity of right,—the right of the parent to govern and the right of the child to be governed. It is similar in its fundamentals to the government of the state and church. It involves the legislative, judicial and executive functions; its elements are law, authority, obedience, and penalties. The basis of its laws is the Word of God. We may consider the whole subject under two general heads, viz., parental authority, and filial obedience.

1. Parental authority is threefold, legislative, judicial and executive. The two latter we shall more fully consider under the head of home-discipline. The legislative authority of the parent is confined to the development of God's laws for the Christian home. He cannot enact arbitrary laws. His authority is founded on his relation to his children as the author of their being; "yet it does not admit," says Schlegel, "of being set forth and comprised in any exact and positive formularies." It does not, as in the old Roman law, concede to the parent the power over the life of the child. This would not only violate the law of natural affection, but would be an amalgamation of the family and state. Neither is the parental authority merely conventional, given to the parent by the state as a policy. It is no civil or political investiture, making the parent a delegated civil ruler; but comes from God as an inalienable right, and independent, as such, of the state. It does not, therefore, rest upon civil legislation, but has its foundation in human nature and the revealed law of God; neither can the state legislate upon it, except in cases where its exercise becomes an infringement upon the prerogatives of the state itself.

Parents are magistrates under God, and, as His stewards, cannot abdicate their authority, nor delegate it to another. Neither can they be tyrants in the exercise of it. God has given to them the principles of home-legislation, the standard of judicial authority, and the rules of their executive power. God gives the law. The parent is only deputy governor, — steward, "bound to be faithful." Hence the obligation of the child to obey the steward is as great as that to obey the Master. "Where the principal is silent, take heed that thou despise not the deputy."

Here, then, we have the extent of the parent's authority, and the spirit and manner in which it should be exercised. His power is grafted on the strength of another, and should not extend beyond it. Its exercise should not run into despotism on the one hand, nor into indifferentism on the other. According to the vagaries of some religious sentimentalists and fanatics, it is supposed that religion supersedes the necessity of parental government. They think that such authority runs counter to the spirit and requisitions of the gospel. But this is asserted in the broad face of God's Word. The promptings of such sentimentalism are to permit children to do as they please, and to bring them up under the influence of domestic libertinism. Honor thy father and thy mother, is a command which explodes such a gaudy theory; and he who does not obey it, brutalizes human nature, dishonors God, subverts the principles of constitutional society, throws off allegiance to the prerogatives of a divinely constituted superior, and overthrows both church and state. Hence the severe penalties attached, in the Mosaic law, to disobedience of parental authority. "He that curseth his father or mother, shall surely be put to death." "The eye that mocketh at his father, and despiseth to obey his mother, the ravens of the valley shall pick it out, and the young eagles shall eat it." And hence also that affectionate obedience which Joseph yielded to his aged father, and that profound veneration with which he kneeled before him to receive his dying blessing.

2. Filial obedience is the correlative of parental authority. If parents have authority, children must yield obedience to it. This is not only necessary to home-government, but also to the proper formation of the character of the child. It must be trained up under law and authority to prepare it for citizenship in the state. This must be the obedience of confidence and love. It does not imply the subordination of the slave.

As the father's authority is not that of the despot, so the obedience of the child is not that of the servile, trembling subject. It is not unnatural,—no infringement upon the rights and liberties of the child. His subordination to the parent is the law of his liberty. He is not free without it. The home in which filial obedience is not yielded to parental authority is "a marvel of permitted chaos," and will soon become desolate, a scene of anarchy and strife. The members live in a state of lawlessness, destitute of reciprocated affection,—the parent unhonored, the father and mother despised and cursed, and the child untrained, uncared for, lawless, and unfit for the state or the church.

If, therefore, God has constituted governmental

relations in the Christian home, and invested the parent with authority over his children, who will deny the coördinate obligations of the child to yield reverence, submission and gratitude to the parent? "Children, obey your parents in all things; for this is well pleasing unto the Lord."

This is called the first commandment with promise. It is one of promise both to the parent and the child. Children are bound to obey their parents in all things, that is, in all things lawful and in accordance with the revealed will of God. The child is not bound to obey the parent's command to sin,—to lie, steal, or neglect the means of grace; because these are express violations of God's law; and in such instances the authority of God supersedes that of the parent. Obey God rather than man.

But, on the other hand, the obligation of the child is, to obey the parent in all things lawful and Christian. Where this is not done the Christian home becomes a curse. What an evil is a refractory child! How often does the parental eye weep in bitterness over such a child! How often have such children brought their parents down in sorrow to the grave! Let them think of this. Let parents think of this before it is too late. Let them think of the fearful criminality which is attached to parental indulgence and filial disobedience.

We may neglect and abuse the home-government in two ways, either by over-indulgence, or by the iron rod of tyranny. When we make it lax in its restraints and requisitions, it becomes merely nominal, and its laws are never enforced and obeyed. Often parents voluntarily relinquish their right and duty to rule their household; and as a consequence, their children abandon the duty of obedience, and grow up in a lawless state; or if they do command, they never execute their commands, but leave all to the discretion of their children. They violate their laws with impunity, until all influence over them is lost, and the child becomes master of the parent. The self-will of the former takes the place of the authority of the latter, until at last the home-government becomes a complete farce and mockery. Such parents are always making laws and giving commands; but never enforce them; they complain that they cannot get their children to obey them; and this cannot is but the utterance and exponent of their unfaithfulness and disgrace.

The opposite abuse of home-government is parental despotism,—ruling with a rod of iron, making slaves of children, acting the unfeeling and heartless tyrant over them, assuming towards them attitudes of hard task-masters, and making them obey from motives of trembling, fear and dread.

There is no christianity in all this. It engenders in them the spirit of a slave; it roots out all confidence and love; their obedience becomes involuntary and mechanical. They shrink in silent dread from the presence of their parents, and long for the time when they can escape their galling yoke. The parental rod destroys the filial love and confidence. Hence the obedience of the latter is servile; and home loses its tender affections and sympathies, and becomes to them a workhouse, a confinement; its restrictions are a yoke; its interests are repulsive, and all its natural affinities give way to complete alienation. The children of such homes, when grown up, are the most lawless and reckless, ready at once to pass over from extreme servitude to libertinism.

The government of the Christian home lies in a medium between these two extremes. It is mild, yet decisive, firm; not lawless, yet not despotic; but combines in proper order and harmony, the true elements of parental authority and filial subordination. Love and fear harmonize; the child fears because he loves; and is prompted to obedience by both. "But give thy son his way, he will hate thee and scorn thee together."

Christian parents! be faithful to the government of your household. Like Abraham, command your household. Without this, your children will be your curse and the curse of the state. Wherever they go they will become the standard-bearer of the turbulent, and brandish the torch of discord, until at last, perhaps, they will die in a dungeon or upon the gibbet. And then the curse will recoil upon you. It will strike deep into your hearts. It will come to you in the darkness of unfulfilled promises and blighted hopes and injured affections and desolated homes and wounded spirits and disgraced names and infamous memories!

And you, in the face of these, will go down with bleeding sorrow to the grave, and up to the bar of God with the blood of your children's destruction upon your skirts, its voice crying unto you from the grave of infamy and from the world of eternal retribution. You will then see the folly and the fruits of your diseased affection and misguided indulgence,—

"A kindness,—most unkind, that hath always spared the rod;
A weak and numbing indecision in the mind that should be master;
A foolish love, pregnant of hate, that never frowned on sin;
A moral cowardice, that never dared command!"

CHAPTER XIX.

HOME-DISCIPLINE.

"In ancient days,
There dwelt a sage called Discipline,
His eye was meek, and a smile
Played on his lips, and in his speech was heard
Paternal sweetness, dignity, and love.
The occupation dearest to his heart
Was to encourage goodness.
If e'er it chanced, as sometimes chance it must,
That one, among so many, overleaped
The limits of control, his gentle eye
Grew stern, and darted a severe rebuke,
His frown was full of terror, and his voice
Shook the delinquent with such fits of awe
As left him not, till penitence had won
Lost favor back again, and closed the breach."

Discipline involves the judicial and executive functions of the home-government. It is the method of regulating and executing the principles and practice of government. It includes the rein and the rod, the treatment of offences against the laws of home, the execution of the parental authority by the imposition of proper restraints upon the child. It involves a reciprocity of duty,—the duty of the parent to correct, and the duty of the child to submit. God has given this discipline; He has invested the parent with power to execute it, and imposed upon the child the obligation to live submissively under it.

All must admit the necessity of home-discipline. "It must needs be that offense come." There is a corresponding needs be in the proper treatment of these offenses when they do come. Law implies penalties; and the proper character and execution of these are as essential to the true object and end of government as is the law itself. The former would be powerless without the latter. Through the agency of home-discipline the proper fear and love of the child are developed in due proportion and brought into proper relations to each other, making the fear filial and the love reverential. There is, therefore, the same call for discipline in the family as there is in the state and the church. It is the condition of true harmony between the parent and child. "The child that is used to constraint, feareth not more than he loveth; but give thy son his way, he will hate thee and scorn thee together."

It is necessary because God commands it; and He commands it because it is indispensable to the security and well-being of the child, and, we might add, of the state and the church. "Withhold not correction from the child; for if thou beatest him with the rod, he shall not die. Thou shalt beat him with the rod, and shalt deliver his soul from hell. He that spareth his rod hateth his son; but he that loveth him chasteneth him betimes." Children are by nature depraved, and if left to themselves, will choose evil rather than good; hence, as foolishness is bound up in the heart of a child, the rod of correction must be used to drive them from it. He must be restrained, corrected, educated under law. In the language of Cowper—

> "Plants raised with tenderness are seldom strong;
> Man's coltish disposition asks the thong;
> And without discipline, the favorite child,
> Like a neglected forester, runs wild."

There are two false systems of home-discipline, viz., the despotism of discipline, or discipline from the standpoint of law without love; and the libertinism of discipline, or discipline from the standpoint of love without law.

Home-discipline from the standpoint of law without love, involves the principle of parental despotism. It is extreme legal severity, and consists in the treatment of children as if they were brutes, using no other mode of correction than that of direct corporeal punishment. This but hardens them, and begets a roughness of nature and spirit like the discipline under which they are brought up. Many parents seek to justify such mechanical severity by the saying of Solomon, "he that spareth the rod spoileth the child." But their interpretation of this does not show the wisdom of the wise man. They suppose the term rod, must mean the iron rod of the unfeeling and unloving despot. Not so; God has a rod for all His children; but it is the rod of a compassionate Father, and does not always inflict corporeal punishment. It is exercised because He loves them, not because He delights in revenge and in their misery. He uses it, not to have them obey Him from fear of punishment, not to force them into a slavish service, and to cause them to shrink with trembling awe from His presence; but to correct their faults by drawing them to Him in fond embrace, in grateful penitence and hopeful reformation, under the deep conviction that every stroke of His rod was the work of love, forcing from them a kiss for His rod, and a blessing for His hand, the utterance of a sanction for His deed, "It was good for me that I was afflicted!"

This rod is very different, however, from that of the despot beneath whom the child crouches with trembling dread, and under the influence of whom he becomes, like the down-trodden subject, servile, brutish and rebellious. You will reap bitter fruits from such a discipline, which is but the exponent of the letter of the law without its spirit, and which has nothing for the child but the scowl and the frown and the cruel lash. You might as well seek to "gather grapes from thorns, or figs from thistles," as to reap from it a true reformation and religious training. Your child will be trained to hate the law, to despise authority, and to regard his obedience as a compromise of true liberty. He will, therefore, seek liberty only in the usurpation of law and government. He will contemn love, because where it should have been disinterested, and shown in its greatest tenderness and purity,—in the parent's heart, it was abused and silenced.

That discipline, therefore, which is ever magnifying trifles, finding fault, scolding and storming, and threatening and whipping, and falling upon the child, like the continual dropping of rain in a winter day, casts a withering gloom over home, makes it repulsive to the child, gives to the parent a forbidding aspect, until the children become provoked to wrath, and regard their home as a prison, their life as a slavery, and long for the time when they may leave home and parents forever. Such discipline makes the reign of the parent a reign of terror. It reminds one of the laws of Draco, written in blood. It produces in the child a broken spirit, a reckless desperation, a hardened contumacy, a deep and sullen melancholy, a mental and moral hardihood which prepares him for deeds of outrage upon law and humanity. It is unnatural, revolting to human nature, to beat and crush, as if with an iron rod, the tender child of our hearts and hopes. It extinguishes natural affection; and no subsequent kindness can rekindle the flame. The child becomes forever alienated, and bears the curse of its maltreatment upon its character and destiny. "Ye parents, provoke not your children to anger, lest they should be discouraged."

The following quaint anecdote is a good commentary upon such discipline: A blacksmith brought up his son, to whom he was very severe, to his own trade. The urchin was, nevertheless, an audacious dog. One day the old vulcan was attempting to harden a cold chisel which he had made of foreign steel, but could not succeed; "horsewhip it, father," exclaimed the youth, "if that will not harden it, nothing will!"

Nothing justifies such cruel discipline. It results in depravity of life. The most notorious criminals began their career under the lash of parental cruelty. If rods and stripes and cries and tears and cruel beating are the first lessons of life we are to learn, then we shall be educated in as well as by these. The Europeans surpass all other nations in cruelty to their offspring. The Arab is tender to his children, and rules them by kindness and caresses. He restrains them by the corrections of wisely exerted love. Cruelty does not become the Christian home. It is revolting to see a parent stand with a rod over his child, to make him read the bible or say his prayers. You cannot whip religion into a child. This is opposite to humanity and religion.

Home-discipline from the standpoint of love without law, is the second false system which we have mentioned, and involves the principle of parental libertinism. It does not consist so much in the want as in the neglect and abuse of discipline. The restraints may be sufficient, and the threats abundant, but they are never executed.

When the children disobey, the parents may flounder and storm, loud and long, but all ends in words, in a storm of passion or whining complaint, and the child is thus encouraged to repeat the misconduct, feeling that his parents have no respect for their word. Such a home becomes scolding, but not an orderly home.

> "Discipline at length,
> O'erlooked and unemployed, grew sick and died,
> Then study languished, emulation slept,
> And virtue fled. What was learned,
> If aught was learned in childhood, is forgot;
> And such expense as pinches parents blue,
> And mortifies the liberal hand of love,
> Is squandered in pursuit of idle sports
> And vicious pleasures."

Parents, through their misguided sympathy, often connive at filial disobedience. Their kindness is most unkind. Their parental love issues forth as a mere burst of feeling, unguided by either reason or law. Hence, their sentimental hearts become an asylum for filial delinquency and criminality. This is no proof of love, but the opposite; for "he that spareth the rod hateth his son; but he that loveth him chasteneth him betimes." Love will thus prompt the parent to chasten his son while there is hope. Eli was an example of extreme parental indulgence. "His sons made themselves vile, and he restrained them not." It was the defect also of David's discipline, and the fruit of this defect caused him to cry out in bitter anguish, "Oh Absalom, my son, my son, would to God I had died for thee!"

That parent who cannot restrain his children, does not bear rule in his house, and as a consequence, cannot bless his household. That parental tenderness which withholds the proper restraints of discipline from an erring child, is most cruel and ruinous. It is winking at his wayward temper, his licentious passions and growing habits of vice. And these, in their terrible maturity, will recoil upon the deluded parent, "biting like a serpent and stinging like an adder." Nothing is more ruinous to a child and disastrous to the hopes and happiness of home, than such relaxation of discipline. "A child left to himself bringeth his mother to shame." How many mothers have bitterly experienced this, and wept bitter tears over the memory of their degraded and wretched offspring! It is ruinous to the parent. He will both curse and despise thee. Your unlawful indulgence, therefore, is infanticide. Your cruel embraces are hugging your child to death. The sentiment of love should never crush the reason and violate the laws of love. Do you permit your sick to die rather than to inflict the pain of giving them the medicine to cure? This would be madness. And yet you do a similar deed when you indulge your child in wickedness. He will grow up lawless, headstrong, rebellious; and these may lead him on to poverty, infamy, crime and perdition, ending thus in total shipwreck of character and soul. You thus make for society bad members, drunkards, blackguards, paupers, criminals; and furnish fuel for the eternal burnings. And will not the curse rest upon you?

It is wonderful to what an extent this extreme indulgence prevails at the present day. Many parents seem insensible even to the necessity of any discipline, and think it is an infringement upon the liberties of the child. Mistaken parents! Such views are opposed to the laws of God and man. By them you sow for yourselves and children the seeds of a future retribution.

Thus we see that there are two dangerous extremes or false systems of home-discipline, viz., the exercise of parental fondness and sympathy without parental authority, on the one hand, and the exercise of parental authority without proper sympathy, on the other. Misguided sympathy and fondness will produce filial libertinism; and despotic authority will beget filial servility.

True Christian home-discipline lies in a medium between these. It involves the union of true parental sympathy and authority, of proper love and proper law; for affection, when not united to authority and law, degenerates into sentimental fondness; and authority and law, when not tempered with love, degenerate into brutal tyranny, and produce inward servility and outward bondage. The parents who are, in discipline, prompted by the first, may be loved, but will not be respected. Those who are ruled by the second, may be dreaded, but will not be loved. The first does violence to law, and ends in the insubordination of the child and the imbecility of the parent. The second does violence to love, makes duty a task, correction a corporeal punishment, the child a slave, the parent a despot, and ends consequently in the destruction of natural affection. Hence, in home-discipline, true severity and true sympathy should unite and temper each other. Without this the very ends proposed will be frustrated.

True home-discipline repudiates the legal idea of punishment as much as of impunity. It lies in a medium between these, and involves the idea of Christian correction or chastisement. We should correct, but not punish our children. Correction is not the mere execution of legal penalties as such, but the fruit of Christian love and concern for the child. It does not mean simple corporeal chastisement, but moral restraints. The impunity is the fruit of love without law; the corporeal punishment is the execution of law without love; Christian correction is the interposition of love acting according to law in restraining the child. Hence, true discipline is the correction of the child by the love of the parent, according to the laws of home-government.

Abraham instituted in his household a model system of home-discipline. "I know him," says God, "that he will command his children and his household after him, and they shall keep the ways of the Lord to do justice and judgment." He was not a tyrant; his comrades did not bear the rough sternness of a despot, neither did his power wear the scowl of vengeance. But these bore the firmness and decision of love tempered and directed by the law of Christian duty and responsibility. They showed his station as a father; they wore the exponent of his authority as a parent, whose love was a safeguard against tyranny on the one hand, and whose accountability to God was a security against anarchy, on the other. Hence, his children respected his station, venerated his name, appreciated his love, confided in his sympathy, and yielded a voluntary obedience to his commands; for they discerned in them the blessing; and when offenses came, they bent in the spirit of loving submission and pupilage, under his rod of correction, and kissed it as the means of their reformation and culture.

Thus does home-discipline involve the firmness of parental authority united with the mildness of parental love. Love should hold the reins and use the rod. Then it will purify and elevate natural affection, and develop in the child a sense of proper fear, without either disrespectful familiarity or mechanical servitude.

The efficiency of home-discipline depends upon its early introduction, upon the decision with which it is administered, upon its adaptation to the real wants of the child, and upon the manner in which it is applied.

It should be commenced in due season, as soon as the child can understand its meaning and object. The child should be made to understand that he lives under authority and restraint. This will prepare him for a profitable correction when necessary. The great fault of many parents is that they begin too late to correct their children, and leave them until then in ignorance of its nature and intent. Hence, the child will not appreciate the parent's motive, and will lack that pliability of spirit which is essential to reformation. "The sceptre," says James, in his Family Monitor, "should be seen by him before the rod; and an early, judicious and steady exhibition of the former, would render the latter almost unnecessary. He must be made to submit, and that while young, and then submission will become a habit; the reins must be felt by him early, and he will thus learn to obey them."

Home-discipline should be steady, uniform, consistent and reasonable. Both parents and children should be guided by the dictates of reason and religion. It should not be administered by the caprice of passion, nor received in the spirit of insubordination. It should be prompted by a parent's heart, and inflicted by a parent's hand. Convince the recreant child that you correct him from motives of love, and for his own good. Let reason and love be at the bottom of every chastisement; let them hold the reins and guide the rod; and when the latter is used, let it be from necessity. Lay no injunction upon your child without the ensurance of a compliance.

Your discipline should never involve impossibilities or uncertainties; neither should you permit your child to sport with your injunctions. Every command should produce either obedience or correction. You should be firm in the infliction of a threatened chastisement, and faithful in the fulfilment of a promise to reward. Many parents are always scolding, threatening and promising, but never execute and fulfil. As a consequence they run from one extreme of discipline to another.

In home-discipline, parents should act harmoniously and coöperate with each other. They should be of one mind and of one heart, and equally bear the burden. The one should not oppose the discipline which the other is administering. This destroys its effect, and leaves the child in a state of indecision, leading to prejudice against one or the other of the parents. It too often happens that parents thus take opposite sides,—the father too severe perhaps, and the mother too indulgent. Thus divided, their house must fall. Nothing is more ruinous to the child than for the mother to counteract by soothing opiates, the admonitions of the father. Children soon see this, and will as soon hate their father. When one parent thus holds the reins without the rod, and the other uses the rod without the reins, the very ends of discipline are frustrated. Sometimes the child is given over to the mother exclusively till a certain age, when the father begins to act without the mother. This is wrong. A child is never too young to be ruled by the father, and never too old to come under the softening influence of the mother.

Discipline should be administered with impartiality. Never make one child a favorite. Favoritism and consequent indulgence, will produce prejudice against the other children. It will introduce dissension among them. This is unworthy the Christian parent and his home. The history of Jacob and Joseph, as regards both the subject and the victim of parental favoritism, is a warning against such partiality. It produces, pride, envy, jealousy, family broils and strife, in which even the parents take a part, and by which the husband is often set against his wife, parents against children, and children against each other.

Correction is an essential element of true discipline. "The rod and the reproof give wisdom." There are two things in correction,—the reins and the whip, or the command and the chastisement. The one should not take the place of the other. The scepter must not be converted into a whip. If the reins are properly held and used, the whip need scarcely ever be required. If the child is timely and properly trained, commanded and chided, he will not require much chastisement,—perhaps no corporeal punishment. It is better to prevent crimes than to punish them; for prevention is more than cure.

Hence the first thing in discipline is timely and wholesome command. Guide and train your child properly, and you need seldom resort to coercion. Training and leading are better than forcing. By the former you establish a habit of systematic obedience which will soon become a pleasure to the child. By the latter you jade and vex and burden him. But when the reins will not do alone, then the whip must be resorted to. And the question at once arises, what kind of a whip? We answer, not such as you use to your horses and oxen in the team,—not the horse-whip. Corporeal punishment should be used only as a last resort, when all other corrections have failed, when the child becomes an outlaw, and his reprobate heart can be reached only through the infliction of bodily pain. As a general thing it is even then unavailing, because too mechanical to produce permanent good, and not adapted to mental and moral reformation.

Sometimes, however, there is necessity in the use of this rod. "Every child," says Dr. South, "has some brute in it, and some man in it, and just in proportion to the brute we must whip it." When thus necessary we should not shrink from this kind of correction. "It is pusillanimity, as well as folly, to shrink from the crushing of the egg, but to wait composedly for the hatching of the viper." Yet, on the other hand, in the language of Dr. Bell, "a maximum of attainment can be made only by a minimum of punishment."

In the discipline of home, whether by guidance or by forcing, whether by the rein or the rod, much depends upon the manner in which it is administered. It should always be adapted to the peculiar character and offense of the child. You can restrain some children better by kind words and promises than by rough admonitions and threats. Study, therefore, the peculiarities of your child, and prudently apportion the correction to the offense. If there are sincere penitence and confession, the correction should be purely moral. Let the object of every correction be to produce penitence and reformation of heart as well as of conduct, and a hatred of the offense. Always execute your threats and fulfill your promises at the time and on the occasion designated. Threaten as little as possible, and be not hasty in your threats. Treat your children as rational and moral beings:

> "Be obeyed when thou commandest, but command not often;
> Spare not, if thy word hath passed for punishment;
> Let not thy child see thee humbled, nor learn to think thee false."

Always examine the offense before you punish. See whether it is of ignorance or not,—whether of the head or the heart,—whether intentional or accidental. Examine his motives in committing the offense. If you find he merits correction, before you inflict it, lay before him the nature and enormity of the offense, wherein he disobeyed, the guilt of that disobedience, its consequences, and your duty to correct him for it.

Never correct in a state of anger. Some correct only when they are in a violent passion. This is ruling from passion, not from principle. It is like administering medicine scalding hot, which rather burns than cures. Be judicious and kind in all your discipline; otherwise you may engender in your child the very propensities and improprieties of action you desire to eradicate.

A mild rebuke in the season of calmness, is better than a rod in the heat of passion. Let your children know and see that all your discipline is for their own good,—to arrest them from danger and ruin, and to train them up in the way God would have them go. Let your words and deeds show this in the form of parental kindness and sympathy and solicitude. This will do more than the angry look, the stormy threat, and the cruel lash.

"By kindness the wolf and the zebra become docile as the spaniel and the horse;
The kite feedeth with the starling, under the law of kindness;
That law shall tame the fiercest, bring down the battlements of pride,
Cherish the weak, control the strong, and win the fearful spirit.
Let thy carriage be the gentleness of love, not the stern front of tyranny."

CHAPTER XX.

HOME-EXAMPLE.

> "EXAMPLE strikes
> All human hearts! A bad example more;
> More still a father's!"

EXAMPLE has much to do with the interests of home. It plays an important part in the formation of character; and its influence is felt more than that of precept. Our object in this chapter is to show the bearing of example upon the well-being of the Christian home. Example may be good or bad. Its power arises out of the home-confidence and authority. Children possess an imitative disposition. They look up to their parents as the pattern or model of their character, and conclude what they do is right and worthy of their imitation. Hence the parental example may lead the child to happiness or to ruin.

> "Lo! thou art a landmark on a hill; thy little ones copy thee in all things.
> Show me a child undutiful, I shall know where to look for a foolish father;
> But how can that son reverence an example he dare not follow?
> Should he imitate thee in thine evil? his scorn is thy rebuke."

The power and influence of the home-example are incalculable. Example is teaching by action. By it the child inherits the spirit and character of the parent. Such is its influence that you can estimate the parent by the child. Show me a child, polite, courteous, refined, moral and honorable in all his sentiments and conduct; and I will point you to a well-conducted nursery, to noble and high-minded parents, faithful to their offspring. Theirs is a holy and a happy home; and the blessing of God rests upon it. But on the other hand, in the wayward, dissolute child I discern unfaithful parents who have no respect for religion, and who take no interest in the spiritual welfare of their children. Thus the child is a living commentary upon its home and its parents. The fruits of the latter will be seen in the character of the former. The child is the moral reproduction of the parent. Hence the pious parent is rewarded in his child, and the immoral parent is cursed in his child. Whatsoever thou sowest in thy child, that shalt thou also reap.

The precepts of home are unavailing unless enforced by a corresponding example. Nothing is so forcible and encouraging as the "Follow me." It proves sincerity and earnestness; and is adapted to the imitative capacity and disposition of the child. It is all-commanding and resistless. Says Solomon, "Iron sharpeneth iron; so a man sharpeneth the countenance of his friend." Says Paul "It is good neither to eat flesh, nor to drink wine, nor anything whereby thy brother stumbleth, or

SUNSHINE OF YOUTH.

is offended, or is made weak." Says Shakspeare, "One drunkard loves another of the name." Says Dr. Young—

> "Ambition fires ambition; love of gain
> Strikes like a pestilence from breast to breast;
> Riot, pride, perfidy, blue vapor's breath;
> And inhumanity is caught from man,
> From smiling man."

If such is the influence of example, we must admit the necessity of a true Christian example in the family. It is necessary because it is the condition of the efficacy of home-precepts. "During the minority of reason, imitation is the regent of the soul, and they who are least swayed by argument are most governed by example." We learn from example before we can speak. Hence if we would have our children walk in the way of God's commandments, we must go before them; we must take the lead; we must exemplify in our action what we incorporate in our oral instructions; our light must shine not only upon, but before them; they must see our good works as well as hear our good precepts. Said a man once to J. A. James, "I owe everything under God, to the eminent and consistent piety of my father. So thoroughly consistent was he, that I could find nothing in the smallest degree at variance with his character as a professor of religion. This kept its hold upon me." It was the means of his conversion to God.

Thus children readily discern any discrepancy

between a parent's teaching and example. If we are professors of religion, and they see us worldly-minded, grasping after riches, pleasures and honors; the dupes of ungodly fashion, manifesting a malicious spirit, indolent, prayerless, and indifferent to their spiritual welfare, what do they infer but that we are hypocrites, and will our precepts then do them any good? No. "Line upon line and precept upon precept" will be given to no purpose. Hence the necessity of enforcing our precepts by Christian deportment. Speak in an angry tone before your child; and what will it avail for you to admonish him against anger? Many parents express surprise that all they can say to their children does no good; they remain stubborn, self-willed and recreant.

But if these parents will look at what they have done as well as said, they will perhaps be less surprised. They may find a solution of the problem in their own capricious disposition, turbulent passions and ungodly walk. The child will soon discard a parent's precepts when they are not enforced by a parent's example. Hence that parent who ruins his own soul can do but little for the soul of his child. The blasphemer and sabbath-breaker is unfit to correct his child for swearing and sabbath-breaking. He alone who doeth the truth can teach his children truth. He only who has good habits can teach his children good habits. "Who loves," says William Jay, "to take his meat from a leprous hand?" A drunkard will make a poor preacher of sobriety. A proud, passionate father is a wretched recommender of humility and meekness to his children. What those who are under his care, see, will more than counteract what they hear; and all his efforts will be rejected with the question, "Thou that teachest another, teachest thou not thyself?" Hence parents should say to their children, "Be ye followers of me, even as I also am of Christ." Their example should include all their precepts. In this way they both hear and see religion in its living, moving and breathing form before them. They should thus go in and out before them, leading them step by step to heaven.

"As a bird each fond endearment tries
To tempt her new-fledged offspring to the skies,
They tried each art, reproved each dull delay,
Allured to brighter worlds, and led the way!"

It is also necessary because of its adaptation to the capacities and imitative disposition of children. They judge by the organs of sense, and by their perceptions of truth through externals. Naked abstract truth does not sufficiently interest them. They are pleased with history, narrative, illustration, more than with philosophy. They are awake to the first and receive from them a lasting impression; while the impression made by the second is dreamy and ephemeral. They will never forget your example because it is adapted to their taste and capacity. Long after they have forgotten your precepts upon the duty and privilege of prayer, will they remember your prayers; and long after the influence of the former has faded, will that of the latter rule and allure them to God. Hence the necessity of a Christian home-example. "If any have children or nephews, let them learn first to show piety at home."

If such, then, are its influence and necessity, we can easily infer the duty of parents to show their children a Christian example. If they form their character upon the approved model of their parents, then the duty to give them a Christian model is very obvious. They will rather follow your ungodly example than obey your godly precepts. "To give children," says Archbishop Tillotson, "good instruction and a bad example, is but beckoning to them with the head to show them the way to heaven—while you take them by the hand to lead them in the way to hell."

This duty is, therefore, enforced by the most powerful motives. The influence and benefit of a pious example; the promised rewards attending it; the deep curse that attends its absence; the misery which a bad example entails upon all the members of the Christian household; and especially the fruits of both a good and bad example, in eternity,—all these considerations should prompt you to the faithful performance of this duty. If the members of your household may be ruined here by a bad example, what will be its consequences in the eternal world?

"If men of good lives,
Who, by their virtuous actions, stir up others
To noble and religious imitation,
Receive the greater glory after death
As sin must needs confess; what may they feel
In height of torment, and in weight of vengeance,
Not only they themselves not doing well,
But set a light up to show men to hell?"

We see a similar inducement to this duty in the blessings and rewards of a pious example. Its blessings are unspeakable both here and hereafter. The temporal and eternal welfare of your home, the hope of meeting your children in heaven, and receiving there the promised reward of your stewardship, depend upon this duty. That family is happy as well as holy, where the parents rear up their children under the fostering influence of a Christian example.

"Behold his little ones around him! they bask in the sunshine of smile;
And infant innocence and joy lighten these happy faces;
He is holy, and they honor him; he is loving; and they love him;
He is consistent, and they esteem him; he is firm, and they fear him.
His house is the palace of peace; for the Prince of peace is there.
Even so, from the bustle of life, he goeth to his well-ordered home."

A serious obstacle to the efficacy of a good example is, the too frequent want of agreement in the example of the parents. That of the father often conflicts with and neutralizes that of the mother. They are not one in their example. This the children soon see, and disregard the good rather than the bad example. "How can two walk together except they be agreed?" The child cannot follow the pious father in the way of life, when the ungodly mother secretly and openly draws him back. Operated upon by two opposite influences, he will move between them.

We are here taught the imprudence, and we might add, sin, of pious persons forming a matrimonial alliance with wicked and ungodly persons. In the choice of a companion for life, we should consider an agreement in religious as well as in social character. How many unhappy matches and homes and children and parents have been made by disobedience to the divine precept, "Be ye not unequally yoked with unbelievers?" Isaac and Rebecca showed their appreciation of this precept in the care they took to procure a pious wife for Jacob. "I am weary of my life," says Rebecca, "because of the daughters of Heth; if Jacob take a wife of the daughters of Heth, such as these, what good shall my life do me?" This should be the solicitude of every Christian parent. Parents should possess unanimity of spirit and practice in making up and giving the home-example. They should walk unitedly, like Zacharias and Elizabeth, in all the ordinances and statutes of the Lord blameless.

CHAPTER XXI.

THE CHOICE OF PURSUITS.

"For what then was I born? to fill the circling year
With daily toil for daily bread, with sordid pains and pleasures?
To walk this chequered world, alternate light and darkness,
The day-dreams of deep thought followed by the night-
dreams of fancy?
To be one in a full procession?—to dig my kindred clay?
To decorate the gallery of art? to clear a few acres of forest?
For more than these, my soul, thy God hath lent thee life!"

The choice of positions and pursuits in life is one important and responsible mission of home. Children look up to their parents to aid them in this. They are to have them prepared for a useful citizenship in the state. Life demands that each of us, in obedience to the law of self-preservation and of our relations to human society, prepare for some useful occupation, not only for a livelihood, but also for the benefit of the state. The duty and the interest of the parent are to bring up the child to such a pursuit as is best adapted to his circumstances and abilities. Our character, success and happiness in life, depend upon our obedience to this law of adaptation.

As such pursuits are chosen and prepared for, while under the guardian care of our parents, it is evident they should take an active part both in the choice and the preparation. They are responsible for these as far as their influence extends. It is their duty to afford their children aid in choosing and preparing for a useful and appropriate occupation, to fit them for the circumstances in which the Providence of God may place them, and to educate them for an efficient citizenship in the state.

This is but developing the principle of self-preservation in the child, and fitting him for a proper adherence to it in after life. The home prepares the individual for his legitimate position in the state as well as in the church; and this implies not only his education in the principles and practice of virtue and religion, but also in some useful and appropriate pursuit, by which he may meet the wants and prepare for the exigencies of life. To rear up your children therefore, in idleness and ignorance of any useful occupation, is not only doing great injustice to the child, but also to human society, subjecting her to expenditure and corruption in the support and influence of paupers and criminals. Every child should learn some trade or profession in order to self-subsistence and to the prosperity and well-being of the state.

Hence it is a breach of moral obligation for parents, whether rich or poor, to permit their children to grow up in idleness and vagrancy. If they do so, and as a consequence, drag out an impoverished and miserable existence, struggling between the importunities of want and those precarious contingencies upon which its satisfaction is suspended; and in the hour of despair and urgent necessity, they resort to crime in order to meet their wants, or to dissipation in order to avert their wretchedness for a time, is it not plain that their parents are responsible to God for all their crime and misery?

Nothing will, therefore, justify them in their omission of this duty. No amount of inherited wealth; no dependance upon wealthy relatives; no honorable station in society, will excuse them from training up their children to some useful employment by which, if circumstances demand, they may secure a subsistence. And even if their legacy render it unnecessary to be followed in order to subsistence, it is a duty which is due to the state. No man can with impunity live in the state without some employment. This would be an infringement upon her rights and an abuse of her privileges. The individual, with all his wealth and talents, belongs to the state, and should, therefore, make such an appropriation of these as will be most conducive to its welfare.

And besides, we know not what disastrous changes may take place in life. The parental legacy may soon be squandered by the child, and he be left without funds or friends; the emergencies of the future may increase beyond all anticipation; sickness and manifold adversities may soon sweep away all his inheritance. And then what will become of your child if he is ignorant of any pursuit in which to engage for a subsistence? Besides, it is a matter of very common observation, that those who receive a large legacy and have been brought up in idleness, become prodigal in their expenditure, and squander their fortune by dissipation more rapidly than their parents amassed it by industry and frugality; and then, ignorant and helpless and profligate, they eke out a wretched existence in abject poverty, resorting to illegitimate means for a living, until the last fruits of their improper training may be seen in the state's prison or upon the gibbet.

History will afford ample illustration of this. From it we may easily infer the duty of parental interposition. The Athenians expressed their sense of this duty in the enactment of a law that, if parents did not qualify their children for securing a livelihood by having them learn some occupation, the child was not bound to make provision for the parent when old and necessitous.

In the selection of an occupation for his children, the parent should consult their taste and talents and circumstances, and choose for them a pursuit adapted to these. If his child is better suited for a mechanical pursuit, he should direct his attention to it, and educate him for it. And thus in all respects he should obey the great law of correspondence between the taste and capacity of the child, and the occupation to be chosen for him.

The violation of this law does great injury to the child and to society, inasmuch as it prevents his success and contentment, and floods the state with quacks and humbuggery. The parent should never compel the child to learn a trade or profession which he dislikes, and for which he shows no talents. Many parents, through a false pride, force their children into a profession for which they have neither inclination nor capacity. While the parent has a right to interfere in the choice of a pursuit, his interference should not be arbitrary, neither should it run counter to the will of the child unless for special moral and religious reasons, or on account of inability to gratify him. However, this is often done. Even though they acknowledge their unfitness for a profession, yet their misguided pride prompts them to drag their children into a calling which in after life they disgrace.

Some parents, on the other hand, through a penurious spirit, refuse to aid their sons in their preparation for a profession for which their talents eminently qualify them. They refuse to educate their sons for the ministry because it is not a lucrative calling, though they give evidence of both mental and moral adaptation for that holy office. Others, through a blind zeal and a false pride, force their sons into this sacred calling. Mistaken parents! rather let your children break stone upon the road, or dig in the earth, yea, rather let them beg their bread, than thrust them into an occupation to which God has not called them, and for which they have neither inclination nor talents, and in which they would, perhaps, not only ruin their own souls, but contribute to the damnation of others. "There are diversities of gifts and of operations." All are not called nor fitted for the ministry. Children soon give indications of specific talents and suitableness for a calling in life. We should critically observe their early propensities. These will indicate their peculiar talents. Unfit for and disliking an occupation, they will become unsettled and dissatisfied, and at best will be but mimics and quacks. Their business will make them sullen slaves. It is because of parental disobedience to this law of adaptation that we have so much humbuggery in the world at the present day. Study, therefore, the infantile predilections of your children to particular employments. These will be an index to their providential calling, and should govern your choice for them.

The social position of the child should also be considered. If possible, the character of his pursuits should not conflict with those social elements in which he has been reared up. It should not detract from his standing in society, nor disrupt his associations in life. Many parents, for the sake of money, will refuse to educate and fit their children for sustaining the position they hold in society. They bring them up in ignorance, and devote them exclusively to Mammon; and then when thrown upon their own resources they are qualified neither in manners nor in pursuit for a continuance in those peculiar relations to society which they at first sustained.

The exigencies of the child should also be considered. If his home can afford him no patrimony, it is then more important to consider the lucrative character of the pursuit chosen, and also the demands of that social position he is to maintain in life. Its profits should then be fully adequate to these demands, and suited to the emergencies which are peculiar to his circumstances. The capital required to engage in it, and its bearing upon the health of body and mind, should also be regarded. This is an important consideration, and not sufficiently attended to by parents. How many children are forced into employments which they have not the means of carrying on, and for which their state of health altogether unfits them! A pursuit involving sedentary habits does not suit a child whose state of health demands exercise.

You should make choice of but one pursuit for your child, and discourage in him the American tendency to be "jack of all trades." One occupation, whatever it may be, whether trade or profession, if properly pursued, will demand all his energies, and give him no time to follow another; and besides, it will afford him an ample subsistence. There is much truth in the two old and quaint adages, "jack of all trades, and master of none;" "he has too many irons in the fire,—some of them must burn!" Show your children the truth and application of these.

But while this is one extreme, and detrimental to the interests of the child, its opposite extreme, viz., that of bringing up the child to no pursuit whatever, is still more injurious. We had better have too many irons in the fire than none at all. It is a base and cowardly desertion of duty to shrink from the task of human occupation. Constituted as human society is, the members of it being mutually dependent upon each other for support, it is evident that our happiness materially depends upon the active concurrence of each individual in the general system of social well-being. He who withholds, therefore, his coöperation and stands aloof from all employment, destroys a link in that chain of things by which the fabric of society is kept together and preserved. He is unfaithful to those sacred obligations which arise out of our relations to the state and the church, and he abuses those inalienable rights with which God has invested the social compact. Besides, he fails to meet those conditions upon which the vigorous development of individual life and character depends. Indolence is no friend either to physical, mental or moral development. The body becomes imbecile, the spirit supine and sentimental, the morals vitiated, and the mind sinks into complete puerility. Activity is a law of all life, and the condition of its healthy development and maturity. Without it we resort to jejune amusement, and from amusement we are hurried on to dissipation, to the card table and dram shop; and from dissipation we sink to degradation, infamy and wretchedness. Idleness is thus the fruitful mother of vice and misery. Our lives cannot exist in a state of neutrality between active good and active evil. It is, therefore, the duty of the Christian home to prepare her young members for some useful calling in life, not only as a means of subsistence, but also as a safeguard against the evils of idleness.

CHAPTER XXII.

THE HOME-PARLOR.

"The foolish floatiness of vanity, and solemn trumperies of pride,—
Harmful copings with the better, and empty-headed apings of the worse;
Vapid pleasures, the weariness of gaiety, the strife and bustle of the world;
The hollowness of courtesies, and substance of deceits, idleness and pastime—
All these and many more alike, thick conveying fancies,
Flit in throngs about my theme, as honey-bees at even to their hives!"

The Christian home includes the parlor. This department we must give but a brief and passing notice. Yet it is as important and responsible as the nursery. In it we have a view of the relations of home to society beyond it. The parlor is set apart for social communion with the world. Much of momentous interest is involved in this relation. The choice of companions, the forming of attachments and matrimonial alliances, the establishment of social position and influence in life beyond the family,—these are all involved in the home-parlor.

If we would, therefore, escape the shackles and contamination of corrupt society, we must hold the parlor sacred and give to it the air and bearing of at least a moral aristocracy. Home is the first form of society. The law of love rules and reigns there. It is enthroned in the heart, and casts light around our existence. In that society we live above the trammels of artificial life. In its parlor the members merge with society beyond its sacred precincts. Hence it is the most beautiful room; the best furniture is there; smiles adorn it; friends meet there; fashion meets there in her silks and jewels, with her circumstance and custom, her sympathies, antipathies and divers kinds of conversation; form and profession reign there; flatteries and hypocrisies intrude themselves there; pledges are given there; attachments and vows are made there; the mind and heart are impressed and moulded there; the cobweb lines of etiquette are drawn there; a panorama of social fascinations pass before the youthful eye there,—these make the parlor the most dangerous department of home. There the young receive their first introduction to society; there they see the world in all the brilliancy of outward life, in the pomp and pageantry of a vanity fair. All seems to them as a fairy dream, as a brilliant romance; their hearts are allured by these outward attractions; their imaginations are fed upon the unreal, and they learn to judge character by the external habiliments in which its reality is concealed. They estimate worth by the beauty of the face and form, by the cost of dress and the genuflections of the body. They form their notions of happiness from fashion, fortune and position. They become enslaved to lovesick novels and fashionable amusements. There, too, they make choice of companions; there they form matrimonial alliances; there their hearts are developed, their minds trained for social life, their affections directed, and influence brought to bear upon them, which will determine their weal or their woe.

If such be the influence of the home-parlor, should it not be held sacred, and made to correspond in all the uses for which it is set apart, with the spirit and character of a Christian family; and should not its doors be effectually guarded against the intrusion of spurious and demoralizing elements of society?

Parents should teach their children all about the character, interests and deceptions of parlor-life. They should undeceive them in their natural proneness to judge people from the standpoint of character assumed in the parlor. They see the lamb there, but not the lion; the smile but not the frown; the affability of manner, but not the tyranny of spirit. They hear the language of flattery, but not the tongue of slander. They see no weak points, detect no evil temper and bad habits. There is an artificial screen behind which all that is revolting and dangerous is concealed. Who would venture to judge a person by his mechanical movements in the parlor? Many are there the very opposite to what they are elsewhere:—

> "Abroad too kind, at home 'tis steadfast hate,
> And one eternal tempest of debate.
> What foul eruptions from a look most meek!
> What thunders bursting from a dimpled cheek!
> Such dead devotion, such zeal for crimes,
> Such licensed ill, such masquerading times,
> Such venal faiths, such misapplied applause,
> Such flattered guilt, and such inverted laws!"

One of the most dangerous periods of life is, when we leave the nursery and school, and enter the parlor. With what solicitude, therefore, should Christian parents guard their parlors from social corruption. They should prepare their children for society, not only by teaching them its manners and customs, how to act in company, how to grace a party, and move with refined ease among companions there, but also by teaching them the dangers and corruptions which lurk in their midst and follow in the train of rustling silks and fashionable denouement. They should never permit their parlor to become the scene of fashionable tyranny. The Christian parlor can be no depot for fashion. It should be sacred to God and to the church. It should be a true exponent of the social elements of Christianity. It should not be a hermitage, a state of seclusion from the world; but should conform to fashion.

yet so far only as the laws of a sanctified taste and refinement will admit.

These laws exclude all compromise and amalgamation with the ungodly spirit and customs of the world. Allegiance to the higher and better law of God will keep us from submission to the laws of a depraved taste and carnal desire. We must keep ourselves unspotted from the world. Whenever we submit with scrupulous exactness to the laws of fashion; whenever we yield a servile complaisance to its forms and ceremonies, wink at its extremes and immoralities and absurd expenditures, seek its flatteries and indulge in its whims and caprices, by throwing open our parlors as the theatre of their denouement, and introducing our children to their actors and master-spirits, we prostitute our homes, our religion and those whom God has given us to train up for Himself, to interests and pleasures the most unworthy the Christian name and character.

There is much danger now of the Christian home becoming in this way slavishly bound to the influence and attractions of society beyond the pale of the church, until all relish for home-enjoyment is lost, and its members no longer seek and enjoy each other's association. They drain the cup of voluptuous pleasure to its dregs, and flee from home as jejune and supine. The husband leaves his wife, and seeks his company in fashionable saloons, at the card table or in halls of revelry. The wife leaves the society of her children, and in company with a bosom companion, seeks to throw off the tedium of home, at masquerade meetings, at the theater or in the ball-room, where

> "Vice, once by modest Nature chained,
> And legal ties, expatiates unrestrained;
> Without thin decency held up to view,
> Naked she stalks o'er law and gospel too!"

The children follow their example; become disgusted with each other's company, and sacrifice their time and talents to a thousand little trifles and absurdities. Taste becomes depraved, and loses all relish for rational enjoyment. The heart teems with idle fancies and vain imaginations. Sentimentalism takes the place of religion; filthy literature and fashionable cards shove the Family Bible in some obscure nook of their parlor and their hearts. The hours devoted to family prayer are now spent in a giddy whirl of amusement and intoxicating pleasure, in the study of the latest fashions and of the newly-published love adventures of some nabob in the world of refined scoundrelism. The parental solicitude, once directed to the eternal welfare of the child, is now expended in match-making and setting out in the world.

Thus does the Christian home often become adulterated with the world by its indiscriminate association with unfit social elements. That portion of society whose master-spirits are love-stricken poets, languishing girls, amorous grandmothers, and sap-headed fiction writers, is certainly unfit for a place in the parlor of the Christian family. We should not permit the principles of common-sense decorum to give place to the lawless vagaries of fancy and the hollow-hearted forms of artificial life. Under the gaudy drapery of smiles and flounces, of rustling silks and blandishments, there are hearts as brutish and stultified, and heads as brainless and incapable of gentle and moral emotion, and characters as selfish and ungenerous, as were ever concealed beneath the rags of poverty, or the uncouth manners and rough garb of the incarcerated villain!

It is, therefore, beneath the dignity of the Christian to permit his home to become in any way a prey to immoral and irreligious associations and influences. Like the personal character of the Christian, it should be kept unspotted from the world; and no spirit, no customs, no companions, opposed to religion, should be permitted to enter its sacred limits. Heedless of this important requisition, parents may soon see their children depart from the ways in which they were trained in the nursery, and at last become a curse to them, and bring down their gray hairs with sorrow to the grave.

Here is indeed the great fault of many Christian parents in the present day. They do not exert that guardian care they should over the social relations and interests of their children. They are too unscrupulous in their introduction to the world, and leave them in ignorance of its snares and deceptions. What results can they look for if they permit their parlor tables to become burdened with French novels, and their children to mingle in company whose influence is the most detrimental to the interests of pure and undefiled religion? Can they reflect upon their daughters for forming improper attachments and alliances? Can they wonder if their sons become desperadoes, and ridicule the religion of their parents? No! They permitted them to dally with the fangs of a viper which found a ready admittance into their parlor; and upon them, therefore, will rest the responsibility,—yea, the deep and eternal curse! Woe unto thee, thou unfaithful parent; the voice of thy children's blood shall send up from the hallowed ground of home, one loud and penetrating cry to God for vengeance; and thou shalt be "beaten with many stripes." It will not only cry out against you, but cling to you!

Guard your parlor, therefore, from the corrupting influence of all immoral associations. Be not carried away by the pomp and glare of refined and decorated wickedness. Let not the ornaments and magnificence of mere outward life divert your attention from those hidden principles which prompt to action. In the choice of companions for your children in the parlor, look to the ornaments of the heart rather than to those of the body. Be not allured by the parade of circumstance and position in life: Be not carried away by that which may intoxicate for a moment, and then leave the heart in more wretchedness than before. Ever remember that the future condition of your children, their domestic character and happiness, will depend upon the kind of company you admit in your parlor. This leads us to the consideration of the part Christian parents should take in the marriage of their children. This we shall investigate in our next chapter under the head of "Match-making."

CHAPTER XXIII.

MATCH-MAKING.

SECTION I.

THE RELATION OF PARENTS TO THE MARRIAGE CHOICE OF THEIR CHILDREN.

"YOUTH longeth for a kindred spirit, and yet yearneth for a
heart that can commune with his own;
Take heed that what charmeth thee is real, nor springeth of
thine own imagination;
And suffer not trifles to win thy love; for a wife is thine unto
death!"

ONE of the most affecting scenes of home-life is that of the bridal hour! Though in one sense it is a scene of joy and festivity; yet in another, it is one of deep sadness. When all is adorned with flowers and smiles, and the parlor becomes the theater of conviviality and parade, even then hearts are oppressed with sorrow at the thought of that separation which is soon to take place.

The bridal is a home-crisis. It is the breaking up of home-ties and communion, a separation from home scenes, a lopping off from the parent vine, an engrafting into a strange vine, and alas! too often, into a degenerate vine. As the youthful bride stands beside her affianced husband, to be wedded to him for life, and reflects that the short ceremonial of that occasion will tear her forever from the loved objects and scenes of her childhood-home, what tears of bitter sorrow adorn the bridal cheek, and what pungent feelings are awakened by her last farewell!

> "'I leave thee, sister! we have played
> Through many a joyous hour,
> Where the silvery gleam of the olive shade
> Hung dim o'er fount and bower.'

"Yes! I leave thee, sister, with all that we have enjoyed together; I leave thee in the memory of our childhood-haunts and song and prayer. We cannot be as we have been. I leave thee now, and all that has bound us together as one; and hereafter memory alone can hail thee, and will do so with her burning tear; therefore, kind sister, let me weep!

> "'I leave thee, father! Eve's bright moon,
> Must now light other feet,
> With the gathered grapes, and the lyre in tune,
> Thy homeward steps to greet.'

"Yes, I leave thee, father! I receive thy last blessing; no longer shall thy protecting hand guide me; no longer shall thy smile be music to my ear. I leave thee, oh, therefore, let me weep!

"'Mother! I leave thee! on thy breast,
Pouring out joy and woe;
I have found that holy place of rest
Still changeless—yet I go!'

"Yes, I go from thee, mother! Though you have watched over me in helpless infancy with all a mother's love and care, and 'lulled me with your strain;' and though earth may not afford me a love like yours; yet I go! Oh, therefore, 'sweet mother, let me weep!'

"'Oh, friends regretted, scenes forever dear
Remembrance hails you with her burning tear;
Drooping she bends o'er pensive fancy's urn,
To trace the hours which ne'er can return.'"

If momentous interests are involved in marriage, then, we think that parents should take an important part in the matrimonial alliances of their children. When they grow up, they naturally seek a companion for life. The making choice of that companion is a crisis in their history, and will determine their future interest and happiness. If separation from home is a great sacrifice, then we should look well to the grounds of our justification in making that sacrifice.

We propose, under the head of "match-making," to consider the part which parents should take in the marriage of their children; and also the false and true standards of judgment both for parents and their children, in making the marriage choice and alliance.

Have parents a right to take any part in the

marriage choice and alliance of their children? Have they a right to interfere in any respect with the marriage of their children? That they do possess such a right, and are justified in the exercise of it within just and reasonable limits, is, we think, undisputed by any one acquainted with the Word of God. It is one of the cardinal prerogatives and duties of the Christian parent. His relation to his children invests him with it. The age and inexperience of the child, on the one hand; and the seductions of the world, on the other; imply it. Children need counsel and admonition; and this is a needs-be for the interposition of the parent's superior wisdom and greater experience.

This right is plainly exemplified in sacred history. Abraham interfered in Isaac's selection of a companion. Isaac and Rebecca aided in the choice of a wife for Jacob. And indeed throughout the patriarchal age, you find this right recognized and practiced. It was also acknowledged and exercised in all the subsequent ages of Judaism, in the age of primitive christianity, and even down to the present time, in every true Christian household. The right still exists, and receives the sanction of the church. The great dereliction of parents now is, that they do not exercise it; and of children, that they do not recognize it. "A wise son heareth his father's instructions." "The eye that mocketh at his father, and despiseth to obey his mother, the ravens of the valley shall pluck it out, and the young eagles shall eat it."

What now is the extent, and what are the duties of that right to interfere? This is a difficult question, and can receive but an imperfect answer. In infancy the authority of the parent is exercised without any reference to the will of the child, because reason is not yet developed. But when he reaches the age of personal accountability, the control of the parent is exercised on more liberal principles; and when, by age, he becomes a responsible citizen, the legal authority of the parent ceases. Still he possesses moral authority, and has a right to exert a restraining influence over the child. This does not, of course, involve a right to compel him to yield to the parent's arbitrary will. He can exert but a moral control over him; and it is the child's duty to yield to this, so long as it is consistent with scripture and the maxims of sound reason and conscience. He should consult his parents, receive them into his confidence, and give priority to their judgment and counsels.

Parents have the right to use coercive measures to prevent an imprudent marriage by their children before they have arrived at age; for until they are of age they are both legally and morally under the authority and government of their parents, who are responsible for them. Hence the child should recognize and submit to their authority. But this right to the use of coercive measures extends only to the prevention of unhappy marriages,—not to the forming of what the parents may regard happy alliances, against the will of the child. No parent has the right to compel a child under age to marry, because the marriage alliance implies the age and free choice of the child.

But when the child reaches legal maturity, the coercive authority of the parent ceases. His interposition then should not involve coercive, but persuasive measures. Then a mere mechanical prevention of an unhappy marriage would have no good moral effect, but would be productive of great evil, inasmuch as it not only involves parental despotism, but the restriction of a manifest and conceded right of the child. It would destroy the sense of personal dignity and responsibility.

Persuasive measures will then accomplish more than all the efforts of the parent to prevent an unhappy union, by threats of disinheritance and expulsion from home. In this way parents often extend their interference to most unreasonable extremes, and to the great detriment of the interests and happiness of their children; while at the same time they often bring disgrace and misery upon their own heads and home. They set themselves up as the choosers of companions for their children, presuming that they should passively submit to their selection whatever it may be. This is taking away the free moral agency of the child, making no account of his taste, judgment, or affections; and forming between him and the object thus chosen a mere outward union, with no inward affinity.

In such cases it most generally happens that parents are prompted by sinister motives and a false pride, as that of wealth, honor, and social position. They do not consult the law of suitability, but that of availability. They think that wealth and family distinction will compensate for the absence of all moral and amiable qualiities, that if outward circumstances are favorable, there need not be inward adaptation of character. Hence they will dictate to their children, make their marriage alliance a mere business matter, and demand implicit obedience on the penalty of expulsion from the parental home, and disinheritance forever. They are thus willing to prostitute the domestic peace and happiness of their offspring to the gratification of their own sordid and inordinate lust for gain and empty distinction.

Who does not perceive and acknowledge the evil of such a course? It involves unfeeling despotism on the one hand, and a servile obedience on the other. The affections are abused; the idea and sacredness of marriage are left out of view; the conditions of domestic felicity are not met. All is supremely selfish; the power exercised is arbitrary; the submission is slavish and demoralizing; the obedience involuntary and degrading; and the result of it all is, an outrage against nature, against marriage, and against God.

On the other hand, the interference of the parent should be persuasive, and the obedience of the child, voluntary. The parent should reason with and counsel the child; and seek by mild and affectionate means to secure obedience to his advice. And if the child then persist in his own course, the parent, we think, has discharged his duty, and the responsibility will rest upon the child. He should not expel and disinherit him, and thus add the hard-heartedness of the parent to the folly and perversity of the child. He should love him still, and seek by parental tenderness to alleviate the sad fruits of filial recklessness. Parents should so train their children in the nursery and parlor, by instilling in them correct principles of judgment in the choice of a companion, as to secure them ever after from an imprudent choice. Here is the place to begin. Parents too often omit this duty, until alas, it is too late.

We have now seen that the parent has no right to destroy the domestic happiness of a child by uniting him forcibly in wedlock to one for whom he has no true affection. On the other hand, the child should pay due deference to the parent's moral suasion, and seek, if possible, to follow his counsels. "A child," says Paley, "who respects his parent's judgment, and is, as he ought to be, tender of their happiness, owes, at least, so much deference to their will, as to try fairly and faithfully, in one case, whether time and absence will not cool an affection which they disapprove. After a sincere but ineffectual endeavor by the child, to accommodate his inclination to his parent's pleasure, he ought not to suffer in his parent's affections, or in his fortunes. The parent, when he has reasonable proof of this, should acquiesce; at all events, the child is then at liberty to provide for his own happiness."

SECTION II.

FALSE TESTS IN THE SELECTION OF A COMPANION FOR LIFE.

Before we advert to some of those biblical principles upon which parents and children should proceed in the marriage choice, we shall take a negative view of the subject, and mention some of those false principles and considerations which have in the present day gained a fearful ascendancy over the better judgment of many professed Christians.

In the matter of marriage, too many are influenced by the pomp and parade of the mere outward. The glitter of gold, the smile of beauty, and the array of titled distinction and circumstance, act like a charm upon the feelings and sentiments of many well-meaning parents and children. But it is not all gold that glitters. We must not think that those are happy in their marriage union, because they are obsequious in their attentions to each other, and live together in splendor, overloaded with fashionable congratulations. We cannot determine the character of a marriage from its pomp and pageantry. We rather determine the many unhappy matches from the false principles upon which the parties acted in making choice of each other. What are some of these? We answer—

1. The manner of paying addresses involves a false principle of procedure. These are either too long or too short, and paid in an improper spirit and manner. There are too much flirtation and romance connected with them. The religious element is not taken up and considered. They do not involve the true idea of preparation, but have an air of mere sentimentalism about them. The object in view is not fully seen. The most reprehensible motives and the most shocking thoughtlessness pervade them throughout. These addresses carry with them an air of trifling, a want of seriousness and frankness, which betrays the absence of all sense of responsibility, and of all proper views of the sacredness of marriage and of its momentous consequences both for time and for eternity.

2. The habit of match-making involves a false principle. This we see more fully among the higher classes of society. It is the work of designing and interested persons, who, for self-interest, intrude their unwelcome interposition. Its whole procedure implies that marriage is simply a legal matter, a piece of business policy, a domestic speculation. It strikes out the great law

of mutual, moral love, and personal adaptation. It makes marriage artificial, and apprehends it as only a mechanical copartnership of interest and life. It is sinister in spirit, and selfish in the end. Many are prompted from motives of novelty to make matches among their friends. All their schemes tend to wrest from the parties interested all true judgment and dispassionate consideration. They are deceived by base misrepresentation, allured by over-wrought pictures of conjugal felicity, so that when the marriage is consummated, they soon find their golden dreams vanish away, and with them, their hopes and their happiness forever.

But there are not only personal match-makers, in the form of tyrannical fathers, sentimental mothers, amorous grandmothers, and obsequious friends; but also book match-makers, in the form of love-sick tales and poetry, containing Eugene-Aram adventures, and scrapes of languishing girls with titled swains running off, calculated to heat the youthful imagination, distort the pictures of fancy, giving to marriage the air of a romantic adventure, and throwing over it a gaudy drapery, leading the young into a world of dreams and nonentities, where all is but a bubble of variegated colors and fantastic forms, which explodes before them as soon as it is touched by the finger of reality and experience.

These are the most dangerous match-makers. Their sister companions in this evil are, the ball-room, the giddy dance and masquerade, the fashionable wine-cup, and the costly apparel. Let me affectionately exhort the members of the Christian home to keep all these at a distance. Touch not, taste not, handle not! They will poison the spirit and the affections, and encircle you with a viper's coil from which there is no hope of escape. Here parents have a right, and it is their duty, to interfere. They can do so effectually by not allowing such filthy match-making intruders to pass the threshold of their homes. What can you expect but an unhappy marriage, if you permit your sons and daughters to spend their time in converse with love-sick tales and languishing swains? They will become love-sick, too, and long for marriage with one who is like the hero of their last-read romance. Perhaps they will not think their matrimonial debut sufficiently flavored with romantic essence, unless they run off with some self-constituted count, or at least with their papa's Irish groom!

3. We might advert, finally, to some of those false influences which are frequently brought to bear upon the children's choice of a companion for life. The term smitten is here significant and deserves our serious consideration. It carries in its pregnant meaning the evidence of a spurious feeling, and a false foundation of love and union. Be it remembered that there must always be something to smite one. We may be smitten by a scoundrel, or by something unworthy our affections. Empty titles and mustaches often smite the susceptible young. Sometimes the heart is smitten by a pretty face and

form; and sometimes by a rod of gold. The simple fact that we are smitten is not enough; we should know who or what it is that smites us. When we are drawn to each other, it should be by a true cord, and by an influence which binds and cements for life. The influènce of mere outward beauty is a false one. Those who are smitten by it, and drawn thus into a matrimonial union by an interest which is but skin-deep, and which may fade like the morning flower, are allured by a dazzling meteor, by a mere bubble, beautifully formed and colored, but empty within. It may dazzle the eye, but it blinds us to all its blemishes and inward infirmities. It is deceptive. Often beneath its gaudy veil there lies the viper, ready to poison all the sweets of home-life, and cause its victim to lament over his folly with bitter tears and heart-burning remorse. How soon may beauty fade; and what then, if it was the only basis of your marriage choice? The union which rested upon it must then be at least morally dissolved; and that which once flitted like an impersonated charm before your admiring eye, now becomes an object of disgust and a source of misery.

To fall in love, therefore, with mere outward beauty is, to dandle with a doll, to fawn upon a picture, to rest your hopes upon a plaything, to pursue a phantom which, as soon as you embrace it, may vanish into nothing. Look not to external beauty alone; but also to the ornaments of an inward spirit, of a noble mind, and an amiable and pious heart. "If," says the Rev. H. Harbaugh, "you will be foolish, follow the gilded butterfly of beauty, drive it a long chase; it will land you at last at some stagnant mud-pond of the highway."

Neither is impulsive passion a true basis of marriage. This is falling in love at first sight, which often proves to be a very dangerous and degrading fall,—a fall from the clouds to the clods, producing both humiliation and misery. It is indeed a fearful leap,—a leap without judgment or forethought; and, therefore, a leap in the dark. It is too precipitate, and shows the infatuation of the victim. Falling in love is not always falling in the embraces of domestic felicity. Such leaping is an act of intoxication. The drunkard, falling in the mire, often thinks that he is embracing his best friend, whereas it is but descending to fellowship with the swine. It is blind love, which is no love, but passion without reason. It is crazy, fitful, stormy, raising the feelings up to boiling point, and bringing the affections under the influence of the high-pressure system. Consequently it is raving, frothy, of a mushroom growth, making mere bubbles, and completing its work in an evaporation of all that it operated upon, passing away like the morning cloud and the early dew.

True love is very different. It is substantial, reasonable, moral, acting according to law, temperate in all things, keeping the heart from extremes, permanent, and based upon principle. Passion, without love, may keep you in a state of pleasurable intoxication until the knot is tied, when you will soon get sober again, only to see, however, your folly and to contemplate the height from which you have fallen, and then, with the recklessness of sullen despair, to pass over into the opposite extreme of stoical indifference and misery. All emotions are transient, and hence no proper standard of judgment in the serious matter of a marriage choice. The heart, unguided by the head, is, in its emotions, like the flaming meteor that passes in its rapid, fiery train across the heavens. It flames only for a time, and soon passes away, leaving the heavens in greater darkness than before.

Neither is wealth a true basis for the marriage choice. "The love of money is the root of all evil;" and when it is the primary desideratum in marriage, it acts like a canker-worm upon domestic peace and happiness. With too many in this day of money-making, marriage is but a pecuniary speculation, a mere gold and silver affair; and their match-making is but a money-making, that is, money makes the match. Many parents (but we don't call such Christians,) sacrifice their children upon the altar of mammon, and prostitute their earthly and eternal happiness to their love of filthy lucre.

Fatal mistake! Will money make your children happy? Is it for money you have them led to the bridal altar? Ah! that sordid dust may cover the grave of their fondest hopes and connubial felicity. Wed not your children to mere dollars and cents. The hand that holds a purse and shakes it before you for your child, may hold also a dagger for both the child and the parent. "Look not only for riches, lest thou be mated with misery." Wealth is good in its place, and we should not object to it, other things being equal. But it never was nor can be good as an inducement to marry. What a miserable policy it is, to make it the test of a proper match! "Do not make the metals of earth the cord of the marriage tie." They are too brittle in their nature to do so. They take to themselves wings and fly away. The fine gold becomes dim; their cords are like ropes of glass-sand,—

> "Like the spider's most attenuated thread,
> They break at every breeze."

Rank also is a false standard of judgment in the forming of a marriage alliance. Many look only to position in society, make it everything, and think that acknowledged social distinction will compensate for the want of all other interests. While there should be a social adaptation of character, and while you should—

> "Be joined to thy equal in rank, or the foot of pride will kick at thee,"

yet there is nothing to justify marrying a person because of his or her social position. The evils of this may be seen in the first classes of English society, where rank is mechanical, and where law forbids a trespass upon its bastard prerogatives; and as a consequence, relatives intermarry, until their descendants have degenerated into complete physical and mental imbecility. Such nepotism as this is replete with untold disaster both in the family and in the state. Too many in our democratic country ape this, look to rank, and are blind to all things else. The fruits of this are seen in that codfish aristocracy which floats with self-inflated importance upon the troubled waters of society, causing too many of the little fish to float after them, until they land themselves in the deep and muddy waters of domestic ruin.

SECTION III.

TRUE TESTS IN THE SELECTION OF A COMPANION FOR LIFE.

Having considered some of the false standards of judgment in the choice of a companion for life, we now revert to those true tests which are given us in the Word of God. There we have the institution and true idea of marriage, and the principles upon which we should proceed in making the marriage choice.

We are taught in the holy scriptures, the primary importance of judicious views of the nature and responsibilities of the marriage institution itself. We should apprehend it, not from its mere worldly standpoint, not as a simple legal alliance, not only as a scheme for temporal welfare and happiness, but as a divine institute, a religious alliance, involving moral responsibilities, and momentous consequences for eternity as well as for time, for soul as well as for body. We are commanded to look to its religious elements and duties; and to regard it with that solemnity of feeling which it truly demands. When the light of the bridal day throws upon the cheek its brightest colors, even then we should rejoice with trembling, and our joy and festivity should be only in the Lord.

> "Joy, serious and sublime,
> Such as doth nerve the energies of prayer,
> Should swell the bosom, when a maiden's hand,
> Filled with life's dewy flowerets, girdeth on
> That harness which the ministry of death
> Alone unlooseth, but whose fearful power
> May stamp the sentence of eternity."

In the days of our forefathers, marriage was thus held sacred, as a divine institution, involving moral and religious duties and responsibilities; and their celebration of it was, therefore, a religious one. They realized its momentous import, and its bearing upon their future welfare. It was not, therefore, without heavings of deep moral emotion and the flow of tears as well as of joyful spirits, that they put the wedding garment on.

> "There are smiles and tears in that gathering band,
> Where the heart is pledged with the trembling hand
> What trying thoughts in the bosom swell,
> As the bride bids parents and home farewell!
> Kneel down by the side of the tearful fair,
> And strengthen the perilous hour with prayer!"

True love in each, and reciprocated by each, must determine the marriage choice. The marriage of children should not be forced. Mutual love is the basis of a proper union, because marriage is a voluntary compact. When parents, therefore, force their children into an alliance, they usurp their undoubted natural and religious rights. Hence there should be no *must*, where there is no *will*, on the part of the child. That choice which is made upon any other than reciprocated affection, is an unreasonable and irreligious one. "Parents have no right," says Paley, "to urge their children upon marriage to which they are averse;" "add to this," says he, "that compulsion in marriage necessarily leads to prevarication; as the reluctant party promises an affection, which neither exists, nor is expected to take place." To proceed to marriage, therefore in the face of absolute dislike and revulsion, is irrational and sinful.

As true, mutual love is the basis of marriage, so also should it be a standard of our judgment in the marriage choice. Without it, neither beauty, wealth nor rank will make home happy. True love should be such as is upheld in scripture. It is above mere passion. It never faileth. It is life-like and never dies out. It is an evergreen in the bosom of home. It has moral stamina, is regulated by moral law, has a moral end, contains moral principle, and rises superior to mere prudential considerations. It is more than mere feeling or emotion; it is not blind, but rational, and above deception, having its ground in our moral and religious nature. It extends to the whole person, to body, mind, and spirit, to the character as well as to the face and form. It is tempered with respect, yea, vitalized, purified, directed and elevated by true piety. Such love alone will survive the charms and allurements of novelty, the fascinations of sense, the ravages of disease and time, and will receive the sanction of heaven.

Mutual adaption of character and position is another scripture standard of judgment. Is that person suited for me? Will that character make my home happy? Could I be happy with such an one? Are we congenial in spirit, sentiment, principle, cultivation, education, morals and religion? Can we sympathize and work harmoniously together in mind and heart and will and taste? Are we complemental to each other? These are questions of far greater importance than the question of wealth, of beauty, or of rank.

Fitness of circumstances, means, and age should be also considered. Am I able to support a family? Can I discharge the duties of a household? Where there is ignorance of household duties, indolence, the want of any visible means of supporting a family, no trade, no education, no energy, and no prospects, there is no reason to think there can be a proper marriage. Thus, then, mutual love, adaptation of character, of means, of circumstances, of position, and of age, should be considered, in the formation of a marriage alliance.

But the standard of judgment to which the scriptures especially direct our attention is, that of religious equality, or spiritual adaptation. "Be not unequally yoked together with unbelievers." The positive command here is, that Christians should marry only in the Lord. Here is a test in the selection of a companion for life, from which neither parents nor children should ever depart. It evidently forbids a matrimonial union with those who have no sympathy with religion. We should make more account of religious equality than of equality of rank and wealth. Is not true piety of more importance than education, affluence or social distinction? When husband and wife are unequally yoked together in soul and grace, their home must suffer spiritually as well as temporally. The performance of religious duties and the enjoyment of religious privileges, will be impossible. The unbeliever will discourage, oppose, and often ridicule, the pious efforts of the believer. Partiality will be produced, and godliness will decline; for, says Peter, unless we dwell as heirs together of the grace of life, our prayers will be hindered. The pious one cannot rule in such a home. Thus divided and striving with each other, their house must fall. Where one draws heavenward and the other hellward, opposite attractions will be presented, and the believer will find constant obstructions to growth in grace, to the discharge of parental duty, and to the cultivation of Christian graces in the heart. How can the unbeliever return, like David, to bless his household? How can he bring up his children in the nurture and admonition of the Lord? Can he be the head of a Christian home? And, tell me, does the true Christian desire any other than a Christian home? "How can two walk together, except they be agreed?" And are you, then, in your marriage, agreed to walk with the unbeliever in the broad road of sin and death? You are not, if you are a true Christian!

We see, therefore, the importance of a rigid adherence to the scripture standard, "Be not unequally yoked together with unbelievers." It is even desirable that husband and wife belong to the same branch of the church, that they may walk together on the sabbath to the house of God. There is indeed something repugnant to the feelings of a Christian to see the husband go in one direction to worship, and the wife in another. They cannot be thus divided, without serious injury to the religious interests of their family, as well as of their own souls. It is impossible for them to train up their children successfully when they are separated by denominational differences. It is a matter of very common observation that when persons thus divided, marry, the one or the other suffers in religious interest. From these and other considerations, we think it is expedient to marry, if possible, within the pales of our own branch of the church. Then, being agreed, they can walk together with one mind and one purpose.

But how much more important that they be united in their pilgrim walk to eternity,—united in the Lord Jesus Christ, by a common life and faith and hope! We believe that Christians commit a sin when they violate this law of religious equality, and unite themselves in matrimony with those who pay no regard to religion. Who can estimate the peril of that home in which one of its members is walking in the narrow way to heaven, while the other one is traveling in the broad road to perdition! Whom, think you, will the children follow? Let the sad experience of a thousand homes respond. Let the blighted hopes and the unrequited affections of the pious wife, reply. Let those children whose infamy and wretchedness have broken the devout mother's heart, or brought the gray hairs of the pious father down with sorrow to the grave, speak forth the answer. It will show the importance of the scripture rule before us, and will declare the sin of violating that rule.

And does not, therefore, a terrible judgment accompany that indiscriminate matrimonial union with the unbelieving world, of which so many Christians, in the present day, are guilty? Parents encourage their pious children to marry unbelievers, though they are well aware that such unholy mixtures are expressly forbidden, and that spiritual harmony is essential to their happiness. "She is at liberty to be married to whom she will, only in the Lord!" Those who violate this cardinal law of marriage, must expect to suffer the penalties attached to it. History is the record of these. The disappointed hopes, and the miseries of unnumbered homes speak forth their execution. This great scripture law has its foundation in the very nature of marriage itself. If marriage involves the law of spiritual harmony; if, in the language of the Roman law, it is "the union of a man and woman, constituting an united habitual course of life, never to be separated;" if it is a partnership of the whole life,—a mutual sharing in all rights, human and divine; if they are one flesh,—one in all the elements of their moral being, as Christ and His church are one; if it is a mystery of man's being, antecedent to all human law; if, in a word, man and woman in marriage, are no more twain, but one flesh; and if the oneness of our nature is framed of the body, the soul, and the spirit, then is it not plain that when two persons marry, who possess no spiritual fitness for, or harmony with, each other, they violate the fundamental law of wedlock; and their marriage cannot meet the scripture conception of matrimonial union or oneness. There will be no adaptation of the whole nature for each other; they will not appreciate the sacred mysteriousness of marriage; instead of the moral and religious development of the spiritual nature, there will be the evolution of selfishness and sensuality as the leading motives of domestic life. We see, then, that the Christian cannot with impunity, violate the scripture law, "Be not unequally yoked with unbelievers."

Shall the Christian parent and child disregard this prohibition of God? Will you ridicule this fundamental principle of Christian marriage?

Will the children of God not hesitate to marry the children of the devil? Can these walk together, in domestic union and harmony? Can saint and sinner be of one mind, one spirit, one life, one hope, one interest? Can the children of the light and the children of darkness, opposite in character and in their apprehension of things, become flesh of each other's flesh, and by the force of their blended light and darkness shed around their home-fireside the cheerfulness of a mutual love, of a common life and hope, and of a progressive spiritual work?

Parents! it is your right and duty to interfere when your children violate this law. Bring them up from infancy to respect it. In the parlor, train them to appreciate its religious importance. Show them that God will visit the iniquity of their departure from it, unto the third and fourth generation. You are stimulated to do so by the divine promise that when they grow old, they will not depart from it.

Such unequal matches are not made in heaven. "God's hand is over such matches, not in them." "What fellowship hath light with darkness?" If love, in Christian marriages, is holy and includes the religious element, then it is evident that the Christian alliance with one between whom and himself there is no religious affinity whatever, is not only an outrage against the marriage institution, but also exposes his home to the curse of God, making it a Babel of confusion and of moral antipathies.

Both the old and the new testaments give explicit testimony to the law of spiritual harmony in marriage. Thus the law of Moses forbid the children of Israel to intermarry among heathen nations. "Neither shalt thou make marriages with them; thy daughter thou shalt not give unto his son, nor his daughter shalt thou take unto thy son."—Deut. vii., 3. Abraham obeyed this law in the part he took in the marriage of his son Isaac, as recorded in the twenty-fourth chapter of Genesis. His obedience was reproduced in Isaac and Rebecca, who manifested the same desire, and took the same care that Jacob should take a wife from among the covenant people of God. See twenty-eighth chapter of Genesis.

The evil consequences of the violation of this law may be seen in the history of Solomon,—i. Kings, chap. 11; also in the case mentioned in the 10th chap.; and in Nehemiah, chap. 13. Paul upholds this law when he exhorts the Corinthians to marry "only in the Lord." Reason itself advocates this law. The true Christian labors for heaven and walks in the path of the just; the unbelieving labor for earth, mind only the things of this world, and walk in the broad road to ruin. Can these now walk together, live in harmony, when so widely different in spirit, in their aims and pursuits? "What fellowship hath righteousness with unrighteousness? What part hath he that believeth with an infidel? And what agreement hath the temple of God with idols? for ye are the temple of the living God; as God hath said, I will dwell in them; and I will be their God, and they shall be my people. Wherefore come out from among them, and be ye separate, saith the Lord, and touch not the unclean thing; and I will receive you, and will be a father unto you, and ye shall be my sons and daughters."

The primitive Christians developed this law in their families. They forbade marriage with Jews, Pagans, Mohammedans, and ungodly persons. With them, piety was the first desideratum in marriage. The sense of the Christian church has ever been against religious inequality in marriage. It has always been felt to be detrimental to personal piety and to the general interests of Christianity. It limits and neutralizes the influence of the church, brings overwhelming temptations to lukewarmness in family religion, and is, in a word, in almost every instance, the fruitful cause of spiritual declension wherever it is practiced.

Let me, then, exhort you to marry only in the Lord. Such an union will be blessed. Daughter of Zion! marry such a man as will, like David, return to bless his household. Son of the Christian home! marry no woman who has not in her heart the casket of piety. Make this your standard; and your home shall be a happy, as well as a holy home, and

> "In the blissful vision, each shall share
> As much of glory as his soul can bear!"

CHAPTER XXIV.

THE CHILDREN'S PATRIMONY.

"GIVE me enough, saith wisdom; for he feareth to ask for more;
And that by the sweat of my brow, addeth stout-hearted independence;
Give me enough, and not less; for want is leagued with the tempter;
Poverty shall make a man desperate, and hurry him ruthless into crime;
Give me enough, and not more, saving for the children of distress;
Wealth oftentimes killeth, where want but hindereth the budding."

THE children's patrimony is a vital subject. It involves the great question, what should Christian parents leave to their children as a true inheritance from the Christian home? We shall return but a very brief and general answer.

The idea of the home-inheritance is generally confined to the amount of wealth which descends from the parent to the child. And this is indeed too often the only inheritance of which children can boast. Many parents, who even claim to be Christians, enslave both themselves and their families, to secure for their offspring a large pecuniary patrimony. They prostitute every thing else to this. And hence it often happens that the greatest money-inheritance becomes the children's greatest curse, running them into all the wild and immoral excesses of prodigality; and ending in abject poverty, licentiousness, and disgrace; or perhaps making them like their deluded parents, penurious, covetous, and contracted in all their views and sentiments.

We think, therefore, that the children's patrimony should be more than gold and silver. This may pamper the body, but will afford no food for the mind and spirit. We do not mean by these remarks, that their patrimony should not include wealth. On the other hand, we believe that parents should make pecuniary provision for them, that they may not begin life totally destitute. But we mean, that when this is the only patrimony they receive, it often proves a curse, because it tends to destroy their sympathy with higher interests, exposes them to the uncertainties of wealth, and makes them dependent upon that alone. If it should elude their grasp, all is gone, and they become poor and helpless indeed.

What, therefore, besides wealth, should be the children's patrimony from the Christian home? We briefly answer.

1. A good character. This is more valuable than wealth; for a good name is rather to be chosen than great riches. This character should be physical, intellectual, and moral. Give your chil-

dren the boon of good health by a proper training to exercise and industry. Transmit to them the patrimony of good physical habits by educating their bodies, and developing their material existence according to the principles of natural law. Develop their intellectual faculties, and enrich them with the treasures of knowledge. Give character to their minds as well as to their bodies; and they will be blessed with an intellectual dowry which cannot be taken from them, and which will bring them an adequate recompense. Give to your children the patrimony of good and just principles. Train the heart to good morals; fill it with the treasures of virtue, of truth, of justice and of honor. Give it moral stamina. Educate the moral sense of your children. Direct the unfolding powers of their conscience; in a word, develop their moral faculties, and supply them with appropriate nutriment; mould their will; cultivate their emotions; rule their desires and passions; and thus unfold their moral nature according to the rules of God's revealed law.

Such a character, involving a true and vigorous evolution of body, mind and spirit, is an effectual safeguard against the evils of prodigality, the disgrace of penuriousness, and the woes of vice and crime. Their property may burn down, and they may be robbed of their gold; but neither the flame nor the robber can deprive them of their character; their intellectual and moral worth is beyond the power of man to destroy; no enemy can rob them of those virtues which a well-developed mind and heart afford; they will be to them a standing capital to enrich them in all that is essential to human happiness.

2. A good occupation is another patrimony which should descend to the children of a Christian home. Bring up your children to some useful employment by which they may be able to make a comfortable living; and you thereby give them hundreds, and, perhaps, thousands of dollars per year; you give them a boon which cannot be taken from them. Many parents, hoping to secure for their children a large pecuniary patrimony, will not permit them to learn either a trade or a profession; but let them grow up in indolence and ignorance, unable as well as unwilling, to be useful either to themselves or to others, living for no purpose, and unfit even to take care of what they leave. And when their wealth descends to them, they soon spend it all in a life of dissipation; so that in a few years they find themselves poor, and friendless, and ignorant of all means of a livelihood, without character, without home, without hope, a nuisance to society, a disgrace to their parents, a curse to themselves! But as we have already dwelt upon this subject in the chapter on the choice of pursuits, we shall not enlarge upon it here.

3. True religion is another inheritance which should descend to the children of the Christian home. This is an undefiled and imperishable treasure, which does not become worthless at the grave, but which will continue to increase in

preciousness as long as the ages of eternity shall roll on. If through the parent's pious agency, the child comes into possession of this invaluable blessing, there is given to him more than earthly treasure, more than pecuniary competency, more than a good name, or a fair reputation, or a high social position in this life; he receives a title to and personal meetness for, the undefiled and imperishable inheritance of heaven, composed of glittering crowns of glory, of unspeakable joys, and sweet communion with all the loved and cherished there. Thus the fruits of a parent's labor for the salvation of his children constitute an infinitely more valuable patrimony than all the accumulated fruits of his industry in behalf of wealth. All the wealth, and rank, and reputation which may descend from parent to child can not supersede the necessity of a spiritual patrimony. It is only, as we have seen in a former chapter, when you minister to the spiritual wants of your children and tinge all their thoughts and feelings with a sense of eternity; when your home is made a spiritual nursery; and you work for their eternal benefit, and thereby secure for them the fulfillment of those blessed promises which God has given concerning the children of believing parents, that you leave them a patrimony worthy the Christian home. Such a spiritual patrimony it is within the power of all Christian parents to bestow. And without its enjoyment by your children, you fail to minister unto them as a faithful steward of God. You may minister to their bodies and minds; you may amass for them a fortune; you may give them an education; you may establish them in the most lucrative business; you may fit them for an honorable and responsible position; you may leave them the heritage of social and political influence; and you may caress them with all the passionate fondness of the parental heart and hand; yet, without the heritage of true piety,—of the true piety of the parent reproduced in the heart and character of the child, all will be worse than vain, yea, a curse to both the parent and the children.

Having thus briefly pointed out some of the essential features of the children's patrimony, as physical, intellectual, moral, and spiritual, we shall now advert to the principles upon which parents should proceed in the distribution of their property to their children.

They should not give them more than a competency. That they should lay by something for them is conceded by all. This is both a right and a duty. It is included in the obligation to provide for them; and he who does it not "hath denied the faith and is worse than an infidel." Natural affection, as well as supernatural faith, stimulates the parent to provide thus for his offspring.

But this does not demand a great fortune; but a simple competency, that is, just enough to meet their immediate wants and emergencies when they enter the world and begin business-life. This competence should correspond with the social position they occupied under the parental roof. It should not go beyond this; it should be just enough to meet the social and financial exigencies of the child. It should be measured also by the peculiar necessities of the child, by his health, abilities, and circumstances. "A parent is justified," says Paley in his Moral and Political Philosophy, "in making a difference between his children according as they stand in greater or less need of the assistance of his fortune, in consequence of the difference of their age or sex, or of the situations in which they are placed, or the various success which they have met with."

Now the law of competence does not demand, yea, it forbids, more than a sufficiency to meet these peculiar exigencies of the child. Those parents who seek for more, become parsimonious, unfaithful to the moral interests of ther household, and indifferent to all legitimate objects of charity and benevolence. These are indeed but the necessary fruits of unfaithfulness to this law; for the course of God's providence indicates the impossibility of our faithfulness to the duty of Christian beneficence, and at the same time lay up for our children more than a sufficiency. We find indeed, that in almost every instance in which parents have transcended the limits of competence, and thus raised their children above the necessity of doing anything themselves for a subsistence, God has cursed the act, and the canker of His displeasure has consumed this ill-saved property. That curse we see often in the prodigality and dissipation of the children. They walk in the slippery paths of sin, kneel at the altar of Mammon, fare sumptuously every day, as prodigal in spending their fortune as their parents were penurious in amassing it, until at last they come to want, rush into crime, and end their unhappy life in the state's prison, or upon the gibbet.

We see, therefore, that when parents give their children more than what they actually need, they place in their possession the instruments with which they ruin themselves. History shows that the most wealthy men started out in the world with barely enough, and some, with nothing; and that generally those who started with an independent fortune ended with less than they started, and many closed their earthly career in abject poverty and misery. Besides, the man who made his fortune knows how to keep and expend it; and in point of happiness derived from property, "there is no comparison between a fortune which a man acquires by well-applied industry, or by a series of success in his business, and one found in his possession or received from another." Let, therefore, the property you leave your children be just enough to meet the exigencies of their situations, and no more; for

> "Wealth hath never given happiness, but often hastened misery;
> Enough hath never caused misery, but often quickened happiness;
> Enough is less than thy thought, O pampered creature of society,
> And he that hath more than enough, is a thief of the rights of his brother!"

Parents should be impartial in the distribution of their patrimony among their children. They should never give one more than another unless for very plausible and Christian reasons, such as bad health, peculiar circumstances, of want, &c. They should have no pets, no favorites among them; and care more for one than for another, or indulge one more than another. Neither should they withhold a dowry from a child as a punishment, unless his crime and character are of such an execrable nature as to warrant the assurance that its bestowment would but enhance his misery. Then indeed, it would be a blessing to withhold it. "A child's vices may be of that sort," says Paley in his Philosophy, "and his vicious habits so incorrigible, as to afford much the same reason for believing that he will waste or misemploy the fortune put into his power, as if he were mad or idiotish, in which case a parent may treat him as a madman or an idiot; that is, may deem it sufficient to provide for his support by an annuity equal to his wants and innocent enjoyments, and which he may be restrained from alienating. This seems to be the only case in which a disinherison, nearly absolute, is justifiable."

Neither should parents be capricious in the distribution of their property among their children. They have no right to withhold a dowry from children because they have married against their will, no more than they have a right, for this reason, to disown them. This would be distributing their property upon the principle of revenge or reward. No parent has a right to indulge a preference founded on such an unreasonable and criminal feeling as revenge. Neither has he a right to distribute his property from considerations of age, sex, merit, or situation. The idea of giving all to the eldest son to perpetuate family wealth and distinction; or of giving all to the sons, and withholding from the daughters; or of giving to those children only who were more obsequious in their adherence to their parent's tyrannical requisitions,—is unreasonable, unchristian, and against the generous dictates of natural affection.

From this whole subject we may infer the infatuation of those parents who toil as the slave in the galley, to amass a large fortune for their children. To accomplish this object they become drudges all their life. They rise early and retire late, deny themselves even the ordinary comforts of life, expend all the time and strength of their manhood, make slaves of their wives and children, and live retired from all society, in order to lay up a fortune for their offspring. To this end they make all things subordinate and subservient; and, indeed, they so greatly neglect their children as to deprive them of even the capacity of enjoying intellectually or morally the patrimony they thus secure for them. They bring them up in gross ignorance of every thing save work and money. They teach them close-fisted parsimony, and prepare them to lead a life as servile and infatuated as their own. Miserable delusion! "What shall it profit a man if he gain the whole world, and lose his own soul?"

> "O cursed lust of gold! when for thy sake
> The fool throws up his interest in both worlds;
> First starved in this, then damned in that to come!"

CHAPTER XXV.

THE PROMISES OF THE CHRISTIAN HOME.

"The promise is unto you, and to your children."
ACTS II., 39.

"PARENT who plantedst in the joy of love,
Yet hast not gather'd fruit,—save rankling thorns,
Or Sodom's bitter apples,—hast thou read
Heaven's promise to the seeker? Thou may'st bring
Those o'er whose cradle thou didst watch with pride,
And lay them at thy Savior's feet, for lo!
His shadow falling on the wayward soul,
May give it holy health. And when thou kneel'st
Low at the pavement of sweet Mercy's gate,
Beseeching for thine erring ones, unfold
The passport of the King,—'Ask, and receive!
Knock,—and it shall be opened!"'

THE promises of the Christian home may be divided into two kinds, viz.: Those which God has given to the family; and those which Christian parents have made to God.

God has not only laid His requisitions upon the Christian home, but given his promises. Every command is accompanied with a promise. These promises give color to all the hopes of home.

When the dark cloud of tribulation overhangs the parent's heart; when the overwhelming storm of misfortune rages around his habitation, uprooting his hopes and demolishing his interests; when the ruthless hand of death tears from his embrace the wife of his bosom and the children of his love;—even in hours of bereavement like these, the promises of God dispel the gloom, and surround his home and his heart with the sunshine of peace and joy.

His promises extend to both the parents and their offspring. "Unto you, and unto your children," "I will pour my spirit on thy seed, and my blessing on thine offspring; and they shall spring up as among the grass, as willows by the water-courses. One shall say, I am the Lord's; and another shall call himself by the name of Jacob; and another shall subscribe with his hand unto the Lord, and surname himself by the name of Israel." His promises extend to children's children; and whatever they may be for the parent, they are "visited upon the children unto the third and fourth generation."

Now these divine promises are of two kinds,—the promise of punishment, and the promise of reward. He promises to punish the unfaithful parent, and to reward the faithful parent. He also promises to visit both the evil and the good of the parents upon their children. Such is the constitution of the family, and such are the vital relations which the members sustain to each other, that by the law of natural and moral reproduction, the child is either blessed or cursed in the parent. What the parent does will run out in its legitimate consequences to the child, either as a malediction or as a benediction.

We have divine promises to punish the unfaithful members of the Christian home. If the parent becomes guilty of iniquity, it will be visited upon the children from generation to generation. There is no consideration which should more effectually restrain parents from unfaithfulness than this. Let them become selfish, sensual, indolent, and dissipated, and soon these elements of iniquity will be transmitted to their offspring. What the parent sows, the child will reap. If the former sow to the flesh, the latter shall of the flesh reap corruption. Thus, whatsoever the parent sows in the child he shall reap from the child. The promised curse of the parent's wickedness is deposited in the child so far as that wickedness affected the child's character. This is all based upon the great principle that the promises are unto you, and to your children.

But while this great principle is ominous of terror to the ungodly, it is a pleasing theme to the pious and faithful. .Home is a stewardship; and if faithful to its high and holy vocation, it has a good reward for its labor of love. "If ye sow to the spirit ye shall of the spirit reap life everlasting." This promise of reward is "to you and to your children." "Many souls shall be given for its hire." Their children shall reap the reward of the faithfulness of the parents. Of them it shall be said, "this is the seed which the Lord hath blessed." Faithful parents have thus a glorious recompense of reward. God shall reward thee openly. Make your household a true nursery for the soul; and He will give thee thy wages. The blessing of the Most High will descend like dew upon you and your children. And when they grow up to manhood, He will make them His agents in rewarding you. They will honor and comfort you in your declining years. They will not depart from the ways of the Lord in which you trained them. Though they may be in a distant land,—far from you and the cherished home of their childhood, yet they will obey your admonitions, gratefully remember your kindness; and their grateful obedience and remembrance will be your great reward from them. They will rise up and call you blessed.

"Though we dwell apart,
Thy loving words are with me evermore,—
Thy precious loving words. Thy hand, and heart,
And earnest soul of love, are here impressed,
For me, a dear memorial through all time.
Mother! I cannot recompense thy love,
But thy reward is sure, for thou hast done
Thy duty perfectly, and we rise up
And call thee blessed; and the Lord shall give
Thy pious cares and labors rich reward."

And when you descend to the grave and are gathered to your fathers, the assurance of fidelity to your home-trust, the prospect of meeting your children in heaven, and all the brilliant hopes that loom up before you, full of the light and glory of the eternal world, will furnish you a great recompense of reward.

Parents can rely upon these promises of God with the full assurance of faith; for His promises are yea and amen. Let them but lay hold upon the promises, and act upon the conditions of their fulfillment, and then leave the rest to God. Abraham and Joshua, and David, acted upon this principle in their families. Let the members of the Christian home do the same, and the blessing of God will rest upon them.

God promises to reward parents in this life. We find their fulfillment in the peace, the hopes, the interests, and the pleasures of the faithful household. The members are happy in each other's love, in each other's virtue, in each other's worth, in each other's hopes, in each other's interests, in each other's confidence, in each other's piety, in each other's fidelity, in each other's happiness. 'Thus God shall reward thee openly. He has never said to the seed of Jacob seek ye me in vain. "Verily there is a reward for the righteous." "This is the seed which the Lord hath blessed."

The promised reward of faithful parents may be seen in their children. They are in the true Christian home a precious heritage from the Lord. Thus a parent's faithfulness was rewarded in the piety of Baxter, and Doddridge, and Watts. What a rich reward did Elkanah and Hannah receive by their training up Samuel! And were not Lois and Eunice rewarded for their faithfulness to young Timothy? What a glorious reward the mother of John Q. Adams received from God, in that great and good man! God blessed her fidelity, by making him worthy of such a mother. He himself was conscious that he was his mother's reward, as may be seen from the following anecdote of him. Governor Briggs of Massachusetts, after reading with great interest the letters of John Q. Adam's mother, one day went over to his seat in Congress, and said to him:

"Mr. Adams, I have found out who made you!"

"What do you mean?" said he.

"I have been reading the letters of your mother," was the reply.

With a flashing eye and glowing face, he started, and in his peculiar manner, said: "Yes, Briggs, all that is good in me, I owe to my mother!"

But God promises to reward faithful parents in the life to come. Their great reward is in heaven. The departure of every pious member of their home but increases the heavenly reward. The little child that dies in its mother's arms, and is borne up to the God who gave it, but increases by its sainted presence there, her joyful anticipations of the eternal reward.

"And when, by father's lonely bed,
You place me in the ground,
And his green turf, with daisies spread,
Has also wrapt me round;
Rejoice to think, to you 'tis given,
To have a ransomed child in heaven!"

And oh, how glorious will be this reward when all the members shall meet again in heaven, recognize each other there, and unite their harps and voices in ascriptions of praise to God. There in that better home, where no separations take place, no trials are endured, no sorrows felt, no tears shed, they shall enjoy the complete fulfillment of divine promises. Heaven, with its unfading treasures, with its golden streets, with its crowns of glory, with its unspeakable joys, with its river of life, and with its anthems of praise, will be their great recompense of the reward. How the anticipation of this should stimulate Christian parents to increased fidelity; oh, what a happy meeting will that be, when husband and wife, parent and child, brother and sister, after many long years of separation, shall greet each other in that glorious world, and feel that parting grief shall weep no more!

> "Oh! when a mother meets on high,
> The child she lost in infancy;
> Hath she not then for pains and fears,
> The day of woe, the watchful night,
> For all her sorrows, all her tears,
> An over-payment of delight?"

With these gracious promises of reward sounding in their ears, Christian parents should never despair; neither should they doubt for a moment the fidelity of God to all his promises. It is true that His promises are conditional, and their fulfillment depends upon the parent's performance of his part as the condition, yet to every duty he has attached a promise; and wherever He has made a promise for us, he has given us the ability to use the means of securing its fulfillment; and as soon as their conditions are thus met, they become absolute. "Train up a child in the way he should go." Here is the duty. "And when he grows old he will not depart from it." Here is the promise. The condition is, that you discharge the duty. If you do so, the promise becomes absolute, and shall with certainty be divinely fulfilled in your child, though the time and manner of this fulfillment may not meet your expectations.

But some may object to this position, and remind us that pious parents are known to have ungodly children who died in their sins. They may refer us to the case of Absalom, and to the sons of Eli. In reply we would state that this is begging the question. It is here taken for granted that these pious parents did fulfill the conditions attached to the above promises. This is a mere assumption; for Absalom was not properly trained; and both he and the sons of Levi, were ruined by the misguided fondness and extreme indulgence of their parents. And thus also does the foolish partiality of many pious parents prevent their fidelity to their children. We must not think that all pious parents are faithful to their duty to their children. The above objection, however, assumes this ground; and, therefore, it is not valid. It is often said that the children of ministers and pious parents are usually more wicked than other children. This is false. The opposite is true. We admit, some have bad children; but it is the fault of the parents; not because God does not fulfill His covenant promises to His people. His people, in these instances, do not meet the conditions upon which His promises are made absolute.

We must not suppose that because a divine promise exists detached from expressed conditions, it will be fulfilled without the use of means. There is a manifest compatibility between the absolute promises of God and the use of the means in our power for their fulfillment. The promise to Paul in the ship in which he was conveyed to Rome, that none of the passengers should perish, was not incompatible with Paul's declaration, "except these persons abide in the ship, ye cannot be saved." Neither were the efforts of the mother of Moses to save him, incompatible with the absolute promise of God that "this babe shall be saved, and be the deliverer of Israel." What she did to preserve his life was accompanied with an active, confiding faith in the divine promise concerning him. And thus should faith in God's promises stimulate Christian parents to zealous activity in the use of all those means which secure their fulfillment.

The Christian home should ever keep in lively remembrance the solemn promises made by her to God. In marriage, in holy baptism, she has made vows unto God, and he says to her, pay thy vows. "When thou shalt vow a vow unto the Lord thy God, thou shalt not slack to pay it; for the Lord thy God will surely require it of thee." These parental promises made to God regard themselves and their children; and their faithful fulfillment brings them within the glorious promise which God gave to Abraham; for, says Paul, "If ye be Christ's, then are ye Abraham's seed, and heirs according to the promise:" Gal. iii., 29.

Christian parents: the promises of God shine forth as brilliantly now as ever they did upon the pages of sacred history. They are as bright for you as they were for Abraham and Joshua, when they trembled in sublime eloquence upon the lips of God. Let them, therefore, be not in vain. The promises are unto you, and to your children. And you in turn have promised God that you would bless your household, and be faithful to your children. Hold fast to these promises without wavering. Hang all your hopes upon them. Cling to them with the wrestling spirit of Jacob. And remember that you cannot shake off your vows and promises made to God. He will surely require it of thee. Therefore pay thy vows unto the Lord. God will reward you for so doing. "The mountains shall depart, and the hills be removed; but my kindness shall not depart from thee, neither shall the covenant of my peace be removed, saith the Lord that hath mercy on thee:" Isaiah liv., 10.

Dan. Huntington.

CHAPTER XXVI.

THE BEREAVEMENTS OF THE CHRISTIAN HOME.*

"Oh, long ago
Those blessed days departed, we are reft,
And scattered like the leaves of some fair rose,
That fall off one by one upon the breeze,
Which bears them where it listeth. Never more
Can they be gathered and become a rose.
And we can be united never more
A family on earth!"

Bereavement involves the providential discipline of home. In almost every household there have been sorrows and tears as well as joys and hopes. As the Christian home is the depository of the highest interests and the purest pleasures, so it is the scene of sad bereavements and of the darkest trials. It may become as desolate as the

---

* In this chapter we have made free use of poetical quotations for the benefit of the afflicted.

home of Job. The Christian may, like the aged tree, be stripped of his clusters, his branches, all his summer glory, and sink down into a lonely and dreary existence. His home, which once rang with glad voices, may become silent and sad and hopeless. Those hearts which once beat with life and love, may become still and cold; and all the earthly interests which clustered around his fireside may pass away like the dream of an hour!

The members of home must separate. Theirs is but a probationary state. Their household is but a tent,—a tabernacle in the flesh, and all that it contains will pass away. The fondest ties will be broken; the brightest hopes will fade; all its joys are transient; its interests meteoric, and the fireside of cheerfulness will ere long become the scene of despondency. Every swing of the pendulum of the clock tells that the time of its probation is becoming shorter and shorter, and that its members are approaching nearer and nearer the period of their separation.

> "There is no union here of hearts,
> That finds not here an end."

Alas! how soon this takes place! The joy of home would be perfect did not the thought of a speedy separation intrude. No sooner than the voice of childhood is changed, than separation begins to take place. Some separate for another world; some are borne by the winds and waves to distant lands; others enter the deep forests of the West, and are heard of no more;—

"Alas! the brother knows not now where fall the sister's tears!
One haply revels at the feast, while one may droop alone;
For broken is the household chain,—the bright fire quenched
and gone!"

What melancholy feelings are awakened within at the sight of a deserted home, in which loved ones once met and lived and loved; but from which they have now wandered, each in the path pointed out by the guiding hand of Providence. How beautifully does Mrs. Hemans portray this separation in the following admirable lines!—

"They grew in beauty side by side,
They filled one home with glee;
Their graves are severed, far and wide,
By mount, and stream, and sea.

The same fond mother bent at night
O'er each fair sleeping brow;
She had each folded flower in sight—
Where are those dreamers now?

One midst the forests of the West
By a dark stream is laid;
The Indian knows his place of rest
Far in the cedar shade.

The sea, the blue lone sea, hath one,
He lies where pearls lie deep;
He was the loved of all, yet none
O'er his low bed may weep.

One sleeps where southern vines are dress'd,
Above the noble slain;
He wrapped his colors round his breast,
On a blood-red field of Spain.

And one—o'er her the myrtle showers,
Its leaves by soft winds fanned;
She faded midst Italian flowers—
The last of that fair band.

And parted thus, they rest, who played
Beneath the same green tree;
Whose voices mingled as they prayed
Around one parent knee!"

It is thus in almost every household. The members may be divided into two classes,—the present and the absent ones. Who may not say of his family—

"We are not all here!
Some are away—the dead ones dear,
Who thronged with us this ancient hearth,
And gave the hour of guiltless mirth.
Fate, with a stern, relentless hand,
Looked in and thinned our little band.
Some like a night-flash passed away,
And some sank lingering day by day,
The quiet graveyard—some lie there,—
We're not all here!"

The bereavements of home are diversified. The reverses of fortune constitute an important class of family afflictions, causing the habits, customs, social privileges and advantages of home to be broken up and changed. Many a family, which, in former days, enjoyed all the pleasures and privileges of wealth and social distinction, have now to struggle with cruel poverty, and receive from the world, scorn and ridicule and dishonor.

But the greatest bereavement of home is, generally, death. They only, who have lived in the house of mourning, know what the sad bereavements are which death produces, and what deep and dark vacancies this last enemy leaves in the stricken heart of home.

> "The lips that used to bless you there,
> Are silent with the dead."

To-day we may visit the family. What a lovely scene it presents! The members are happy in each other's love, and each one resting his hopes upon all the rest. No cares perplex them; no sorrows corrode them; no trials distress them; no darkness overshadows them! What tender bonds unite them; what hopes cluster around each heart; what a depth of reciprocated affection we find in each bosom; and by what tender sympathy they are drawn to each other!

But alas! in an hour of supposed security, that loving group is broken up by the intrusion of death, and some one or more carried from the bosom of love to the cold and cheerless grave. The curfew-bell speaks the solemn truth, and warns the members that "in the midst of life they are in death." Where is the home that has not some memorial of departed ones,—a chair empty, a vacant seat at the table,—garments laid by,—ashes of the dead treasured up in the urn of memory! What sudden ravages does this ruthless foe of life, often make in the family! The members are often taken away, one by one in quick succession, until all of them are laid side by side beneath the green sod.

What a memorable epoch in the history of home is that, in which death finds his first entrance within its sacred enclosures, and with ruthless hand breaks the first link of a golden chain that creates its identity! We can never forget that event. It may be the first-born in the radiant beauty of youth, or the babe in the first bursting of life's budding loveliness, or a father in the midst of his anxious cares, or the mother who gave light and happiness to all around her. Whoever it is, the first death makes a breach there which no subsequent bereavement can equal; new feelings are then awakened; a new order of associations is then commenced; hopes and fears are then aroused that never subside; and the mysterious web of family life receives the hue of a new and darker thread.

What a sad bereavement is the death of the husband and father! Children! there is the grave of your father! You have recently heard the clods of the valley groan upon his coffin. The parent stem from which you grew and to which you fondly clung, has been shattered by the lightning-stroke of death, and its terrible shock is now felt in every fiber of the wrenched and torn branches. Yours is now a widowed and an orphaned home. The disconsolate members are left helpless and hopeless in the world; the widowed mother sits by the dying embers of her lonely cottage, overwhelmed with grief, and poor in everything but her children and her God. These orphans are turned out upon the cold charities of an unfriendly world, neglected and forlorn, having no one to care for them but a poor, broken-hearted mother, whose deathless faith points them to the bright spirit-world to which their sainted father has gone, where parting grief shall weep no more.

But a greater bereavement even than this, is, the death of a wife and mother. Ah! here is a bereavement which the child alone can fully feel. When the mother is laid upon the cold bier, and sleeps among the dead, the center of home-love and attraction is gone. What children are more desolate and more to be pitied than the motherless ones? She, who fed them from her gentle breast and sung sweet lullaby to soothe them into sleep, —she, who taught them to kneel in prayer at her side, and ministered to all their little wants, and sympathized with them in all their little troubles, —she has now been torn from them, leaving them a smitten flock indeed, and the light of her smile will never again be round their beds and paths. As the shades of night close in upon that smitten home, and the chime of the bell tells the hour in which the mother used to gather them around her for prayer, and sing them to their rosy rest, with what a stricken heart does the bereaved husband seek to perform this office of love in her stead; and as he gathers them for the first time around him, how fully does he feel that none can take a mother's place!

"My sheltering arms can clasp you all,
My poor deserted throng;
Cling as you used to cling to her
Who sings the angel's song.
Begin, sweet ones, the accustomed strain,
Come, warble loud and clear;
Alas, alas! you're weeping all,
You're sobbing in my ear;
Good night; go, say the prayer she taught,
Beside your little bed.

The lips that used to bless you there,
Are silent with the dead.
A father's hand your course may guide
Amid the storms of life,
His care protect those shrinking plants
That dread the storm of strife;
But who, upon your infant hearts,
Shall like that mother write?
Who touch the strings that rule the soul?
Dear smitten flock, good night!"

Who can forget a mother, or lose those impressions which her death made upon our deeply stricken hearts? None,—not even the wretch who has brutalized all the feelings of natural affection. The memory of a mother's death is as fadeless as the deep impress of a mother's love upon our hearts. As often as we resort to her grave we must leave behind the tribute of our tears. Who can read the following beautiful lines of Cowper, and—if the memory of a sainted mother is awakened by them,—not weep?

"My mother! When I learned that thou wast dead,
Say, wast thou conscious of the tears I shed?
Hovered thy spirit o'er thy sorrowing son,
Wretch even then, life's journey just begun!
Perhaps thou gav'st me, though unfelt, a kiss;
Perhaps a tear, if souls can weep in bliss—
Ah, that maternal smile! it answers—yes!
I heard the bell toll on the burial day,
I saw the hearse that bore thee slow away,
And, turning from my nurs'ry window, drew
A long, long sigh, and wept a last adieu!
But was it such? It was. Where thou art gone
Adieus and farewells are a sound unknown.
May I but meet thee on that peaceful shore,
The parting word shall pass my lips no more!"

The death of children is a great bereavement of home. Behold that little blossom withered in its mother's arms! See those tears which flood her eyes as she bends in her deep grief over the grave of her cherished babe! Go, fond parents, to that little mound, and weep! It is well to do so; it is well for thee in the twilight hour to steal around that hallowed spot, and pay the tribute of memory to your little one, in flooding tears. There beneath those blooming flowers which the hand of affection planted, it sweetly sleeps. It bids adieu to all the scenes and cares of life. It just began to taste the cup of life, and turned from its ingredients of commingled joy and sorrow, to a more peaceful clime. Cold now is that little heart which once beat its warm pulses so near to thine; hushed is now that sweet voice that once breathed music to your soul. Like the folding up of the rose, it passed away; that beautiful bud which bloomed and cheered your heart, was transplanted ere the storm beat upon it:—

"Death found strange beauty on that polished brow,
And dashed it out—
There was a tint of rose
On cheek and lip. He touched the veins with ice,
And the rose faded.
Forth from those blue eyes
There spake a wishful tenderness, a doubt
Whether to grieve or sleep, which innocence
Alone may wear. With ruthless haste he bound
The silken fringes of those curtained lids
Forever.
There had been a murmuring sound,
With which the babe would claim its mother's ear,
Charming her even to tears. The spoiler set
His seal of silence.
But there beamed a smile
So fixed, so holy, from that cherub brow,
Death gazed—and left it there.
He dared not steal
The signet-ring of heaven!"

The death of such an infant is indeed a sore affliction, and causes the bleeding heart of the parent to cry out, "Whose sorrow is like unto my sorrow!" Unfeeling Death! that thou shouldst thus blight the fair flowers and nip the unfolding buds of promise in the Christian home!

"Death! thou dread looser of the dearest tie,
Was there no aged and no sick one nigh?
No languid wretch who long'd, but long'd in vain,
For thy cold hand to cool his fiery pain?
And was the only victim thou couldst find,
An infant in its mother's arms reclined?"

Thus it is that death often turns from the sickly to the healthy, from the decrepitude of age to the strong man in his prime, from the miserable wretch who longs for the grave to the smiling babe upon its mother's breast, and there in those "azure veins which steal like streams along a field of snow," he pours his putrefying breath, and leaves within that mother's arms nothing but loathsomeness and ruin! It was thus, bereaved parents, that he came within your peaceful home, and threw a cruel mockery over all your visions of delight, over all the joys and hopes and interests of your fireside, personifying their wreck in the cold and ghastly corpse of your child. All that is now left to you is, the memorials around you that once the pride of your heart was there;—

"The nursery shows thy pictured wall,
Thy bat, thy bow,
Thy cloak and bonnet, club and ball,
But where art thou?
A corner holds thine empty chair,
Thy playthings idly scattered there,
But speak to us of our despair!"

How sad and lonely especially is the mother who is called thus to weep the loss of her departed infant. Oh, it is hard for her to give up that loved one whose smile and childish glee were the light and the hope of her heart. As she lays it in the cold, damp earth, and returns to her house of mourning, and there contemplates its empty cradle, and that silent nursery, once gladsome with its mirth, she feels the sinking weight of her desolation. No light, no luxury, no friend, can fill the place of her lost one.

And especially if this lost one be the first-born,—the first bud of promise and of hope, how doubly painful is the bereavement. It makes our home as dark and desolate as was the hour when Abraham with uplifted knife, was about to send death to the throbbing heart of his beloved Isaac. Nothing can supply the place of a first-born child; and home can never be what it was when the sweet voice of that first-born child was heard. The first green leaf of that household has faded; and though leaves may put forth, and other buds of promise may unfold, and bright faces may light up the home-hearth, and the sunshine of hope may play around the heart; but—

"They never can replace the bud our early fondness nurst,
They may be lovely and beloved, but not like thee—the first!"

Your heart continues lonely and desolate; its strings are broken; its tenderest fibers wrenched; you continue to steal "beneath the church-yard tree, where the grass grows green and wild," and there weep over the grave of your first maternal love; and like Rachael, refuse to be comforted because he is not. Your grief is natural, and only those who have lost their first-born can fully realize it:—

"Young mother! what can feeble friendship say,
To soothe the anguish of this mournful day?
They, they alone, whose hearts like thine have bled,
Know how the living sorrow for the dead;
I've felt it all,—alas! too well I know
How vain all earthly power to hush thy woe!
God cheer thee, childless mother! 'tis not given
For man to ward the blow that falls from heaven.
I've felt it all—as thou art feeling now;
Like thee, with stricken heart and aching brow,
I've sat and watched by dying beauty's bed,
And burning tears of hopeless anguish shed;
I've gazed upon the sweet, but pallid face,
And vainly tried some comfort there to trace;
I've listened to the short and struggling breath;
I've seen the cherub eye grow dim in death;
Like thee, I've veiled my head in speechless gloom,
And laid my first-born in the silent tomb!"

Now in all these bereavements of the Christian home we have developed the wisdom and goodness of God; and the consideration of this we commend to the bereaved as a great comfort. They are but the execution of God's merciful design concerning the family. Pious parents can, therefore, bless the Lord for these afflictions. It is often well for both you and your children that bereavements come. They come often as the ministers of grace. The tendency of home is to confine its supreme affections within itself, and not yield them unto God. Parents often bestow upon their children all their love, and live for them alone. Then God lays his rod upon them, takes their loved ones to his own arms, to show them the folly of using them as abusing them. If home had no such bereavements, eternity would be lost sight of; God would not be obeyed; souls would be neglected; natural affection would crush the higher incentives and restraints of faith; earthly interests would push from our hearts all spiritual concerns; and our tent-home in this vale of tears would be substituted for our heavenly home. We see, therefore, the benevolent wisdom of God in ordaining bereavements to arrest us from the control of unsanctified natural affection. When we see the flowers of our household withered and strewn around us; when that which we most tenderly loved and clung to, is taken from us in an unexpected hour, we begin to see the futility of living for earthly interests alone; and we turn from the lamented dead to be more faithful to the cherished and dependent living.

Let us, therefore, remember that in all our afflictions God has some merciful design, the execution of which will contribute to the temporal and eternal welfare of our home. He designs either to correct us if we do wrong, or to prevent us from doing wrong, or to test our Christian fidelity, or to instruct us in the deep mysteries and meandering ways of human life, and keep before us the true idea of our homes and lives as a pilgrimage. Nothing, save supernatural agencies, so effectually removes the moral film from our intellectual eye as the hand of bereavement. Death is a great teacher. Sources of pensive reflection and spiritual communion are opened, which none but death could unseal. A proper sense of the spirit-world is developed; life appears in its naked reality; heaven gains new attractions; eternity becomes a holier theme,—a more cheerful object of thought; the true relation of this to the life to come, is realized; and the presence of the world of the unseen enters more deeply into our moral consciousness.

Though our loved ones are gone, they are still with us in spirit; yea, they are ours still, in the best sense of possession; our relationship with them is not destroyed, but hallowed. Though absent, they still live and love; and they come thronging as ministering spirits to our hearts; they hover near us, and commune with us. Though death may separate us from them, it does not disunite us. Your departed children, though separated from you in body, are still yours, are with you in spirit, and are members of your family. They represent your household in heaven, and are a promise that you will be there also. You are still their parents; you are still one family,—one in spirit, in faith, in hope, in promise, in Christ. You still dwell together in the fond memories of home, and in the bright anticipation of a coming reünion in heaven. Oh, with this view of death, and with this hope of joining love's buried ones again, you can gather those that yet remain, and talk to them of those you put, cold and speechless, in their bed of clay; and while their bodies lie exposed to the winter's storm or to the summer's heat, you can point the living to that cheering promise which spans, as with an areole of glory, the graves of buried love; you can tell them they shall meet their departed kindred in a better home. Oh, clasp this promise to your aching heart; treasure it up as a pearl of great price. Your departed children are not lost to you; and their death to them is great gain. They are not lost, but only sent before. "The Lord has taken them away." With these views of death before you, and with the moral instructions they afford, you cannot but feel that your children, though absent from you in body, are with you in spirit,—are still living with you in your household, and are among that spirit-throng which ever press around you, to bear you up lest you dash your foot against a stone. Such were the feelings of the Christian father, as expressed in the following touching lines:—

"I cannot make him dead!
When passing by his bed,
So long watched over with parental care,
My spirit and my eye
Seek it inquiringly,
Before the thought comes that—he is not there!

When at the day's calm close,
Before we seek repose,
I'm with his mother, offering up our prayer,
Whate'er I may be saying,
I am, in spirit, praying
For our boy's spirit, though—he is not there!

Not there? Where, then, is he?
The form I used to see
Was but the raiment that he used to wear.
The grave, that now doth press
Upon that cast-off dress,
Is but his wardrobe locked;—he is not there!

He lives! In all the past
He lives; nor, to the last,
Of seeing him again will I despair;
In dreams I see him now,
And on his angel brow,
I see it written, 'Thou shalt see me there!'

Yes, we all live to God!
Father, thy chastening rod
So help us, thine afflicted ones, to bear,
That in the spirit-land,
Meeting at thy right hand,
'Twill be our heaven to find that—he is there!"

From this view of the educational principle involved in all our bereavements, we may easily infer that God designs to benefit us by them. There is an actual usefulness in all the bereavements of the Christian home. They are but the discipline of a Father's hand and the ministration of a Father's love. Though His face may wear a dark frown, or be hid behind the tempest-cloud, and His rod may be laid heavily upon you, yet you are not warranted to believe that no sweet is in the bitter cup you drink, that no light shines behind the cloud, or that no good dwells in the bursting storm around you. The present may indeed be dark; but the future will be bright and laden with a Father's blessing. The smile will succeed the frown; the balm will follow the rod. The good seed will be sown after the deep furrows are made. "No chastening for the present seemeth joyous, but grievous, yet it worketh out a far more exceeding and eternal weight of glory to them that are exercised thereby." The memory that lingers around the grave of our loved ones, is sad and tearful. The stricken heart heaves with emotions too big for utterance, when we hear no more the sound of their accustomed footsteps upon the threshold of our door. Oh, the cup of bereavement is then bitter, its hour dark, and the pall of desolation hangs heavily around our hearts and homes.

But this is only the dark side of bereavement. The eye which then weeps may fail at the time to behold through its tears, the quickening, softening, subduing and resuscitating power which dwells in the clouds of darkness and of storm; and the heart, wounded and bleeding, too often fails to realize the light and glory which loom up from the grave. But when we look upon the cold, pale face of the dead, in the light of a hopeful resurrection; when their silent forms move in the light of those saving influences which have been exerted upon us, we learn the necessity of bereavement; the mournful cypress will become more beautiful than the palm tree, and in view of its saving power over us, we can say, "it is good for us that we have been afflicted!"

"The path of sorrow, and that path alone,
Leads to the land where sorrow is unknown.
No traveler e'er reached that blest abode,
Who found not thorns and briers in his road.
For He who knew what human hearts would prove,
How slow to learn the dictates of His love;
That, hard by nature and of stubborn will,
A life of ease would make them harder still;
Called for a cloud to darken all their years,
And said, 'Go, spend them in the vale of tears!'"

Who will not admit that it is an act of real kindness for God to remove little children from this world, and at once take them as His own in heaven? This is surely an act of His mercy, and for their benefit. It arrests them from the perils and tribulations of mature life; it makes their pilgrimage through this vale of tears, of short duration; they escape thereby the bitter cup of actual sin, and the mental and moral agonies of death. It is well with them. How true are the following beautiful verses on the death of children, from the pen of John Q. Adams:—

"Sure, to the mansions of the blest
When infant innocence ascends,
Some angel brighter than the rest
The spotless spirit's flight attends.

On wings of ecstasy they rise,
Beyond where worlds material roll,
Till some fair sister of the skies,
Receives the unpolluted soul.
There at the Almighty Father's hand,
Nearest the throne of living light,
The choirs of infant seraphs stand,
And dazzling shine, where all are bright!"

Christ became a little child, that little children might receive the crown of their age and be eternally saved. He took them in His arms, blessed them, and said, "of such is the kingdom of heaven." And we are told that "out of the mouths of babes and sucklings He has ordained strength." The sweetest hosannas before His throne, doubtless proceed from cherub-lips, and they glow nearest to the bright vision of the face of unveiled glory.

"Calm on the bosom of thy God,
Young spirits! rest thee now!
Even while with us thy footsteps trod,
His seal was on thy brow."

They stand before the throne in white robes, with palms in their hands, and crowns of glory on their heads, crying out, "Salvation to our God, which sitteth upon the throne, and unto the Lamb!" Tell me, does not this view dilate the parent's heart, and make him thankful that he has a sainted child in heaven? Weep for those you have with you, who live under the shades of a moral death, who have entered upon a thorny pilgrimage, and are exposed to the ravages of sin; oh, weep for them!—

> "But never be a tear-drop given
> To those that rest in yon blue heaven."

The sainted dead of your home are more blessed than the pilgrim living. Weep not, then, that they are gone. Their early departure was to them great gain. Had they been spared to grow up to manhood, you then might have to take up the lamentation of David, "Would to God I had died for thee!" While they, in the culprit's cell, or on the dying couch of the hopeless impenitent, would respond to you in tones of deepening woe,—

> "Would I had died when young!
> How many burning tears,
> And wasted hopes and severed ties,
> Had spared my after years!"

Would you, then, to gratify a parent's heart, awake that little slumberer from its peaceful repose, and recall its happy spirit from its realms of glory? There the light of heaven irradiates it; its visions are unclouded there; and from those battlements of uncreated glory it comes to thee on errands of love and mercy. Would you, now, that this inhabitant of heaven should be degraded to earth again? Would you remove him from those rivers of delight to this dry and thirsty land? Would not this be cruel?

When, therefore, your babe is taken from you, regard it as a kind deed of your heavenly Father, and say, "even so it seemeth good in thy sight:"

"Pour not the voice of woe!
 Shed not a burning tear
When spirits from the cold earth go,
 Too bright to linger here!
Unsullied let them pass
 Into oblivion's tomb—
Like snow-flakes melting in the sea
 When ripe with vestal bloom.
Then strew fresh flowers above the grave,
 And let the tall grass o'er it wave."

But the death of little children is a great mercy, not only to themselves, but also to the living. Those that remain behind are greatly benefited thereby. It exerts a sanctifying, elevating and alluring influence over them. As they pass in their bright pathway to heaven, they leave a blessing behind. God takes them in goodness to us. The interests of the parents are not different from, or opposed to, those of their offspring. The happiness of the latter is that of the former. If, therefore, their death is their blessing, it must be the parent's blessing also. "If love," says Baxter, "teaches us to mourn with them that mourn, and rejoice with them that rejoice, then can we mourn for those of our children that are possessed of the highest everlasting happiness?"

It is true, their sweet faces, unfurrowed by guilt

or shame, we shall never more gaze upon; the sound of their happy lullaby we shall never again hear. They are gone now to the spirit-land. But a parent's care and solicitude are also gone. All alarm for their safety is gone; and you now rejoice in the assurance that they have gone to a higher and happier home; and can joyfully exclaim now with Leigh Richmond, "My child is a saint in glory!" His infant powers, so speedily paralyzed by the ruthless hand of death, are now expanding themselves amidst the untold glories of the heavenly world, and are enlisted now in ministering to his pilgrim kindred on earth.

It is true, your children were a source of great joy to you here. Insensibly did they entwine themselves around your heart, and with all the wild ecstasy of maternal love, you embraced them, as they attached themselves, like the slender vine, to you. They were indeed, the life and light of your home, and the deepest joy of your heart. But if they had lived, might they not also have been a source of the deepest sorrow and misery? Might they not have drawn your souls from God and heaven, causing you to live alone for them, and bringing eventually your gray hairs down with sorrow to the grave?

But you have watched at their dying couch, and seen them die; and in that death you have also seen the departure of all such fears and dangers. They are now transplanted to a more congenial clime, where they will bloom forever in unfading loveliness, and from which they will come on errands of ministering love to your household:—

> "They come, on the wings of the morning they come,
> Impatient to lead some poor wanderer home;
> Some pilgrim to snatch from his stormy abode,
> And lay him to rest in the arms of his God!"

One of the greatest blessings which the death of our pious kindred confers upon their bereaved friends is, that they hold a saving communion with them, and are ministering spirits sent to minister salvation and consolation unto them.

> "The saints on earth, and all the dead,
> But one communion make."

They constitute our guardian angels; they witness our Christian race; they commune with our spirits; they link us to the spirit-world; they impress us with its deep mysteries; they stimulate our religious life, and bear us up lest we dash our feet against the pebble which lies in our pathway to the mansions of the blest. The mother who bends in the deep anguish of her soul, over the little grave in which her infant slumbers, has in heaven a cherub spirit to minister to her. And oh, could the veil which wraps the spirit-world from our view, be now removed, and we permitted to catch a glimpse of the heavenly scene there displayed, we should doubtless behold on the threshold of that better home, an innumerable host witnessing with intensity of interest, the scenes of human life; and no doubt to you, bereaved friend, the most conspicuous among that celestial throng, would be the sainted form of that dear one whose grave you often adorn with the warm tribute of memory's gushing tears. And oh, could you understand the relation in which that sainted one stands to you, you would doubtless be conscious that over and about you it hovers from day to day as your guardian spirit, watching all the details of your life, soothing the anguish of your troubled heart, and ministering unto you in holy things!

"The spirits of the loved and departed
  Are with us; and they tell us of the sky,
A rest for the bereaved and broken-hearted,
  A house not made with hands, a home on high!
They have gone from us, and the grave is strong!
  Yet in night's silent watches they are near;
Their voices linger round us, as the song
  Of the sweet skylark lingers on the ear."

The whole dispensation of grace is like the ladder set up on earth, whose top reached heaven, and upon which Jacob saw the angels ascending and descending. As the Christian pilgrim in his spiritual progression mounts each round of this ladder, he finds himself in the midst of a spirit-throng ascending and descending on errands of love and mercy to him; yea, the canopy of the sky seems lined with so great a cloud of witnesses and ministering spirits; and among them we behold our sainted friends bidding us climb on to their lofty abodes; they beckon us to themselves; their voices animate us, as they steal down upon our spirits in solemn and beautiful cadence.

"Hark! heard ye not a sound
Sweeter than wild-bird's note, or minstrel's lay!
I know that music well, for night and day
I hear it echoing round.

It is the tuneful chime
Of spirit-voices!—'tis my infant band
Calling the mourner from this darkened land
To joy's unclouded clime.

My beautiful, my blest!
I see them there, by the great Spirit's throne;
With winning words, and fond beseeching tone,
They woo me to my rest!"

Weeping mother! that little babe, whose spirit has been borne by angels to heaven, where it now glows in visions of loveliness around God's throne, comes often as a ministering spirit to thee, whispers peace and hope to thy disconsolate heart, and with its tiny hands bears thee up in thy dark and troubled path! And my dear bereaved young friend! that mother, who nursed you on her knee, who taught your infant lips to lisp the name of Jesus, and amid whose prayers you have grown up to maturity,—that sainted mother over whose grave you have often wept in bitter anguish, hovers over you now with all the passionate fondness of a mother's love, guides and impresses you, attends you in all your walks, takes charge of you in all your steps; soothes you in your sorrows; and when burning with fever on the sick bed, fans you with angel wing and breath, and warms your chilled nerves with an angel's heart!

Now when we regard the departed of our homes in this light, shall we not admit that the death of those who go to heaven is a blessing, not only to them, but to those they leave behind! And especially when we remember that they return to us in spirit to minister to our wants even unto the smallest details of life, that they are our guardian angels, are with us wherever we go, to warn and deliver us from temptation and danger, to urge us in the path of duty, to smooth our pillow when thrown upon beds of languishing, and then, when the vital spark has fled, to convey us to the paradise of God,—oh, when we remember this, we say, shall we not rather bless God that He has afflicted us? Though our hearts may be lonely, yet with this view of the departed ones of our home, we can feel that we are, nevertheless, not alone.

"I am not quite alone. Around me glide
Unnumbered beings of the unseen world;—
And one dear spirit hovering by my side,
Hath o'er my form its snow-white wings unfurled,
It is a token that when death is nigh,
It then will wait to bear my soul on high!"

What afflicted heart will not respond with deep and grateful emotion, to the following beautiful address of a bereaved pilgrim to his sainted loved ones in heaven:—

"Gone!—have ye all then gone,—
The good, the beautiful, the kind, the dear?
Passed to your glorious rest so swiftly on,
And left me weeping here?

I gaze on your bright track;
I hear your lessening voices as they go;
Have ye no sign, no solace to fling back
To those who toil below?

Oh! from that land of love,
Look ye not sometimes on this world of wo?
Think ye not, dear ones, in brighter bowers above,
Of those you left below?

Surely ye note us here,
Though not as we appear to mortal view,
And can we still, with all our stains, be dear
To spirits pure as you?

Is it a fair, fond thought,
That you may still our friends and guardians be;
And heaven's high ministry by you be wrought
With objects low as we?

May we not secretly hope,
That you around our path and bed may dwell?
And shall not all our blessings brighter drop
From hands we loved so well?

Shall we not feel you near
In hours of danger, solitude, and pain,
Cheering the darkness, drying off the tear,
And turning loss to gain?

Shall not your gentle voice
  Break on temptation's dark and sullen mood,
Subdue our erring will, o'errule our choice,
  And win from ill to good?

Oh, yes! to us, to us,
  A portion of your converse still be given!
Struggling affection still would hold us thus,
  Nor yield you all to heaven!

Lead our faint steps to God;
  Be with us while the desert here we roam;
Teach us to tread the path which you have trod,
  To find with you our home!"

What a comfort does this view of the pious dead afford the pious living. We commend it now to you. What consolation to the bereaved parents is the assurance that all infants are saved! This gives them "beauty for ashes, the oil of joy for mourning, and the garment of praise for the spirit of heaviness." Your infant has gone to heaven; for "of such is the kingdom of heaven." Zuinlius was perhaps the first who proclaimed salvation for all who died in infancy. He based this doctrine, so comforting to the afflicted parent, upon the atonement of Christ for all; and he believed that Christ made provision for infants in this general atonement or redemption of human nature. This is the general belief now. Calvin declared that "God adopts infants and washes them in the blood of his son," and that "they are regarded by Christ as among His flock." Dr. Junkin says, "It is not inconsistent with any doctrine of the bible, that the souls of deceased infants go to heaven." Newton says, "I hope you are both well reconciled to the death of your child. Indeed, I cannot be sorry for the death of infants. How many storms do they escape! Nor can I doubt, in my private judgment, that they are included in the election of grace." This is the opinion, too, of all evangelical branches of the Christian church. If so, you have here a source of great consolation.

> "Though it be hard to bid thy heart divide,
> And lay the gem of all thy love aside—
> Faith tells thee, and it tells thee not in vain,
> That thou shalt meet thy infant yet again."

What, oh, what, if you had not the assurance of the salvation of all infants? What if your faith would tell you that all children who die before they can exercise faith would be lost or annihilated! Then indeed you might well refuse to be comforted because they are not. But your child is not lost,—but only removed to a better home:—

> "A treasure but removed,
> A bright bird parted for a clearer day—
> Yours still in heaven!"

And yours to meet there! The hope of a glorious reünion with departed friends in heaven, lifts the afflicted Christian into regions of happiness never before enjoyed. And as he contemplates their better state, and muses over the trials and sorrows of his pilgrim land, he longs to pass over the stream which divides that happy home from this. He is grateful to God that heaven has thus become doubly attractive by his bereavement, and that he can look forward with fond anticipation, to the time when he shall there become reünited with those who have gone before.

> "Oh! I could weep
> With very gratitude that thou art saved—
> Thy soul forever saved. What though my heart
> Should bleed at every pore—still thou art blessed.
> There is an hour, my precious innocent,
> When we shall meet again! Oh! may we meet
> To separate no more. Yes! I can smile,
> And sing with gratitude, and weep with joy,
> Even while my heart is breaking!"

We infer from the whole subject, that we should not murmur against God when afflicted, however great our bereavements may be. This does not, of course, forbid godly sorrow and tears. It is not inconsistent to weep; neither does sorrow for the dead, as such, imply a murmuring spirit. Christ himself invited to tears when he wept over the grave of his friend Lazarus. It is meet that we pay our tribute to departed kindred, in falling tears. These are not selfish; neither is the sorrow they express, a sin, nor an evidence of filial distrust, or of reluctant submission to the will of God. The unfeeling stoic may regard it such; but he outrages the generous impulses of humanity. Undefiled religion does not aim to cancel natural affection. Our piety, if genuine, will not make us guilty of crimes against nature, and prompt us to bend with apathy over the grave of buried love. The mother of Jesus wept her pungent woes beneath the Cross; and the Marys dropt the tear of sorrowing love and memory at the mouth of his sepulchre. And shall we refuse the tribute of sorrow to the memory of those dear ones who sleep beneath the sod? To do so would but unchristianize the deep grief which bereavement awakens, and which true piety sanctifies; it would unhumanize the very constitution of home itself. To be Christians, must the unnumbered memories of life be all without a tear? When we walk in the family grave-yard, and think of the loved who slumber there; when we open the family bible, and read there the names of those who have gone before us, say, shall this awaken no slumbering grief, invite no warm, gushing tears, and not bear us back to scenes of tenderness and love?

Ah, no! The gospel encourages godly sorrow over the dead. We are permitted to sorrow, only not as those who have no hope, as not being cast down, and as not being disquieted within us. Such godly sorrow is refreshing, and the tears it sheds are a balm to the wounded spirit. They refine our sentiments, and beget longings after a better country. The memory of bereaved affection is grief. In traversing the past, our thoughts glide along a procession of dear events arrested by the tomb; and we become sad and weep. But this is not inconsistent with a confiding faith in God, nor with a meek resignation to His afflicting providence. Faith was not designed to overpower a visible privation. When death enters our home we should feel pungently, though we have the faith of an angel, and weep before the smile of God. The evidences of faith, and the brilliant idealities of hope will hush the voice of murmur, and incite us to kiss the rod that is laid upon us.

It is, therefore, a Christian privilege to weep over the death of our departed kindred, yea, who can stifle the anguish of the heart when the tender flowers of home sink into the waxen form of death? when the flickering flame of infant life burns lower and weaker; when the death-glazed eye is closed, and the little bosom heaves no more, and that lovely form becomes cold as the grave, what parental heart can then remain unmoved, and what eye can then forbid a tear? Not even the assurance of infant salvation and the hope of reünion in heaven, can prevent sorrow for the dead.

> "To think his child is blest above,
> To pray their parting grief,
> These, these may soothe, but death alone,
> Can heal a father's grief."

But this grief should never amount to dissatisfaction with God. Though it is right to weep, it is wrong to murmur. Many parents murmuringly mourn the loss of their children, and in wrestling with God to spare them, betray the want of a true submission to His will. It is sinful to murmur at the decrees of God. We have seen that they are wise, and all designed for our good. Methinks if your dying babe could respond to your murmuring sighs and tears around its crib, it would thus reprove you:—

"Nay, mother, fix not thus on me
 That streaming eye,
And clasp not thus my freezing hand;
 For I must die.
To Him ye gave the opening bud,
 The early bloom;
Then grieve not that the ripened fruit
 He gathers home."

But we should not only refrain from murmuring, but meekly submit to the providential afflictions of our home. We should remember that all the adversities of life are from the Lord, and that when death invades our household, and crushes the fond hopes of our hearts, it is for some wise and good purpose. Though we may not understand it here, where we look through a glass darkly; but eternity will reveal it. Though the dying of a child is like tearing a limb from us; but remember God demands it. Surrender it to Him, therefore, with Christian resignation. He does not demand it without a cause. It may offend thee, though it be a right hand or a right eye. Let the branch be cut off. At the resurrection you shall see it again. Give it up willingly; for it is the Lord's will that you should. Have the meek submission to exclaim, "Not my will, but Thine be done!" Whatever may be your pleas to the contrary, they are all selfish; when you come to look at your bereavement, with the candid, discerning eye of faith, you cannot murmur; but will bend under the stroke with silent tears and with grateful submission. Faith in God, the hope of reünion in heaven, and true Christian love for the object taken from us, will effectually quell every uprising of complaint in our hearts:—

"My stricken heart to Jesus yields
Love's deep devotion now,
Adores and blesses—while it bleeds—
His hand that strikes the blow.
Then fare thee well—a little while—
Life's troubled dream is past;
And I shall meet with thee, my child,
In life—in bliss, at last!"

CHAPTER XXVII.

THE MEMORIES OF HOME.*

"The home of my youth stands in silence and sadness;
None that tasted its simple enjoyments are there,
No longer its walls ring with glee and with gladness;
No strain of blithe melody breaks on the ear.
. . . . .
Why, memory, cling thus to life's jocund morning?
Why point to its treasures exhausted too soon?
Or tell that the buds of the heart at the dawning,
Were destined to wither and perish at noon?

On the past sadly musing, oh pause not a moment;
Could we live o'er again but one bright sunny day,
'Twere better than ages of present enjoyment,
In the memory of scenes that have long passed away.

But time ne'er retraces the footsteps he measures;
In fancy alone with the past we can dwell;
Then take my last blessing, loved scene of young pleasures;
Dear home of my childhood—forever farewell!"

Chief Justice Gibson.

The bereavements of home fill up the urn of memory with its most hallowed treasures. Though these memories of the household have

---

* In this, as in the preceding chapter, we have introduced poetry, for the same reason.

an alloy of sorrow and are the product of its adversities, yet there is no pleasure so delicate, so pure, so painful, so much longed after, as that which they afford. They bring to our hearts the purest essence of the past, and cause us to live it over again. They come over us like the "breath of the sweet south breathing over a bed of violets." When we revert to the happy scenes of our childhood, we live amid them in spirit again, and remembrance swells with many a proof of recollected love; sweet ideals of all that lived under the parental roof spring up within us, and pass before us in visions of delight; the home of the past becomes the home of the present. The things of that home are spiritualized and changed into the thoughts of home; we enjoy them again; and we live our life over again with those we loved the most.

"Why in age
Do we revert so fondly to the walks
Of childhood, but that there the soul discerns
The dear memorial footsteps, unimpaired,
Of her own native vigor; thence can hear
Reverberations, and a choral song
Commingling with the incense that ascends,
Undaunted, towards the imperishable heavens,
From her own lonely altar?"

The memories of home are both pleasing and painful. When we leave the parental home for some distant land, how many pleasing recollections sweep over our spirits then. Even when tossed to and fro upon the angry wave, far from our native land,

> "There comes a fond memory
> Of home o'er the deep."

The memory of departed worth is a kind of compensation for the loss we sustain. The pious mother's recollection of her sainted husband or child becomes the soother of her grief, and casts a pleasing light along her pathway, and awakens a new joy in her widowed heart. Pious memories, when they reflect the hope of reünion in heaven, are like the radiant sky studded with brilliant stars, each shining through the clouds which move along the verge of the horizon. They sweep as gently over the troubled heart as the summer zephyr over the blushing rose, touching all the chords of holy feeling, making them vibrate sadly sweet, in blended tones, too sweet to last.

> "Here a deeper and serener charm
> To all is given,
> And blessed memories of the faithful dead
> O'er wood and vale, and meadow-stream have shed
> The holy hues of heaven."

How indelibly does memory paint the image of a departed child upon the mother's heart! No flight of years; no distance from the grave in which he slumbers, can erase the image. It will be ever fresh, and, with awakening power, mingle with her tears and glow in her fondest hopes. Though time and distance and vicissitudes may calm her troubled heart, and cause her to settle down into tranquility of feeling; but these can never destroy the tenacity and vividness of her memory. Even then those objects to which it fondly clings, become the theme of her holiest and her happiest thoughts; and she retains them with a passionate ardor, exceeded only by that with which she clung to the living child. Her greatest pleasure is, to retire from the busy cares of the world, to some solitude where she may sit among flowers that remind her of the one that withered in her arms, and meditate upon him who slumbers beneath the clods of the valley. Oh, these are sweet and precious moments to her; and the tears which are then drawn from the deep well-springs of reminiscence, are sacred to him with whom she in spirit there communes. There with rapture she remembers

> "All his winning ways,
> His pretty, playful smiles,
> His joy, his ecstasy,
> His tricks, his mimicry,
> And all his little wiles;
> Oh! these are recollections
> Round mothers' hearts that cling—
> That mingle with the tears
> And smiles of after years,
> With oft awakening!"

Memory links together the loved ones of home, though they be widely separated from each other, some on earth, and some in eternity. There is a mystic chain which binds them together, and brings them in spirit near to each other, and infuses, as it were, with electric power, a realizing sense of each other, while their past life under the same roof, "like shadows o'er them sweep." In the light of memory their faded forms are vividly brought back to view; they see each other as when they rambled over their childhood haunts; and the echo of their playful mirth comes booming back in deep reverberations through their souls. In this respect the memory of the dead is a pleasure so deep and delicate, and withal so melancholy, yea, so painful, that the heart shrinks from its intensity. This we experience when we ramble through the family graveyard, and bring within the sweep of recollection our past communion with the loved who slumber there. There is a mysterious feeling awakened in our hearts,—a feeling of peculiar melancholy, which combines two opposite emotions,—that of pleasure and that of pain. These seem to embrace each other, and their union in our hearts affords us a strange enjoyment. We enjoy the pain; the agony awakened by the remembrance of those who lie beneath the sod is pleasing to us. It is a bitter cup we love to drink; we love to keep open the wounds there inflicted. The sadness we then feel we dearly cherish; and we linger around these tombs as if bound to them by some mystic chord we could not break; we are loth to leave a spot in which are accumulated the fondest associations of early life. Would the mother, if she could, forget the child that slumbers beneath the flower-crowned sod of the family cemetery? "Where," in the beautiful language of Irving, "is the child that would willingly forget the most tender of parents, though to remember be but to lament? Who, even in the hour of agony, would forget the friend over whom he mourns? Who, even when the tomb is closing upon the remains of her he most loved and he feels his heart, as it were, crushed in the closing of its portals, would accept consolation that was to be bought by forgetfulness? And when the overwhelming burst of grief is calmed into the gentle tear of recollection, when the sudden anguish and the convulsive agony over the present ruins of all that we most loved, is softened away into pensive meditation on all that it was in the days of its loveliness, who would root out such a sorrow from the heart? Though it may sometimes throw a passing cloud even over the bright hour of gayety, yet who would exchange it even for the song of pleasure or the burst of revelry? No; there is a voice from the tomb sweeter than song; there is a recollection of the dead to which we turn even from the charms of the living!" How passionately we cling to those memories of a sainted mother, which crowd in rapid succession upon our minds!

"Weep not for her! Her memory is the shrine
Of pleasing thoughts, soft as the scent of flowers,
Calm as on windless eve the sun's decline,
Sweet as the song of birds among the bowers."

What a purifying and restraining influence does

the memory of a pious parent's love, exert upon the wayward child! When he bends in mournful recollection over the grave of a sainted mother, how must every heart-string break, and with what remorse he reviews his past life of wickedness and filial disobedience. The memory of that mother's love and kindness to him, haunts him in all his revels, and draws him back, as if by magnetic force, from scenes of riot and of ruin. Can he think of that mother's prayers and teachings and tears of solicitude, and not feel deeply, and often savingly, his own guilt and ingratitude? If there is a memory of home-life which allures him to heaven, it is the recollection of her love and pious efforts to save him.

The child who lives in exile from his country and his home, is soothed in the midst of his cares and disappointments, by the stirring imagery of his far-distant friends and home. And oh, if he has been unfaithful to the ministrations of that home; if he has trodden under foot the proffered love of his parents, and repulsed all the overtures of their pious solicitude, will not the memory of their anguish haunt his soul, and plough deep furrows of remorse in his conscience? The sense of past filial ingratitude, and the recollection of a parent's injured love and disappointed hope, constitute one of the most powerful incentives to repentance and reformation. It was thus with the prodigal son. As soon as he came to himself, he remembered the dear home of his youth, the kind love of his father, and his own unworthiness and ingratitude; and this brought him to repentance and to the resolution to return to his father, confess his sin, and seek pardon. How many now, in thus looking back upon the home of their childhood, do not remember their abuse of parental love and kindness!

"Oh! in our stern manhood, when no ray
Of earlier sunshine glimmers on our way;
When girt with sin and sorrow, and the toil
Of cares, which tear the bosom that they soil;
Oh! if there be in retrospection's chain
One link that knits us with young dreams again—
One thought so sweet we scarcely dare to muse
On all the hoarded raptures it reviews;
Which seems each instant, in its backward range,
The heart to soften, and its ties to change,
And every spring untouched for years to move,
It is—the memory of a mother's love!"

We see, therefore, that there are painful, as well as pleasant, memories of home. When the absent disobedient child remembers how he abused the privileges of the parental home, and brought the gray hairs of his parents down with sorrow to the grave, and turned that household into a desolation; when

"Pensive memory lingers o'er
Those scenes to be enjoyed no more,
Those scenes regretted ever,"

how dark and painful must be the shadows which then sweep over his penitent spirit! "If thou art a child, and hast ever added a sorrow to the soul or a furrow to the silvered brow of an affectionate parent; if thou art a husband, and hast ever caused the fond bosom that ventured its whole happiness in thy arms, to doubt one moment of thy kindness or thy truth; if thou art a friend, and hast ever wronged the spirit that generously confided in thee; if thou art a lover, and hast ever given one unmerited pang to that true heart that now lies cold and still beneath thy feet; then be sure that every unkind look, every ungracious word, every ungentle action, will come thronging back upon thy memory; then be sure that thou wilt lie down sorrowing and penitent on the grave!"

If we would avoid the agony of declining age, let us be faithful to our childhood-home. What must be the anguish of that wretch who has brought infamy upon it; how painful must be every recollection of it, when in the distance of years and of space, from its scenes and its loved ones, his remembrance hails them with its burning tear.

"I am far from the home that gave me birth,
    A blight is on my name;
It only brings to my father's hearth
    The memory of shame;
Yet, oh! do they think of me to-day,
    The loved ones lingering there;
Do they think of the outcast far away,
    And breathe for me a prayer?
That early home I shall see no more,
    And I wish not there to go,

For the happy past may nought restore—
The future is but woe.
But 'twould be a balm to my heavy heart
Upon its dreary way,
If I could think I have a part
In the prayers of home to-day!"

Every thing within the memory of home will question our hearts whether we have been faithful to her parental ministry. Every cherished association; every remembered object, and even the old scenes and objects around the homestead, will challenge our faithfulness. The trees under whose shade we frolicked and of whose fruit we ate; the streams that meandered through the meadow; the hills and groves over which we gamboled in the sunny days of childhood; the old oaken bucket and the old ancestral walls that yet stand as monuments of the past,—these will all question your fidelity to the training you received in their midst; and oh, if they assume, in the courts of memory, the attitude of witnesses against you; if nursery recollections speak of forgotten prayers and abandoned habits, what a deep and painful sense of guilt and ingratitude will this testimony develop in your bosom, and

"Darken'd and troubled you'll come at last,
To the home of your boyish glee."

How precious are the mementoes of home! Memory needs such auxiliaries. That lock of silken hair which the mother holds with tearful contemplation, and wears as a precious relic, near her heart, what recollections of the buried one it awakens within her!

> "Thou bringest fond memories of a gentle girl,
> Like passing spirits in a summer night!
> Oh, precious curl!"

And that picture of a departed mother which the orphan child presses with holy reverence to her bosom! As she gazes upon those familiar features, and reads in them a mother's love and kindness, what scenes of home-life rise upon the troubled thought, and what echoes of love come through the lapse of years from the old homestead, touching all the fires of her soul, and causing them to thrill with plaintive sadness and with painful joy. What mementoes of a sad, yet pleasing memory are found in the chamber of bereavement, where death has done his work; the empty chair; the garments laid by; playthings idly scattered there;—these are pictures upon which the eye of memory rests with pensive meditation. And our letters from home! What sweet recollections they awaken as we read line after line; and what volumes of love they contain from those dear ones who now moulder in the narrow vaults of death! Oh, how miserable must he be who has no recollections of home, who is not able to revert to the scenes of childhood, and amid whose cherished memories of life, the image of a mother does not glow!

Let us lay the foundation of a joyful, grateful memory. Let us be faithful to home, that when we leave it, and when the members of it leave us, we may delight in all the memories which loom up from the scenes of home-life:

> "Oh, friends regretted, scenes forever dear,
> Remembrance hails you with her burning tear!
> Drooping she bends o'er pensive fancy's urn,
> To trace the hours which never can return;
> Yet with retrospection loves to dwell,
> And soothe the sorrows of her last farewell!"

CHAPTER XXVIII.

THE ANTITYPE OF THE CHRISTIAN HOME.

"Oh, talk to me of heaven! I love
To hear about my home above;
For there doth many a loved one dwell
In light and joy ineffable.

O! tell me how they shine and sing,
While every harp rings echoing,
And every glad and tearless eye
Beams like the bright sun gloriously.

Tell me of that victorious palm,
  Each hand in glory beareth;
Tell me of that celestial calm,
  Each face in glory weareth!"

The Christian home on earth is but a type of his better home in heaven. The pious members feel the force of this. Every thing within their earthly homes reminds them of that happy country which lies beyond the Jordan. Besides, they behold the impress of change upon every aspect of their home. All that is near and dear to them there is passing away. It is but the shadow of better things to come. And as the type bears some resemblance to that which it typifies, we may understand both by considering the relation they sustain to each other. We may gain a new view of the Christian home by looking at it in the light of its typical relation to heaven; and we have a transporting view of our heavenly home when we contemplate it as the antitype of our home on earth.

The Christian home on earth is a tent-home, a tabernacle adapted to the pilgrim-life of God's people, set up in a dreary wilderness, designed to subserve the purposes of a few years, as a preparation for a better home. The Christian, amid all his domestic enjoyments, does not realize that his home is his rest, but that it is only a probationary state, the foretaste and anticipation of the rest that remaineth for the people of God. It is but the emblem,—the shadow of his eternal home; and it is, therefore, unsatisfying; it does not meet all the wants of our nature; there is a yearning after a better state; the purest happiness it affords proceeds from the hopes and longings it begets, and the interests it is transferring to eternity, laying up, as it were, treasures in a better home. Our home here, develops our wants, inflames our desires, excites our expectations, educates, and points us to the realities of which it is an emblem; but it does not fully satisfy our desires, it only increases their intensity. The pilgrim soul of the child of God pines and frets amid all

> "Her sylvan scenes, and hill and dale
> And liquid lapse of murmuring streams."

These afford him no satisfaction; they only develop in him the saving sense of earth's insufficiency; all the scenes of this wilderness state are but those of thorns, and desert heath, and barren sands; and he cries out in the midst of his happy home,—"This is not your rest!" Our tent-home may include every earthly cup, and all the riches and honors of the world, yet it satisfies not, and the Christian turns from it all to rest and expatiate in a life to come. Every home here is baptized with tears and scarred with graves. Its poverty is a burden, its riches are snares, its friends are taken from us; broken hearts agonized there; restlessness is tossed to and fro there; and disappointment reigns in every member there. Hence in our wilderness-home we hunger and thirst, and pine for something more satisfying. We turn from the shadow to the reality; and realizing the insufficiency of home as a mere type, we turn with anxious hope to that which it typifies—our heavenly home.

Heaven is the antitype of the Christian home. There the latter reaches its consummation, and reaps the rich harvest of its great reward. The Father; the Mother of us all; our Brethren; our inheritance; our all sufficiency are there. Yea, all that is included in the dear name of home, is treasured up there, for the child of God. In that better land he finds the reality of his home on earth; the latter is but the prophecy of the former:—

> "There is my house and portion fair,
> My treasure and my heart are there,
> And my abiding home."

That better home is radiant with light and love. There you shall not see through a glass darkly, but shall behold all things face to face. You shall not merely know in part, but even as you are known. There you shall realize in all its fulness what you dimly taste here. We have a hunger here which is not fully satisfied till in heaven we pluck the fruits of the tree of life. We have a thirst here which is not fully quenched till in heaven we drink of the waters of the river of life which flows fast by the throne of God. In our tent-home here, we eat and drink, but hunger and thirst again; we are healed, but we sicken again; we live in the light of truth, but darkness and clouds intervene; we are comforted by the spirit and by friends; but we sorrow and weep again.

But in heaven "sighing grief shall weep no more;" and we "shall hunger no more, neither shall we thirst any more; and we shall not say I am sick; and there shall be no night, nor sorrow, nor tears, nor sighing, nor death; for the former things are passed away." Love will then be perfect; there will be no heart-burnings and disappointments there. There you shall enjoy the honey without the sting, and the rose without the thorn. "Earth hath no sorrows that heaven cannot heal." All care and toil, and tears, and orphanage, and widowhood, shall drop and disappear at the threshold of heaven. If our tent-home stirs up within us imperishable joys, by the power of anticipation and foretaste, what joy will not that better land afford? If the promise is so cheering, what must the fulfillment be! If the pursuit is so inspiring, what must the possession be! If our home on Tabor, where we have but a distant view of home-life, affords us so much happiness, what must our home on the eternal throne of God be? There your intercourse with the loved ones of earth will not be clogged by pain and infirmities. Your society there will be the most endearing, and with "a great multitude which no man could number, of all nations, and kindred, and people, and tongues, standing before the throne, clothed with white robes, and palms in their hands." You shall there hold fellowship with the fathers of a thousand generations, with the patriarchs, and prophets, and apostles, and martyrs, and reformers, and the "innumerable company of angels." With these you shall engage in the most delightful avocation. There will be no indolence there, as we often find in earthly homes; but all will be continually engaged. "They serve Him day and night in His temple." There will be one unbroken worship, which will afford you rapturous delight. You shall be presented before God's glory, with exceeding joy; for "in His presence is fullness of joy, and at His right hand are pleasures for evermore." These joys will be eternal,—forever and ever. That better home will never be dissolved, cannot be shaken, and your crown of glory there is a crown which fadeth not away.

But this happiness and glory of heaven are not only eternal but progressive,—ever increasing. There is nothing stationary there with the saints; but their powers will ever expand and their glory increase. New songs will be ever bursting in new strains from the celestial choir; new discoveries and fresh exclamations of praise and gratitude will be continually made. Here on earth they were "by nature the children of wrath even as others;" they had their tribulations and often murmured at God's dealings with them. But there in that heavenly home they will understand the reason for all this. The deep mysteries of the Christian life are now revealed, and they see that a father's chastisements are the work of a father's love, and worketh out for them that are exercised thereby, an "exceeding and eternal weight of glory." They now see that while in their tent-home they lived in the center of a grand system of natural, providential and spiritual things, all of which were working in beautiful harmony together for "the good of them that loved God and were the called according to His purpose;" and with rapturous gratitude they cry out, "Marvelous are thy works, Lord God Almighty; just and true are all thy ways, O thou King of Saints!"

Here, too, they will fully realize the wisdom of the Christian home and life; they will now see how wise it was for them as a family, to serve the Lord. In their earthly home, they "knew whom they believed, and were persuaded that he was able to keep that which they committed unto Him against that day." They did this in the midst of fiery trials. They were unknown. The world hated and despised them as she did their divine Master. But they persevered unto the end; and now they "shine forth as the sun in the kingdom of their Father." We shall not there, as we do here, eat the bread of care and drink the waters of bitterness. Here thunders spend their echoes and lightnings gleam in fierce wrath around our homes. There such sounds and storms never come.

"No sickness there,
No weary wasting of the frame away;
No fearful shrinking from the midnight air;
No dread of summer's bright and fervid ray.

No hidden grief,
No wild and cheerless vision of despair;
No vain petition for a swift relief,
No tearful eye, no broken hearts are there

Care has no home
  Within that realm of ceaseless praise and song;
Its tossing billows break and melt in foam,
  Far from the mansions of the spirit-throng.

The storm's black wing
  Is never spread athwart celestial skies;
Its wailings blend not with the voice of spring,
  As some too tender floweret fades and dies."

Christ is the great center of heaven's glory and attraction. "Whom have I in heaven but thee?" It would not be heaven if He were absent. Its harps would become unstrung, and its voices would lose their tune. When eternity dawns upon our disembodied spirits, and the heavenly home appears in view, with its golden streets, and living temples, and crowns, and thrones, and joys, bursting on our sight; while seraphim and cherubim, and angels, and the sainted spirits of departed friends—our parents and children, and kindred, bend over its threshold to hail our entrance with songs and shouts of everlasting joy,—oh, what a glorious heritage will this be! But all this will fade into insignificance before the Lamb on the throne. He will absorb all interest; and will be all and in all to its unfading treasures. Oh, there is much in that celestial home to allure us there. Its "fields arrayed in living green, and rivers of delight." Its blood-washed throng, its crowns and peace, the angelic choir, our friends and relations,—perhaps a father and a mother, perhaps a husband or wife, perhaps a brother or a sister, or a child,—a lovely babe;—all these make heaven dear, and draw us there. They beckon us to themselves; they are waiting for us now, and on the glowing pinions of love they come thronging as ministering spirits, to our hearts.

But what are all these attractions of that spirit-home, compared with Jesus there as the crowning glory of them all! other things are stars and streamlets. He is the central sun,—the source of all. Take Him away, and all the brightness and the glory of that heavenly world would become shrouded in darkness and desolation.

There is a living union between the Christian's home on earth, and his home in heaven. Christ represents our nature and advocates our cause there. The saints on earth and the inhabitants of heaven "but one communion make." The latter minister to the former. "Are they not all ministering spirits, sent to minister unto them who shall be the heirs of salvation?"

"Oh! a mother's spirit hung
  O'er her last pledge of earthly love,
And, while attending angel's sung,
  Welcom'd her dear one home above.

Gentle babe, I come for thee:
  I did come to bear thee home,
Far from mortal agony;
  Come, then, gentle infant, come.

Yes; while o'er thy mouldering dust
  Falls the tear of earthly love,
Thou shalt live amidst the just,
  Brighter life in heaven above."

Every thing good in our earthly home has its echo in heaven, and sweeps like the breath of God over the harps of the blessed. When the pious mother kneels with her child in prayer to God, it sends a thrill of new ecstasy into the bosom of the redeemed around His throne. When the child gives its heart to Christ, each harp bursts forth with a new anthem of joy at the prospect of that accession to their happy band. And oh, what unspeakable joy must thrill the bosom of a sainted mother when the news of her child's conversion reaches her there!—

. . . . "A new harp is strung, and a new song is given
To the breezes that float o'er the gardens of heaven."

And there, too, sainted relations continually warn the impenitent members of the tent-home. "Though dead they yet speak." "Turn ye, turn ye; for why will ye die?" "The spirit and the bride say, come!" Oh, regard those solemn admonitions which come to you from the spirit-world! With unearthly eloquence they urge you to "lay aside every weight and the sin that doth so easily beset you, and run the race set before you, looking unto Jesus, the author and finisher of your faith." And oh, if you, in obedience to these angelic persuasives to piety, yield yourself unto the Lord, all the arches of that eternal home will reverberate with the sound of jubilee over your salvation, until its echo from harp to harp shall be borne up to the throne of God.

And as there is a living union of the Christian's home on earth and in heaven, so also will there be a conscious union and recognition of the members of the Christian home, when they enter that better land. When the tent-home is broken up, and its members take their place and enter upon their joys in the heavenly home, they will recognize each other, and exchange congratulations. The bonds of natural affection which bound them together here will bind them also there. They will possess the same home-feeling and sympathy; they will love each other as members of the same household; the parents will know and love their children as parents; and the children will feel towards their parents as children. Thus in the clear light of that blessed land we shall see and know our kindred, and shall be recognized and known by them. All family ties will be re-knit; all home-relationships will be restored; all the links of affection will be renewed. The babe that withered in your arms like a frost-stricken flower in winter, will come forth clad in redemption robes, to embrace you there; and one of your joys will be a conscious reünion with him:—

"We shall go home to our Father's house:
To our Father's house in the skies,

> Where the hope of our souls shall have no blight,
> Our love no broken ties;
> We shall roam on the banks of the river of peace,
> And bathe in its blissful tide;
> And one of the joys of our heaven shall be,
> The little boy that died!"

And that sainted mother of yours shall greet you there. In your earth-home, you and she were united in faith and love and hope; and in the morning of the resurrection you shall ascend together from the family grave-yard; and together bow in grateful adoration before the throne of God.

And oh, what a glorious meeting in heaven that will be, when all the members of the Christian household shall unitedly surround the marriage supper of the Lamb! It will be joyful beyond conception. There they "shall meet at Jesus' feet,—shall meet to part no more!" No one is absent. Bright faces will meet there; bounding hearts will meet there; and on the banks of the river of life they will walk hand in hand, as they did unitedly in this vale of tears. "There is hereafter to be no separation in that family. No one is to lie down on a bed of pain. No one to wander away into temptation. No one to sink into the arms of death. Never in heaven is that family to move along the slow procession, clad in the habiliments of woe, to consign one of its members to the tomb!"—Rev. A. Barnes.

If heaven is our better home, where the members of Christian families meet to part no more; if dreams cannot picture a world so fair; and if eye has not seen, nor ear heard, nor human heart conceived the felicity of its peaceful inhabitants, then we should greatly rejoice that our pious kindred have been taken there, and that we are blessed with the hope of reünion with them in that heavenly home:—

. . . "If to Christ, with faith sincere,
Your babe at death was given,
The kindred tie that bound you here,
Though rent apart with many a tear,
Shall be renewed in heaven!"

In our tent-home, we should cultivate spiritual longings after heaven, and live in the true hope and assurance of entering there. The soul of the Christian, conscious of the emptiness of all things here, rests and expatiates in a life to come. In proportion to his preparation for it, and his nearness to it, will be the depth of his aspirations and the assurance of his hope. The widowed mother, who feels that part of her household is in heaven and that soon she will join them there, yearns with all the pining of home-sickness, for departure to the promised land, which is far better.

"When shall my labors have an end,
In joy and peace and thee!"

Even these hopes and longings after reünion with the departed in heaven, afford her joy, and open in her panting spirit a foretaste of unearthly bliss. To her aspiring faith all things look heavenward. The stars of the sky, and the flowers of the field smile their blessings upon her; and she welcomes death to break off her chains, to draw the bolts and bars, and open the prison doors of her house of clay, that her home-sick spirit may go up to that happier land where her possessions lie:—

"Let me go! my heart is fainting
'Neath its weight of sin and fears,
And my wakeful eyes are failing
With these ever-falling tears!
For the morning I am sighing,
While I earth's long vigils keep;
Here the loved are ever dying,
And the loving live to weep!

Let me go! I fain would follow,
Where I know their steps have passed—
Far beyond life's heaving billows,
Finding home and heaven at last!
While my exiled heart is pining
To behold my Father's face,
They, in His own brightness shining,
Beckon me to that blest place!

Let me go! I hear them calling,
'Ho! thou weary one,—come home!'
Words which on mine ears are falling,
Wheresoe'er my footsteps roam,
I can catch the far-off murmurs
Of life's river, sweet and low,
Calling, from earth's bitter waters,
Unto me—O let me go!"

Gentle reader! seek that better land. Let your home be a preparation for, and a pilgrimage to, a home in heaven. You are now in the wilderness beset on every side by enemies. Go forward! You are now in the deep vale,—in the low retreats of pilgrim life. "Friend, go up higher!" "Be thou faithful unto death, and you shall receive a crown of life." Be patient in tribulation. The storms that swell around your pilgrim home will soon subside, and a cloudless sky will burst upon you; the winter gloom and desolation will soon pass away; and "sweet fields arrayed in living green and rivers of delight," will spread out themselves before your enraptured vision. Remember that "the sufferings of the present time are not worthy to be compared with the glory that shall be revealed in us." In a few years at most the conflict shall end, and sighing grief shall weep no more; the wormwood and the gall will be exchanged for the cup of salvation; the armor and the battle-field will be exchanged for the white garment, the crown and the throne. Soon your typical homestead shall be exchanged for your antitypical home; and we shall unite in the home song of everlasting joy,—the song of, "unto Him that loved us and washed us in His own blood, to Him be praise and glory and dominion forever!"

Let the hope of soon entering that happy home, stimulate you to increased ardor in the cause of your Master. Methinks, some who will read these pages, have snow-white locks and wrinkled brows and faded cheeks; and these tell you that soon your pilgrim journey will be ended, your tent-home dissolved, and your staff laid aside; and oh, if you have made God the strength of your heart and your portion forever, you shall welcome death with joy; yea, you will now be anxious to lay aside these garments of toil and conflict, and soar away to that better country, where the wicked cease from troubling, and the weary are at rest. With holy pantings after God you will say, "Come, Lord Jesus, come quickly!"

"Let me go! my feet are weary,
In the desert where I roam.
Let me go! the way is dreary—
Let the wanderer go home!
I am weary of the darkness
Of these lonely, failing streams—
Let me go where founts are flashing
In the light of heaven's beams!

Let me go! my soul is thirsting
For those waters, bright, and clear,
From the fount of glory bursting—
Ah! why keep the pilgrim here?
Let me go! O, who would linger,
Fainting, fearing, and athirst,
When before us lies a region
Where undying pleasures burst?"

We have now enumerated some of the elements of the Christian home—its constitution, its ministry, its trials, its joys, and its relation to a better home in heaven. But we have not exhausted this interesting subject; we have given but a very general and imperfect sketch. If this our first effort will contribute to the salvation of one soul, we shall be compensated; and should our encouragement justify it, we may continue the effort, in the preparation of a work on the historical development of the Christian home.

FINIS.

and as affectionately as he may the memory of that immortal man—in whose serene and majestic presence, it seems to us, common men must have felt emotions approaching even to awe—the reader cannot peruse this excellent work without having his reverence and affection heightened. In these days of degeneracy, when the wise and sagacious counsels of Washington appear to be forgotten, and men are threatening the destruction of the free institutions for which we owe him so much, it would be well for all to refresh themselves in the pure waters of his patriotism."

[*From the Savannah Republican.*]

"This work is profusely and handsomely illustrated, beginning with an excellent likeness of Washington. All who have read 'Washington and his Generals' by the same author, will be certain to buy this. Those who have not are the losers. Mr. Headley's style is popular and would sell any book; but a book on a subject so dear to every American heart cannot fail to please and interest."

[*From the Presbyterian.*]

"Mr. Headley's glorious pen finds an appropriate theme in the character and History of Washington. He professes to have had access to new material, in various papers which came into his possession, the substance of which he has embodied in his narrative. The author's reputation as a portrayer of battle scenes is fully sustained by the dashing and brilliant pictures he here presents of the great conflicts of 'the times that tried men's souls.' It is a volume admirably suited to the popular taste. It is illustrated with a profusion of engravings."

[*From the New York Observer.*]

"Every thing that increases our *knowledge* of Washington, adds to the *reverence* in which his name is held, and in this day we hail the repeated efforts to illustrate the life of Washington, and to exhibit it to the country as the most cheering signs of the times. The great popularity of Mr. Headley as a writer appears to be well sustained, and we think that he has never employed his pen to better advantage than in the preparation of this work. It is elegantly published in a large octavo volume, with numerous fine engravings."

[*From the Boston Journal.*]

"The work is written in Headley's usual dramatic and somewhat florid but attractive style, presenting, as it were panoramic pictures of many of the leading events of Washington's career. That it will find its way into thousands of families and become a popular work, we are justified in believing by the uniform success of Mr. Headley's works, as well as by the intrinsic merits of the book itself. It is profusely illustrated with engravings on steel and wood."

[*From the New York Post.*]

"Mr. Headley is certainly a clever writer. His Life of Washington is, on the whole, a strong and lucid record of the great man's career; we see in his vivid prose the long lines of the sweeping squadrons and the gleam of the dancing flags, and are borne excitedly through the rush and shock of the charge. He certainly has the power of stirring the blood in one's heart. It is accurate and interesting, has facts and incidents not elsewhere recorded."

[*From the New York Picayune.*]

"Headley has many of the characteristics of Macaulay. He is voluble and epigrammatic, pouring out epithets with a rapidity and force that never fail to produce their effect. He groups skillfully and paints vividly. The volume before us is a very complete one, Mr. Headley having had access to a large quantity of new material, including the papers, correspondence and diary of Rufus Putnam. The paper is stout, the type clear, and altogether in matter and appearance it is worthy of a place in every American library."

[*From the New York Evangelist.*]

"It is brief and comprehensive, yet written with an animation of style which makes the great story interesting, and adapted for popular effect. Some of the battle scenes of this book have great energy and life. We doubt not it will find public favor, and will be read with an interest that few romancers could excite, and with new admiration of the consummate character it portrays."

[*From the Chautauque Democrat.*]

"A Magnificent Book.—J. T. Headley's Illustrated Life of Washington is one of the most magnificent books that has been added to the literature of this country for many a year. It is written in the graceful and deeply interesting style of the author, and illustrated by splendid steel plate and wood engravings. It is published in the best style—large octavo, thick white paper, large and beautiful type, and neatly and richly bound."

www.ingramcontent.com/pod-product-compliance
Lightning Source LLC
LaVergne TN
LVHW020119110826
845151LV00001B/204

* 9 7 8 1 4 2 5 5 4 1 8 7 3 *